T0316461

FURRY NATION

FURRY NATION

The True Story of America's Most Misunderstood Subculture

by Joe Strike

CLEiS
PRESS

Copyright © 2017 by Joe Strike.

All rights reserved. Except for brief passages quoted in newspaper, magazine, radio, television, or online reviews, no part of this book may be reproduced in any form or by any means, electronic or mechanical, including photocopying or recording, or by information storage or retrieval system, without permission in writing from the publisher.

Published in the United States by Cleis Press, an imprint of Start Midnight, LLC, 101 Hudson Street, Thirty-Seventh Floor, Suite 3705, Jersey City, NJ 07302.

Printed in the United States.
Cover design: Scott Idleman/Blink
Cover photograph: "Madelein the Lynx" © Breanna Smalser;
    constructed and photographed by Temperance
Text design: Frank Wiedemann
Back cover illustration: "Just Desserts" © Kacey Miyagami

First Edition.
10 9 8 7 6 5 4 3 2 1

Trade paper ISBN: 978-1-62778-232-6
E-book ISBN: 978-1-62778-233-3

Library of Congress Cataloging-in-Publication Data is available on file.

www.furrynation.com

TABLE OF CONTENTS

Preface

THE BOOK YOU'RE HOLDING is quite different from the one I set out to write.

Furry Nation's original title was *ANTHROPOMOR-PHISM: Furries, Funny Animals and Dogs Playing Poker.* While my original goal was to explain furry fandom to the world at large (and to my fellow furs curious about our history), I was planning to downplay Furry itself to focus on anthropomorphism as a primal form of self-expression, with Furry as its modern manifestation.

An editor at a publishing house was interested but said there were two things missing from my book proposal: "[myself] and other furries."

I put the proposal down and didn't touch it again for years. I wasn't ready to share what Furry means to me or the (large) role it plays in my life.

But times change, I've changed and Furry has grown from a fandom into a community. It's bigger than ever before, attracting more people every day and—thanks to occasionally accurate media coverage—beginning to seep into the public consciousness. That consciousness has changed as well, as people (especially millennials) embrace ideas and lifestyles previously shunned or scorned.

Furry Nation isn't really about the costumes, the

conventions or even the kinks. *Furry Nation* is about people: the people who birthed the community, wear the costumes, create the art, attend the conventions—and maybe enjoy a furry kink or two.

    Furry Nation is their story—and it's also mine.

    It's a very human story.

Definition

furry [**fur**-ee]

Noun: 1. a fan of anthropomorphic animal characters;
2. a self-identified member of the contemporary subculture known as "furry fandom" [plural: furries; synonyms: fur, furfan, furfag (derisive)];
3. a fictional or imaginary being combining human and animal appearance, abilities or traits; an anthropomorphic animal character [plural: furries; synonyms: anthro, morph];
4. furry fandom itself [concise].

Adjective: 1. favorably inclined towards the concept of anthropomorphic animals;
2. covered in fur [archaic].

CHAPTER ONE

In the Beginning . . .

Every animal knows more than you do.
— NATIVE AMERICAN PROVERB

IT WAS A TALKING ANIMAL that got us into all this trouble. If only that snake had kept its mouth shut, if only Eve hadn't listened, we'd still be living in that peaceable kingdom known as Eden, our arms around our fellow creatures in a comradely hug: lions and tigers and bears— oh boy!

We're animals too, in case you've forgotten. Want proof? Check your pulse; if you don't have one you're either a vegetable or a mineral. But we've got it all compared to other animals, don't we? Where are *their* mega-malls, SUVs, Internet, all those material things that make our lives worth living?

On the other hand, there's a definite shortage of crooked politicians, greedy CEOs and financial swindlers in the animal world. They're living *la vida loca*, the primal, sensual life we've traded in for a big brain and a thumb. There they are, naked and unashamed, screwing and shitting (and when they're predators, killing) without a second thought, free of the neurotic baggage, social inhibitions and technological trinkets that weigh us down.

Who wouldn't envy that?

Way back when, the hard-and-fast line between people and animals wasn't so hard or fast. It was natural to feel a kinship with your cattle if something out there in the dark would just as soon eat you as it would eat them. Shamans spoke with animals and even turned into them on occasion. It was easy to imbue animals with powers far beyond those of mortal men, or imagine them as strange visitors from another world: turtles who carry the Earth on their backs, jackals who ferry the dead to the afterlife. At the same time, people living eye-to-eye with animals saw them as behaving like people: sly foxes, stubborn mules, deceitful serpents, regal lions and loyal dogs. We're doing it to this day. We can't help it—it's hard-wired into our brains. There's a word for it, giving animals human qualities: *anthropomorphism*.

If anthropomorphism is an elevator raising animals up to our level, then *zoomorphism* is the same elevator heading down—with us on board. Suddenly, as if touched by Circe, humans become those clever foxes, greedy pigs, total jackasses and treacherous snakes; and as every tyrant knows, people are sheep.

Our evolutionary need to reproduce turns men into predatory wolves and tomcats, women into vixens, birds, chicks and (if they stand up for themselves) bitches. Husky gay men are bears, older women with a taste for young males, cougars. Our sexual organs, the most animalistic part of ourselves, are beavers, pussies, lizards and trouser snakes, and it's a lucky man who's hung like a horse.

There may not be cattle in the backyard, chickens in the living room or wolves howling in the night any more (at least not where I live), but we're still surrounded by animals: Mustangs on the highway, Pumas on the sidewalk and Broncos butting heads with Rams on the gridiron, while donkeys and elephants take turns running the country. America itself is a bald eagle, Britain (once upon a time) an imperial lion and scrappy bulldog, France a rooster and Russia a bear. (Kangaroos still = Australia, and the koalas are getting mighty pissed about it.) Animals sell cereal to kids, entertain them in cartoons and picture books and their huggable plush forms keep them company at night.

But anthropomorphic animals aren't just for kids. They can be found in serious novels, sporting ids and libidos for the occasion; on pedestals and canvases in art galleries; and on Broadway, where performers pretending to be all manner of beasts sing and dance for audiences eagerly shelling out $100 a pop.

Artists and entertainers aren't the only ones embracing their inner animal. Plenty of average, walking-around people have been using anthropomorphic animals to express themselves on an emotional, intellectual and even physical level for years—but it's the kind of thing you don't talk about in polite company, unless you enjoy having people give you funny looks. Then they started running into each other at animated film clubs and sci-fi and comic book conventions where they could talk all they wanted about Uncle Scrooge and the Kzinti and who's sexier, *Pogo*'s Miss Mam'selle Hepzibah or Thumper's girlfriend in *Bambi* . . .

Then the Internet came along and people didn't have to run into each other anymore—all they had to do was go online. They discovered they weren't just a few dozen people at a convention, but a few *thousand*, and a lot more than that; people who'd never dreamed, *my God, other folks are into this stuff too!* They've been multiplying like [culturally entrenched animal metaphor] ever since, and for better or worse they've crossed a threshold, reached critical mass and made it onto the cultural radar.

I'm one of those people. Perhaps you've heard of us. We're called furries.

What *is* a furry? Since I'm an inclusive kind of guy, I go broad brush. For me:

- A furry human is anyone with an above-average interest in anthropomorphic characters, whether or not they consider themselves furry—or have ever even heard of the fandom (a.k.a. "furry but doesn't know it yet");

- A furry animal is *any* animal with *any* human characteristics, no matter what its origin: entertainment, mythology, advertising, kids' books or adult literature. To put it simply, Furry is about the *idea* of animals—what they represent in our minds—not their reality.

A lot of furfans are not as small-c catholic as I am. For some, a furry is strictly a cartoon or comic book "funny animal" invented to entertain people, while others only use the word to describe fan-created characters. Some "fursuiters" believe that if you're not in an animal costume, you're not really a furry. Others take their Furry with a dose of mysticism, feeling a link with a personal spirit animal, or believing themselves therian or otherkin: at heart an animal or dragon, trapped in a human body. And quite a few people who enjoy anthro characters no longer call themselves furry due to a certain reputation we've somehow acquired. (More on that later.)

In other words, there's no one way to be furry—which is how it should be. Furry fandom is a huge, growing and self-created world. No single TV show or movie, no *Star Trek* or *Star Wars*, no corporate-owned intellectual property or entertainment brand brought us together.

You might be a furry if you've been doodling your own imaginary menagerie for years, and they all have names, personalities and backstories . . . if you wonder what cartoon animal characters do between cartoons, or if Bugs and Daffy are secretly lovers . . . if you've always had a secret desire to wear one of those sports-team mascot suits . . . if you feel spiritually connected to a particular animal . . . or if there happens to be a fox or a tiger or a wolf or a rabbit trapped inside you, waiting to escape. Yes, that could all mean you are furry. And it's time to embrace your furriness.

From this point on I'll be calling furry fans "furs" as often as possible and save "furries" for the animals themselves, along with the occasional "anthro." Apart from avoiding confusion between the animals and the people, "-ie" is a diminutive; "fur" sounds way more sophisticated than "furry," the same way "kid" sounds better than "kiddie" or "Trekker" sounds better than "Trekkie," at least in my humble opinion.

Which brings us back to our image problem: adults watching cartoons, drawing furry pictures and playing animal dress-up—don't they know that's kid stuff? And exploring the physicality, the sensuality and even the *sexuality* of imaginary animals—That's just wrong, wrong, *wrong* . . . right?

Actually, the human race has been taking anthropomorphic animals seriously for a very long time; it's only in the last few centuries these particular furries have largely been banished to kiddieland.

In fact, the oldest known work of art in existence depicts a furry. He's 40,000 years old and was found deep in a cave in Germany. The broad-shouldered "Lion Man" (*Löwenmensch*)[1] sports a leonine head above a human body. The slender figure, almost a foot tall, was carved out of a mammoth tooth by a flint-wielding Stone Age sculptor.

A teenager by comparison, the cave painting known as "The Sorcerer"[2] dates back a mere 140 centuries. Discovered in a cave beneath the French countryside, "The Sorcerer," like his older brother the Lion Man, is a therianthrope—a combination of man and beast. A gently curving tail and dangling genitalia adorn an otherwise human rump. His upper arms are pressed tightly against his torso while his forearms, thrust straight out, end in paws. His head sports antlers, tufted animal ears—and a pair of human eyes, round and looking over his shoulder as if startled.

The Lion Man and the Sorcerer: half-human,

---

1   http://www.theartnewspaper.com/articles/Ice-Age-iLion-Mani-is-worlds-earliest-figurative-sculpture/28595

2   *Trois Frères*. www.britannica.com, both retrieved February 16 2016.

half-animal deities? Or shamans, shape-shifters at home in both the human and animal worlds? Ten thousand years later the artwork became more impressive: three-dimensional statues and friezes of solid stone depicting the Egyptians' animal-headed gods.

The biggest and best-known of these depictions is so large you can, as they say, see him from space: a human-faced lion sitting in noble repose like the ones in front of the New York Public Library—only this one is 241 feet long, twenty-feet wide and taller than a six-story building.

The Egyptians revered the lion as a god; the Great Sphinx of Giza was built by a Pharaoh who wanted to be remembered forever as a half-human, half-animal deity. (His wish came true—at least the half-human, half-animal part.)

Furry images can be found in many religions. Believing the Bible forbade graven images not just of God but humans as well, medieval Jews illustrated a fourteenth-century *Haggadah* with depictions of bird-headed people,[3] In India, elephant-headed Ganesha is the bringer of wisdom, prosperity and good fortune, and a widely beloved Hindu deity. Hollywood cartoon elephants jump on a chair shrieking at the sight of a mouse, but not Ganesha: he pals around with a friendly rodent who helps himself to the food at the big guy's feet.

If anyone proves Jung's theories about the collective unconscious, it's the trickster—the in-your-face wise guy and often-too-clever-for-his-own-good mischief-maker. He shows up wherever he pleases: in ancient Egypt he

---

3   "The Birds' Head Haggadah." jhom.com. Retrieved November 24, 2016. (http://jhom.com/topics/birds/haggadah.htm)

was a patchwork beast named Set; in Africa the spider Anansi; in France the miscreant fox Reynard. In Celtic folklore, there's the Púca, a part-time horse, goat, dog or any number of beasts. In America, there's an invisible six-feet, three-and-a-half-inch tall rabbit named Harvey.[4] For Native Americans, the trickster's a coyote (often very often horny and likely to get his penis caught in places it doesn't belong), or a rabbit in legends that merged with African tales of their own long-eared smart aleck. The love child of this union is the very American Br'er Rabbit. His DNA turns up in his modern descendants, disguise-loving lapines like Bugs Bunny and the Trix Rabbit, not to mention the battery-powered Energizer Bunny.

In twelfth-century Japan, Animal Scrolls[5] depicted frogs, rabbits and monkeys fighting and praying human-style. In their folklore, shape-shifting foxes known as *kitsune* sometimes befriend, sometimes prank and some-times take human form to bed an infatuated lover. (*Kitsune* translates as "come and sleep."[6]) Trees grow more rings as they age, people grow nose hairs, but *kitsune* acquire additional tails, each a measure of its increasing power and wisdom. (Fans of Sonic the Hedgehog are probably unaware his double-tailed pal, Tails, is a young *kitsune*.

The *tanuki*—a Japanese raccoon-dog—is another shape-shifting trickster, but more of the Adult Swim variety—it's difficult to be taken seriously when you're

---

4   The 1944 play starring said rabbit won the Pulitzer Prize for Drama.

5   Their title literally translates as "Animal-person Caricatures," and the work has sometimes been described as the very first manga. "Chōjū-jinbutsu-giga." Wikipedia. (https://en.wikipedia.org/wiki/Chōjū-jinbutsu-giga)

6   Smyers, Karen Ann. *The Fox and the Jewel: Shared and Private Meanings in Contemporary Japanese Inari Worship*. Honolulu: University of Hawaii Press, 1999. pg 72. Both retrieved November 23, 2016.

dragging an enormous pair of testicles around. A real *tanuki* has a healthy set, but a mythical one can use his as a drum or a blunt instrument to clobber people. Look for him (in statue form) in front of noodle shops: he'll be sporting a bamboo hat, holding a bottle of sake in one hand and an empty purse in the other. Who needs cash when you have sake—and magic that turns leaves into paper money long enough to fool gullible shopkeepers?

The 16th century Chinese novel *Journey to the West* (based on even older legends) stars Sun Wukong, the "monkey awakened to emptiness." A real bad-ass, he learned (or swiped) magical secrets that made him immortal and invulnerable, not to mention king of the monkeys. Pushing his luck, he challenged Buddha himself—and wound up humbled, imprisoned and forced to serve as a holy man's bodyguard until he acquired a bit of humility.

Ancient Greece's top god, Zeus, had a unique appreciation of anthropomorphism and practiced bestiality the old-fashioned way, turning himself into a bull or a swan and getting it on with easily impressed mortal babes like Europa and Leda. The Greeks were also responsible for the story of Circe, who transformed (un)lucky visitors to her island into various animals. (Her preference for pigs is wildly exaggerated; if you were a class act you might wind up a wolf or lion.) Half-and-half minotaurs, satyrs, and centaurs show up as supporting players in Greek mythology as well. While centaurs have made a huge pop-culture comeback in recent years, appearing in everything from big-budget fantasy movies to TV commercials, the satyrs' non-stop licentiousness didn't go over too well with the no-sex-please early Christians. Animals from the waist down? It wasn't long before goat-god Pan got a name change and makeover into Evil Incarnate Satan.

Folk tales dating back to medieval times featuring talking animals were sanitized and prettified into "fairy tales" by Perrault and the Brothers Grimm and sold to parents seeking G-rated reading material for their children. Lewis Carroll's *Alice* books made him a nineteenth-century celebrity; at the dawn of the twentieth, Baum published his first *Oz* books, followed shortly by Peter Rabbit's first raid on Mr. McGregor's garden. Cheshire cats, cowardly lions and hungry rabbits . . . as the century rolled along, the idea that talking animals were kid stuff grew from a presumption into a rock-ribbed certainty. Modern marketers and advertisers did their part, using furry mascots and cartoon celebrities to sell toys, breakfast cereal and kidswear. The juvenilization of anthropomorphic characters and storytelling had officially taken hold.

So here we are today, furs trying to free anthropomorphic animals from their cultural dungeon, not because we're immature, overgrown children (well, maybe some of us are, just a little), but because like those artists, writers and pious souls of days gone by, we take them seriously. We know they're metaphors for ourselves—particularly parts of ourselves we might otherwise never experience. We envy their freedom and enjoy the anarchy trickster furries happily unleash. And when we draw them or dress up like them, we're claiming a little of that freedom for ourselves.

This touches a raw nerve in a *lot* of people. They can't handle the willingness (and, occasionally, eagerness) to take what's supposed to be child-safe, family-friendly characters and explore their implicit, sometimes blatant, sexuality (have you ever seen Minerva Mink vamp it up on *Animaniacs*?). Anthropomorphic beings combine human intellect and animal instinct just as we do—and like Zeus and the tricksters, have every right to behave like we do. Cartoon animals mimicking flirtatious human behavior is one thing; endowing them with actual sexual urges and functioning genitalia is a whole other animal.

But culture in general and entertainment in particular has grown increasingly uninhibited—and sexualized. Language and subject matter that would've been unimaginable on television a generation ago are now fodder for prime-time cartoon shows. Sexual kinks once barely whispered about are now sitcom laugh lines.

Cartoon animals aren't immune to this evolution. Things have changed since 1961, when the spiciest joke Disney could insert into *101 Dalmatians* is Pongo earning a rub on the head and "you old rascal!" from his admiring master when he returns home with ninety-nine puppies in tow. (That he's actually fathered only a handful of them safely neuters the joke.) Fast forward to 1994: a cartoon lioness is lying on her back with an unmistakable and very human do-me look in her eyes while Elton John croons "Can You Feel the Love Tonight." (On the film's DVD commentary track one of its directors boasted they had come up with "the most steamy love scene in any Disney film ever," to which his partner could only respond "Wooo!")

Had Walt been around at the time he might have vetoed the scene, but audiences didn't mind one bit; *The Lion King* was that year's number-two box office champ. (On the other hand, Mr. Disney did let Thumper get seduced into an orgasmic thumping frenzy by a voluptuous lady rabbit in 1942's *Bambi*, but unless some hitherto unseen outtake surfaces, that's as far as those particular bunnies went.) Today, *Family Guy*'s family dog Brian can sleep with human women and even father a human child without a single bestiality gag in sight. Can you blame a certain percentage of the population if our imagination travels in the same direction—or takes things further?

And there's a lot more reasons why furs identify with animals on a deeper level: a growing awareness of how a ravaged environment threatens everyone (are we any safer than that polar bear clinging to a melting ice floe?) and a way to distance ourselves from the humans who seem intent on destroying the planet; a sense of kinship with the natural world springing from alternative spiritual beliefs; and scientific research revealing animals are far more intelligent—and genetically linked to us far more closely—than we had previously imagined.

But then, it's also just fun to pretend you're someone—or something—else. For some people it might be a Hollywood celebrity, a rock star, a superhero, a pro athlete or a business tycoon, and—save for a favorite T-shirt or Halloween party—that alter ego stays closeted.

For us, it's animals: natural ones in the wild, but with human awareness and intelligence, relishing their freedom and power; imaginary ones who walk upright, sharing our world and much of our physiognomy, or living in a nearly identical but human-free anthropomorphic universe. We might draw them, watch their cartoons and read their books, roleplay them online, adopt them as our spirit animals—or wear fursuits to *become* them. We've slipped the surly bonds of reality and chosen to celebrate, not repress or ignore, our collective imagination.

Why not join us?

CHAPTER TWO

"I'm Not the Only One!"

IT WAS A FEW DAYS AFTER Halloween 1988 when the envelope—a plain white #10 with a Philadelphia return address—arrived. Inside was a single sheet of paper; on it, a drawing of festive cartoon animals. Not Disney or *Looney Tunes* celebrities either, but characters I'd never seen before, someone's personal creations.

A typical furry party flyer
Illustration courtesy of and © Peter Stoller

There was something different about them. They were somehow more *animalistic*, yet at the same time more human than the ones populating standard Hollywood cartoons, sporting realistic yet expressive animal heads on accurately drawn human bodies.

The animals wanted me to join them at something called a "furry party" at the city's annual sci-fi convention. I instantly knew, as if I'd known all along, exactly what the flyer meant:

I wasn't the only one.

There were people out there just like me, adults who liked anthropomorphic animals, animals with human qualities—and I mean *really* liked them. Not just owning a VHS of *Dumbo* or a Bugs Bunny mug they picked up at Six Flags, but people who created their own characters and believed in them, identified with them and very often, yes, wanted to *be* them.

They didn't call their anthropomorphic creations "cartoon characters" either; they called them (and as I soon learned, themselves) "furries."

I knew I had found my peer group. I was one of them. *I was a furry*—and I'd been one all along.

I finally understood why I preferred the "funny animal" comics over the superhero books that lined the shelves of my parents' candy store (that's right, I was that kid in the candy store). Why, as a ninth-grader, I pretended to be going to the library when I was really heading to see *The Sword in the Stone* (because in that pre-*Little Mermaid* era, only *babies* went to Disney movies) and relish Wart's transformation into fish, squirrel and bird. Why, as a college freshman, I'd leave the dorm one night to see *The Jungle Book* without telling my roommates.

(On my return one of them accused me of sneaking off to find a Times Square prostitute; was my furtiveness *that* obvious?) Or why, in my twenties, I enhanced the bottom of the shaggy brown socks I wore to work with circles of black electrical tape, took my shoes off under my desk, rubbed my feet on the cheap industrial carpeting and thought, "No one knows I have *paws*."

That unexpected Philadelphia letter was still fourteen years in my future, though for thousands of others, and possibly more, it would take another decade or two until they could google their most obscure interests and discover they too were furries. I was lucky—I'd gotten in on the ground floor.

I rediscovered comic books in my college years, thanks to a pal's collection of Ditko-era *Doctor Strange* stories and the underground comics of Robert Crumb and friends (very often featuring funny animals who indulged in much more adult behavior than their 1950s selves). By the mid eighties, however, the undergrounds were all but extinct, and overexposure to superheroic rock 'em, sock 'em stories left me yawning. Even so, I wasn't ready to give up on the medium; I continued to prowl the comic shops, now in search of something new and/or different.

The eighties were the age of "zines" (as in "magazines"), self-published mini-comics photocopied onto sheets of typing paper that were folded in half or quarters and sliced into individual pages. They were personal, idiosyncratic efforts capable of telling all sorts of stories— biographical, whimsical, fantastical—in tiny form.

One in particular caught my eye: *Centaurs Gatherum*, a zine devoted to fan art of those mythological creatures who straddled the human and animal worlds.

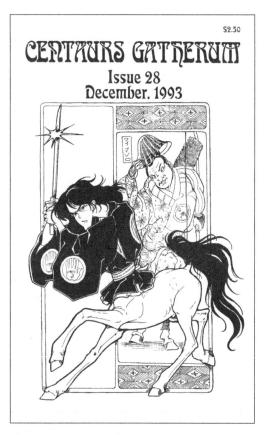

Illustration courtesy of and © Vicky Wyman

Centaurs were definitely among my furry interests, thanks to multiple *Fantasia* viewings—and in my younger days, a particularly mediocre Hercules cartoon series that burdened its hero with a bare-assed adolescent centaur sidekick who had the annoying habit of saying everything twice, *everything twice!*

Being one myself (a fan, not a centaur), I bought a copy and took out a subscription. It was a minor "I'm not the only one" moment compared to what was to follow, but a profound one nonetheless.

As I later learned, *Gatherum*'s publisher shared his subscriber list with various interested parties—which is how my name wound up in a phone-book–thick national directory of science fiction fans.

That's where Ray Rooney found it.

In the late 1980s, Ray belonged to the Philadelphia chapter of the C/FO—the Cartoon/Fantasy Organization. Animation of all stripes was screened at the group's monthly meetings, but a lot of folks were there for one genre in particular: Japanese animation, or as we know it now, anime.

Back in the day, this stylized, high-energy animation was barely a blip on the pop culture radar screen. It first gained a foothold with American audiences in the 1960s with shows like *Astro Boy, Kimba the White Lion* and *Speed Racer.* These cartoons were like nothing tube-watching baby boomers had ever seen. Their limited, almost jagged animation was more than made up for with dynamic posing and fast-paced storytelling. (Their off-kilter, equally fast-paced English dialog, a necessity of matching the replacement script's line readings to Japanese "lip flap," is being spoofed to this day.)

In the seventies, however, anime was known only to a below-the-radar fandom tired of the bargain basement Saturday morning animation of the era. In 1977 a handful of Los Angeles fans organized themselves into the first C/FO and began meeting to watch rare videos of those series. They linked up with video collectors in Japan and swapped American TV shows for anime episodes, traded tapes with Hawaiian anime fans who recorded newer series broadcast to the state's Japanese population and purchased VHS tapes from video stores in L.A.'s Japantown.

Astroboy

Kimba the White Lion

Bagi

The Amazing 3

©Tezuka Productions

Two of those early series—*Astro Boy* (known in Japan as *Tetsuwan Atomu*, "The Mighty Atom") and *Kimba the White Lion* (*Junguru Taitei*, "Jungle Emperor") were created by the legendary Osamu Tezuka. In his day Tezuka was considered the Walt Disney of Japan[7]. He drew thousands of comic book pages, becoming the country's most

---

7   An unofficial honorific inherited by Hayao Miyazaki, director of the Oscar®-winning *Spirited Away*; his films (like many of Tezuka's manga) often include humans who have been transformed into animals.

popular cartoonist and resuscitating the then-moribund art of manga.

Tezuka's drive and talent took him into Japan's at-the-time stagnant animation industry. His cinematic style and inventive storytelling wrote the anime rulebook. Tezuka also deserves credit for anime characters' signature big-eyed look—inspired, interestingly enough, by Disney's *Bambi*.[8]

A third Tezuka series isn't as well known these days. *The Amazing 3* (called *W3* in Japan) concerned three aliens who come to Earth and take on the forms of a rabbit, duck and horse, respectively, in order to study our planet. Captain Bokko (Bonnie Bunny in the English version), the trio's leader, was quite a cutie, with a narrow waist, wide hips and a puffball tail larger than her body. Characters like Bokko and Kimba (and Bagi, another Tezuka creation: a female, semi-feral, genetically engineered human-panther hybrid) began attracting cartoon animal fans (many of whom were already creating art of their own furry characters) to the C/FO screenings. Out of town anime fans began showing up too, including a Philadelphian and railroad hobbyist named Bill Thomas.

Bill was plugged into the informal network of anime collectors communicating and sharing tapes via mail. He'd been holding informal, standing-room-only screenings in his tiny Philadelphia apartment, and in 1978 he flew to L.A. and dropped in on a C/FO meeting. A year or so later, Bill launched the Philadelphia C/FO, the first chapter outside southern California, and began holding

---

8   Tezuka acknowledged Walt's animation as a major influence; the Disney studio returned the favor (unintentionally, or so they claimed) by creating a story for *The Lion King* closely paralleling Kimba's origin. *The Simpsons* took note of the similarity in one episode, animating a ghostly lion head in the night sky intoning, "you must avenge my death Kimba—I mean Simba."

monthly screenings at the Chestnut Street YWCA—screenings that also attracted Bill's fellow railroad buffs.

"There was always something of a furry connection with the [Philadelphia C/FO] chapter," longtime fur and railroad fan Mitch Marmel remembers. "At first I didn't pay much mind to it. I was there for anime stuff. One room had the furries, one room had the anime fans and one room had some guys who were into trains. "I mostly concentrated on anime and train stuff; I didn't get much into the furry thing. I was never averse to anthros though. I grew up reading Richard Scarry; I liked Bugs Bunny, Mickey Mouse comics, Daffy Duck and all that good stuff." (Exposure to a voluptuous variety of furry babes eventually turned Mitch into a full-fledged fur himself.)

"Bill wasn't really into fur—'Lordy, there go them goddamn skunk fuckers again,' he'd say in a midwestern twang. It was tongue in cheek of course; he was an anime and railroad fan, and nice enough to put up with us being in the back room. In a way he was a facilitator; the space he let us use was like a Petri dish the fandom could grow in."

Putting aside the metaphor of Furry as a mold or bacteria, the fandom did indeed begin spreading through the northeast, thanks in no small part to the Philadelphia C/FO screenings.

Meanwhile, Ray Rooney was paving the way for the very first East Coast furry gathering. Ray was both an anime and fur fan with a collection of mainstream and mini-comics featuring animal characters and definitely recognized the importance of such creations. At a 1984 gathering he met someone carrying xeroxed pages from a fan publication with the unlikely name *Rowrbrazzle*;

among them was a flyer for a furry party to be held at the upcoming San Diego Comic-Con.[9]

Ray had been considering traveling to the San Diego convention for a long time to attend the annual furry party. In 1988 he decided to make the trip—thanks to the Caped Crusader:

"Tim Burton's first Batman movie was in the works and a local museum was planning an exhibit about Batman through the decades. I had a couple of connections to the movie business back then so the museum asked me to help.

"Doing stuff by phone was difficult—people just wouldn't call back. The studio was trying to avoid connections with past silly versions, especially the sixties TV series. But I did get one callback; my mother answered the phone and found herself talking to Adam West!

"I decided I'd have to go to the West Coast to avoid a telephone brush off. Since the movie's promotion people were going to be at San Diego Comic-Con, I figured I could kill two birds with one stone: get a hold of them—and meet the people in furry fandom who I had been corresponding with or who made the art I loved."

In truth, Furry was neither a mold nor bacteria. It was a virus—one Ray would be bringing back east.

---

9 In 1988 the San Diego Comic-Con was strictly a small-bore affair held in a dilapidated downtown hotel, years away from its evolution into the pop culture mega-event it is today.

21

CHAPTER THREE

The Many Flavors of Fur

SOME FURS (and quite a few onlookers) compare ourselves to the football fans who paint themselves in their team's colors and go bare-chested in thirty-degree weather hoping to be seen on TV.

It's a not-quite-adequate comparison that only covers a single flavor of fur: the fursuiters, people who dress in full-body animal costumes. Like the football face painters, the 'suiters are the ones most likely to wind up in the media, thanks to TV directors and newspaper editors on the lookout for the most engaging visual imagery. But unlike 'suiters, the facepainters are not seen as representing football fans in general.

Those face painters are a microscopic minority—a mere handful of the 60,000 or so people who pack a football stadium on any given Sunday, versus the 59,990 there to just enjoy game. But of that 59,990 you'll find no small number of fans with their own unique interest in the sport: team loyalists who know every player's statistics by heart; memorabilia collectors whose homes overflow with dozens of knickknacks, doodads and miscellaneous items sporting their team's name; fantasy football obsessives determined to win the virtual equivalent of the Super Bowl; stadium enthusiasts who can recite the dimensions and seating capacity of every arena ever built.

It's the same way with furs. Convention fursuit parades usually attract between 20–25% of the crowd on hand, a figure that probably holds true for the fandom as a whole. In other words, if you meet a fur, there's only a one-in-four chance—at *most*—that person wears a fursuit. That means about 75% of the furry fandom express their furriness in other ways.

Take Kathy Gerbasi, for example. Kathy is a social psychologist who has been studying furries for so long (since 2006) that's she's actually turned into one. You could say her "flavor of fur" is research and study.[10]

"I have a background in what's called anthrozoology," she explains. It was her original connection to furry fandom. "It's the study of human/animal relationships—broadly construed, any way you can think about human animals interfacing with other species. In that capacity I was a moderator of an academic online discussion group. It was kind of my job to answer the questions no one else knew [the answers to].

"One day somebody posted a question, this was probably in the early 2000s: did anybody know anything about furries? Nobody answered the question, and these were all professors, grad student types. There's a resource called Psycinfo, a professional database of all the psychological

---

10 Kathy is a psychology professor at Niagara County Community College in upstate New York, not far from the Falls.

Photograph courtesy of and © Dr. Gerbasi; "Fur Science!" cover illustration by Echo of Justice

[reports and studies]. I'm like, okay, I'll Psycinfo it and enlighten somebody. So I went to Psycinfo; there was stuff about how much fur mice had and whether they were this, that or the other. It was totally not what they were looking for. There was nothing, zero research—no scientific reference whatsoever.

"I still didn't know what they were looking for. So I decided to do some research. This was back when people didn't spend all day Googling things—I just had to search and see what I could find. And I got the *Vanity Fair* article [a sensationalistic look at the fandom that appeared in a 2001 issue of the high-society magazine]. And I'm like, wow, if this article is remotely true somebody should be doing some research on this, and if it isn't true, somebody should be doing some research to say this is bullshit.

I teach at a community college and my job is not to do research—my job is to teach a whole bunch of classes, be an advisor, go to dumb committee meetings . . . But the essence of my *training* is to be an inquisitive scientist.

"I saw this as an opportunity in a very low-tech sort of way because I wasn't going to get funding from my college to do pretty much *anything*—all I needed to do was find some of these [furries] and do a survey sort of thing. I didn't need to buy a $5 million machine. Thus began a quest.

"It ebbed and flowed for a while. I didn't have really good access as to where these people were. Very, very early on, before we even had an ethics review board or anything like that, I was teaching a very small research methods class. I told the students 'there are these people called "furries" and I don't really know exactly what it means, but here's what this crazy magazine says.' We came up with a little survey and we tried to put it on a furry website. The furries had a fit, saying that we would wind up making them look bad. And, you can't blame them. So that really didn't go anywhere.

"A couple of years later, a kid at my college who is a furry ends up in my human animal relations class. I was sharing an office with his advisor at the time, and he was in our office before class signups. He had a big art portfolio with him and asked if I wanted to see his drawings. It was filled with drawings of anthropomorphic characters. I'm like, 'Oh, that looks like furry art!' He did a double take, like 'You know what furry art is?' And I'm like, '*Holy shit, I finally met a furry!*'

"I told him if he could change his schedule he could take my human-animal relations class and write a paper about furries. He jumped all over that. At the end of the semester he was graduating and asked if the college might send him to a furry convention. This was in 2006, when Anthrocon [the world's largest furry convention] was moving from Philadelphia to Pittsburgh, which is less than four hours from home. We had a limited budget, so I said, 'maybe we could get permission to go there and do some research, and you could go because you would be a helper.' Oh, he was all for that!

"I got ahold of Sam Conway, the incredible CEO of Anthrocon, and told him that I'd like to come do a survey. He said, 'Here's the deal: you can come, you can pass it out—but no one will do it.'

"As it turned out I couldn't go that year [but my student could]. A friend on the faculty went in my place, but she was only able to stay for part of the weekend . . . Still, she came home with a couple hundred surveys. I was ecstatic!"

With Conway's permission, Kathy's survey questionnaires were included in the con bags containing the convention guidebook and other goodies given to attendees at the registration counter. They wound up including the survey in the con bags for several years.

"A lot of people wouldn't look in the con bag until they get home—they're too busy enjoying the convention. But we'd see these long lines of people waiting to register. We begged, 'please, *please* let us pass out the surveys to people waiting on line.' I think they initially thought it would be obtrusive, which I can understand. But finally they said okay. And it was perfect: people are standing in line with nothing to do. That's the plan I will probably stick with until I don't know when."

Kathy didn't realize it at the time, but her transformation from objective observer to full-fledged furry was already underway.

My Secret Identity: The Fursona

We might not all wear fursuits, but just about every fur has a "fursona"—an animal alter ego to represent themselves to the fandom. It's customary, nearly mandatory, to wear a badge featuring yours at furry conventions. (And quite often, clipped to your belt, your fursona's tail as well.)

Fursona beasts aren't generic animals; they rarely resemble their real-world counterparts, and they'll never be mistaken for the average TV cartoon critter. It's hard to say if any one species populates the most badges; foxes, wolves and canines of all sort are ubiquitous, but there's no shortage of dragons (not many other reptiles however), along with felines large and small. Rodents and rabbits and otters are present, as are raccoons, birds, bears and hybrid beasts.[11] They can be dripping with muscles or bulging with fat. Attitude is all: sly, self-confident, leering, adorable, sinister.

When you adopt a fursona, you put both human species and real life name on hold: "Axikor," "Jayron," "Savanti," "Caltroplay," "Wibble," "Fulgur" all hold significance to the human behind the fursona, whether spun from thin air or borrowed from elsewhere.

---

11 According to *Fur Science!*, the 2016 International Anthropomorphic Research Project report (http://furscience.com, retrieved October 14, 2016), imaginary hybrid beasts accounted for more than half of all fursonas. The report lists the most popular hybrids (dragon/wolf, fox/tiger, etc.) and breaks down the most popular fursona animals into their respective subspecies. (e.g., A fur's fox fursona might be a red or an arctic fox, a fennec or even a mythological Japanese kitsune.) Much more about *Fur Science!* ahead.

The idea of having a fursona may have been inspired by the imaginary identities *Dungeons & Dragons* players constructed for their quests, but it truly began when artists—the earliest furs—created animal alter egos to represent themselves to each other or in their art.

The practice took root in the fandom and today it is the rare fur who does not have at least one. It's an arbitrary decision for some; for others it connects to something deep inside, something known to indigenous peoples around the world as a "power animal," a totem connecting them to a primal, spiritual source of energy and wisdom represented by a particular beast.

One such fursona belongs to "Rant," a twenty-six-year-old nurse working the night shift in a Midwest hospital. Her fursona is a pheodra—a phoenix/dragon hybrid. "Her name is 'Al-D-Natch,' which is Egyptian for Thunderstorms," Rant explains. "She evolved over the last fifteen years. When I was twelve, my friends and I loved [the video game character] Spyro the dragon and

Illustration by Voegel,
courtesy of Rant

dragons in general." The tweens loved dragons so much, in fact, they all wanted to be one. "I wanted to be a red dragon," Rant continues, "but another kid pitched a fit. He said there can't be two red dragons, and he was more 'special' so he deserved to be the red dragon.

"So the character I created, Natchy, was a red-backed, blue-fronted dragon. She looked pretty noobish so I kept going back and changing the design until I was satisfied with it. She became feathered and more organically designed. I have a deep love of birds so I chose the swallow-tailed kite as the bird base. That tail design is aerodynamically superior to others, offering the greatest speed, agility and control in the air—it's bad ass. I mixed in a velociraptor for a more 'realistic' dragon form, and the phoenix has fire-related abilities that I figured would pair well with a fire dragon.

"Personality wise, she's very much like me, or the me I want to be. I guess for lack of a better word, she's bolder. Even a little rude and honest without real-life repercussions or backlash. Outside the fandom I'm rather timid and a people-pleaser to a painful fault. I use Natchy as a mask to say and do the things I can't do in real life. She's not a super-powered fursona like many dragons you see— she's full of faults and weakness. She's more human than I am at times."

While similar themes ring true for many furs, most fursonas aren't as exotic as a dragons or phoenixes.

Take "BlueWorrior" (not a typo) for example, whose fursona seems to be a more accurate representation of his true self than any photograph.

"My fursona's name is 'Danni Taw.' It's a combination of who I am and where I'm from. It [blends] my middle name, Daniel, and 'Tawel,' the Welsh word for quiet," Blue reveals.

"Danni's a husky because I just really love huskies; simple as that, really. I was gonna go for a wolf but I decided not to because Danni doesn't really have many wolf-like characteristics. He's pretty much a distillation of who I am, taking my good and bad traits and exaggerating them: Danni is kind, understanding, sensitive and creative, but also lazy, clumsy and very emotional."

Some fursonas extend into science fiction and beyond, as in the case of "ChapterAquila92," a twenty-something member of the Canadian armed forces. He started developing his fursona as a high-school student in 2007. "My goal was to create a symbolic reflection of who I am in real life, and I think it still holds true.

"Initially, I went with a kentrosaurus [a type of dinosaur] cyborg whose bionic arm and eye were the result of some injury that I've never quite fully explained to this day, but I realized the defensive nature of that prehistoric herbivore didn't really suit me all that well.

"Then I discovered *Dungeons & Dragons*. I became intrigued by some of the aspects of bronze dragons as described in the v3.5 Monster Manual: inquisitive, fascinated by warfare, a desire for order. It left a pretty strong impression on an intelligent, structured army brat like myself.

"The bionics and the injuries that they made up for were initially an expression of how far I was willing to push myself to accomplish whatever I wanted to do and overcome obstacles that could hinder my progress. I still hold this mentality today, which is why bionics are still present on my fursona," like the robotic left arm on the

Illustration by Kojiro-Brushard, courtesy of and © ChapterAquila92

dinosaur who serves as his online avatar. "The symbolism now extends into my advocacy for the ethical forms of transhumanism[12] as well; I see a lot of good that can come out of the technologies involved with the ideology, but I'm aware of their possible abuse as well; I want to do what I can to mitigate those risks."

---

12   Wikipedia defines transhumanism as "an international and intellectual movement that aims to transform the human condition by developing and making widely available sophisticated technologies to greatly enhance human intellectual, physical and psychological capacities." "Transhumanism" (https://en.wikipedia.org/wiki/Transhumanism) Retrieved November 16, 2016.

Illustration by Lord Fenrir,
courtesy of Bob Nelson

There are no age limits on adopting a fursona; Bob "Anthrocoon" Nelson is a fifty-four-year-old radio DJ. Long before furry fandom he, like his fellow baby boomers, watched just about every cartoon from Hanna-Barbera, Warner Brothers and others on TV back in the day.

"I knew a cartoonist named Don Fields who drew a character called Shmuck-O Rat. I don't think Don considered himself a furry, but he said something like 'Shmuck-O is in *Giant Shanda Animal* from Shanda Comics.' I sent away for it and when it came back there was a flyer with it for Albany Anthrocon.

"I was already doing a personal fanzine called *Raccoon Times*; I like drawing raccoon characters, they're probably my favorite species. I had a little bit of everything I thought was interesting in there: my travels, CD reviews, a few furry comics and a friend tossed in some movie reviews. I wrote a short story or two—one was about a man landing on a planet of giant raccoons—and I reviewed furry comics *like Shanda, Hey Neeters!, Mad Raccoons* and so on.

"I'd already done a fanzine about giant and tiny people and animals in fact and fiction. Since I like raccoons and was getting a bit into the furry fandom I figured I could connect the two. Originally I called myself Rac Cooney but changed it later to Anthrocoon, a play on Anthrocon and man-raccoon. I use the screen name 'raccoonradio' because I'm into both.

"When the [Anthrocon] convention heard I called myself Anthrocoon they let me in for free two years in a row. I've been to every single one since then, and I've had a great time at all of them. When [I'm away] someone else hosts my show [and I've] called in from both Anthrocon and Furpocalypse to do live reports. [I've] also played songs like 'Try Everything' from *Zootopia,* of course."

An animal fursona expresses an inner, often truer self- -but sometimes it takes a while to discover who that beast really is. When I first joined the fandom I figured I needed a fursona of my own—but what? For quite a few years I considered myself a bear. I was fairly husky at the time and their ability to switch from a four-legged stance to an upright, humanlike posture (not to mention that luxurious head-to-toe fur coat) appealed to me. Then I grew a beard, let my hair grow out and became a lion.

Finally it was time for a badge. I went to Jim Groat (aka "Rabbi Tom,") one of the first furs, a "greymuzzle" (the term for an older furry) like myself whose furry roots go back to the dawn of the fandom. Jim is an accomplished cartoonist—not to mention instigator, troublemaker, ringleader, organizer of garage-roof Smurf baseball games and late-night White Castle runs. His fursona is, of course, a goat. You can see him done up in fancy Old West duds getting shoved out of a dance-hall chair in 1993's *Tombstone*.

"Jim, can you do a badge of me as a lion?" Groat the goat takes one look at me and says, "No, Joe, that's not you," and proceeds to draw me as an alligator—a glasses-wearing, goateed gator with lengthy jaws, holding a camcorder (I was never without one back in the day) and sporting an amused sneer. It was me, the essence of me. It turned out I already had a fursona—my inner reptile. But how did Jim know? For that matter, how did my niece Sammi know back before the fandom even existed? She could still count her age on the fingers of one hand, when out of the blue one day she told me, "You're an alligator!" ("Watch out, I bite!" I snapped back.)

Perhaps they both knew something about me, something I had yet to learn.

Illustration by Jim Groat/Rabbi Tom, courtesy of and © the author

The Hobbyist vs. the Lifestyler

Or, how seriously do you take Furry? Is it a hobby you indulge in occasionally but don't take particularly seriously? Or is it an interest to the point of an obsession that all but defines you—*literally* the style in which you live your life?

At best, "lifestyler" is an amorphous term that still carries negative connotations within the fandom. Perhaps a few questions will reveal whether or not you're a lifestyler; the more you answer "yes" (particularly to the later questions) the more likely you are one. Do you:

- have a fursona
- collect or draw furry art
- attend the occasional furry convention
- own a fursuit
- commission artists to create furry art to your specifications
- decorate your living space with furry art or images of your fursona animal
- live with or do almost all of your socializing with other furs
- chat online with other furs as your fursona
- wear your fursuit around the house
- own *several* fursuits
- attend more than two or three furry conventions per year
- think of yourself interchangeably or simultaneously as your human self and your fursona . . .

You probably get the idea. The concept of a furry lifestyle originated in the mid-1990s on alt.fan.furry, a Usenet board, in its day Discussion (not to mention Argument) Central for the furry community.[13] The hobbyists (mostly artists) weren't particularly fond of people who took it *too far*, in their humble opinion; your obsession makes the more "normal" of us look bad, they said.

Furry fandom was born of a cluster of sci-fi, animation and funny animal fans and cartoonists. Furs who wanted to talk about what Furry meant to them personally, not just who drew the sexiest vixens or whether *The Rescuers Down Under* was better than *The Rescuers*, were "encouraged" via a quaint Internet custom known as a flame war to start their own message board—which they did.

Thus alt.lifestyle.furry was born. The new group's charter described "furry lifestyle" as:

> *a definition [encompassing] a broad range of activities, interests and beliefs. Such topics include, but are not limited to, animal identities, alter egos and spirit guides, the wearing and making of fursuits, collars and other furry clothing, plush toys, theriomorphosis,[14] and general philosophical discussion—and the personal experience of being furry: socially, sexually and psychologically.[15]*

---

13 "Alt" stood for "alternative," as in alternative points of view and subject matter. Usenet groups are all but extinct, replaced by Facebook, Twitter and other social media platforms.

14 "Theriomorphosis" is not to be found in the dictionary. Dictionary.com defines "theriomorphic" as "thought of or represented as having the form of beasts"; in all likelihood "theriomorphosis" refers to the idea of assuming the form of an animal.

15 "Alt.lifestyle.furry" WikiFur. (http://en.wikifur.com/wiki/alt.lifestyle.furry). Retrieved November 1, 2016.

It's interesting to note in 1996 little of the above, apart from fursuiting were considered legitimate forms of furry self-expression by the furs of the day. Twenty years later the furry umbrella has opened wide, far wider than they could have imagined—or wanted.

Not that they had any choice in the matter. No one is in charge of Furry: there's no governing body, no test to pass, no membership dues to pay. Basically, anyone who wants to call themselves a fur or a furry, be they a hobbyist or lifestyler, is free to do so.

In fact, the distinction between hobbyist and life-styler has blurred to the point of invisibility. It's no longer a straight-line progression from hobbyist to full-fledged lifestyler, but a pick-and-choose shopping list to determine not your degree of furriness, but rather, your *unique* furriness.

Perhaps the most unique example of this is Boomer the Dog.

Boomer made me nervous. A far as I was concerned, he's one of those furs who "takes it too far," who makes the rest of us look ridiculous with his creepy shredded paper dog suit and dreamy, almost simple-minded smile. Somehow he's all over the media; in fact, he may be one of the better known furs out there.

He's been seen on TV trying (without success so far) to have his name legally changed to Boomer the Dog. His website boomerthedog.net has links to his numerous video appearances and media articles, scads of photographs of him all dogged up and several pages where he explains himself and his canine interests.

Boomer was the focus of *Fursonas*, a 2016 documentary about the fandom that earned mainstream attention

Photograph courtesy of and © Boomer the Dog

when it played at the Slamdance Film Festival. He was also the subject of a Bill O'Reilly segment and appeared in a high-profile *Dr. Phil* episode.

What changed my mind and made me respect him wasn't his *Dr. Phil* appearance, but what came afterwards.

Boomer appeared on "Animal Obsessed," a 2014 *Dr. Phil* episode which began with a bit of stand-up by the good doctor. "You may learn something today from our guests who say they are obsessed . . . with different animals." A video of his dog appears on the screen behind him, evoking a heartwarming "awww" from the mostly female audience. "I love her, we're very close, and she is family."

The video is replaced by a photograph of Dr. Phil's face . . . photoshopped onto the dog's head. "But never once have I wanted to *be* her!" The audience bursts into laughter while the camera seeks out several women who look particularly shocked.

Boomer's appearance is bracketed by a woman who treats her pet rabbits like her children and a mother upset that her daughter is a furry, but Boomer is the episode's centerpiece. His ruddy face is framed by bangs covering his forehead and, except for two loops resembling dog ears pinned atop his head, cascades of chest-length hair. Around his neck is a dog collar sporting a bone-shaped tag.

Dr. Phil's discomfort while interviewing Boomer[16] is palpable, perhaps magnified by Boomer's serene self-confidence. "If anyone at home is still watching the show today," he says nervously, "a lot of them are thinking that you're weird."

"I know what I look like to the outside world," Boomer responds. "I think a good word is 'eccentric.'"

"Whatever floats your boat, as long as you're not hurting someone else," Dr. Phil magnanimously offers before asking, "Do you consider yourself what's called a 'furry?'" There we are, I sigh, all of us defined by this . . . "eccentric" character in his paper dog suit.

Sure enough, Boomer admits: "Furry is the scene that I'm in. I found it after I discovered I was a dog and I kind of fit in there." After quizzing Boomer about his penchant for eating "disgusting" dog food out of a dish ("I do, once in a while," he tells Phil. "I tried kibble but I prefer canned food") Phil asks, "Do you date?"

---

16   Two clips from the interview (featuring video of Boomer gallivanting about his neighborhood in his shaggy paper dog suit) can be seen on Dr. Phil's website at http://www.drphil.com/shows/2191/. (Retrieved December 26, 2016.)

"I don't date. I've never been on a date, ever," Boomer answers unapologetically.

"Sure, go figure," is Dr. Phil's sympathetic response.

The next link on Boomer's website goes to a Jimmy Kimmel show segment featuring Dr. Phil. Kimmel asks him if he's ever rejected any of the "nuttier" ideas for guests on his show. No, he answers, but "there are a few things I did that I wish I hadn't [aired. My staff said] we can't be serious every day, we have to lighten things up, so we have a guy who thinks he's a dog."

Dr. Phil grows flustered remembering Boomer. "He didn't, I guess he goes out in the yard, I don't know. We had the guy on and . . . " he ends his sentence with a face palm and an "Oh my God . . . "

"You have no tolerance for that guy," Kimmel sagely observes.

"And then we had an adult baby on," Dr. Phil continues. "If I could erase two shows from the vault it would be those two." The Kimmel clip ends with an in-studio surprise: a guy in a saggy, baggy, long-eared open-face dog suit, and a second wearing nothing except a diaper and a baby bonnet, crawl across the stage on their hands and knees.

Boomer's next link connects to Jimmy Fallon doing his top-of-the-show monologue setting up Dr. Phil's appearance later. "He's a doctor, he talks about serious issues, the stuff we want to learn more about. Well, this week he had a guy on who likes to pretend that he's a dog. Check it out." A few clips of Boomer follow, beginning with one of him standing upright in what looks like his attic, wearing his paper dog suit and waving his front paws. Goofy, polka-type music plays in the background, most likely a

Fallon add-on. The last clip is Boomer saying "I've never been on a date, ever."

Back on camera, Fallon has a smirk on his face wide enough to bridge continents. "See, ladies, there are interesting single guys out there . . . Even Sarah McLachlan is like 'this is too sad for me.'"

Both shows went out of their way to mock and humiliate Boomer. Personally, I would never link my website to these kinds of follow-ups to something I had done on TV—but Boomer has.

You have to be extremely comfortable with who you are to share this kind of stuff about yourself with people—and to be unperturbed by the mockery.

Boomer has never let others' opinions of him deter his fascination, even when he was a kid. It was watching Dean Jones vanish under layers of special effects sheepdog fur in Disney's *The Shaggy D.A.* that first intrigued the eleven-year-old Boomer (then Gary) with the idea of being a dog, or turning into one. (Boomer and I communicated via email; in his messages the word "Dog" was always capitalized.)

"I made different Dog masks out of paper, mop strings stapled onto paper, fur from coats and old stuffed toys that had been trashed. I'd put them on and play Dog after school, before my parents came home, then I'd hear someone at the door and rush to put the masks away.

"I started out wanting to be like Elwood [*The Shaggy D.A.*'s canine star]. I could see that as the breed to transform into, and imagined it in the weeks after seeing the movie—and after that too, when I was playing Dog and transformation. I was also the Dalmatian Pongo [from Disney's *101 Dalmatians*], or at least I used the name, [as well as] Muffin and a few other Dogs. I guess I was switching around, finding myself. Then *Here's Boomer* came out."

Here's Boomer aired on NBC from 1980 through 1982. The series was sort of a canine version of *The Fugitive* or *Kung Fu,* with Boomer travelling from town to town, helping people with their problems before moving on at the end of the episode.

"I think I related to Boomer most because he was a tramp Dog, a vagabond traveling the country, and I related to that where I was at the time—thinking of being away from family and on the road. Other Dogs like Elwood and Pongo were decidedly family Dogs, so I switched to the name Boomer, and his breed, Pyrenean Shepherd, which is a kind of Sheepdog after all. I felt at home there and never changed afterwards."

While Boomer is the name he's adopted for himself, his shredded paper sheepdog suit has a name all its own, a very logical one: Papey.

"When I went to a convention in Papey for the first time, it got a good reception, better than I anticipated. I thought it would be a funny take on a suit to other furs, but many people thought it was a clever idea. The difference from what other furs have is part of the story, a DIY 'punk rock' ethic. I did it on the cheap, and it's like no other costume. I like that it could be considered trash materials, while at the same time to me it's worth a million bucks for all of the fun, connections and goodwill it's generated.

"In my town people love it, and when I go out, especially on Halloween, I have the greatest time meeting the neighbors in my Dog suit. Papey is a touchstone for people; he's been a pivotal connection with others and the media with me being a Dog. I give Papey a lot of credit for bridging the gap between my Doggishness and other folks. It will start conversations when I go out and I'm not in Papey. On the street or at the supermarket, people will start talking to me about the costume. It happens frequently, and some [people] are so supportive."

Boomer's first inkling of furry fandom was a 1997 newspaper article about the increasing number of special interest conventions. "They mentioned 'anthropomorphic conventions, anything having to do with animals with human characteristics.' [I] didn't have a computer at that time, and I didn't know how to find out more about it. I concluded it must be a scientific conference; it had to be different than my personal take on being Dog. I'd been doing art, wearing Dog collars and broadcasting about it on my [Internet] radio show, and I never heard from anyone else who really related to it. Later that year I went to a gallery show of Dog paintings. A friend asked about it and I explained they were portraits that the artist had painted Dog heads over the people's faces. My friend said, 'There are these people online called furries.' We looked at them at his house; it was exciting, and I was online in days!"

On his website Boomer tried to answer the people who ask: "Why are you a dog?"

"It's one of the hardest questions, and it's something I've been trying to figure out myself. If you're a Human, think about how hard [it would be] to answer if you were asked, 'Why are you a Human?' The question is just too big if you think deeply about it."

I tell him it wouldn't be hard at all for me to answer to the question; I'd simply quote Lady Gaga, "I was born this way," no big deal, nothing existential to think about.

I was not expecting him to quote Lady Gaga back to me: "She says 'everybody put your paws up' in that song too.

"I've tried to figure out why I'm a Dog over the years. I've gone soul searching about why and what the point of it might be. I've had conversations with several Therians and know some Weres,[17] and yeah, I connect, but haven't really gotten into those communities. It used to be easier to find them too; now there's not as much information out in the open. They've had their share of media attention and I think they're laying low.

"When I found furries in 1997 there were lifestyler discussions going on pretty openly, and I was enjoying the mix with the fandom. I was at the point where I wasn't just wondering about being a Dog; I was interested in doing more things with it. I was probably farther along than those who come in now with more nebulous feelings of being another animal and are looking for others who are being creative with their knowledge about themselves. I met others on similar paths right away. I was kind of hooked in by that."

There was a particularly rough patch in Boomer's journey from adolescence to adulthood, the kind of thing TV's Boomer might've helped him with had he actually existed.

"Early on when I called myself a Dog or behaved like one, adults didn't care too much. They probably saw it as a kid's imagination, but I kept doing it and it went against adult expectations as I got older. A big deal was made about how wrong it was to want to be a Dog. I didn't

---

17 Therians believe they have an animal soul or spirit and have been born into a human body in error; "weres" are shapeshifters of various species, not just wolves.

45

believe it—how could it be wrong to want to be such a wonderful creature? I knew of other students getting in trouble with smoking or with girls, or guys in upper grades dropping out. I just wanted to be a Dog. What could be so wrong with that? It's a victimless crime. I saw it as hypocrisy, the big people wanting you to be good—but not if you want to be a friendly tail-wagging Dog!

"At home I was fighting with my dad over everyday things: my behavior and the future, everything colliding . . . It's the people who are most in your life making the biggest fuss, asking big questions, [and] not giving you a way out. . . . Maybe adults can handle the hard questions, but I just clammed up.

"When things got really rough at school I ran away with one of my Dog buddies and stayed away all day without catching the bus. The next week the school took me to Western Psych for evaluation. I was there for weeks while they tried to find out what was going on and straighten me out."

"I ran away with one of my Dog buddies..." Boomer's recollection brought to mind something he had said earlier: "I think I related to Boomer most because he was a tramp Dog, a vagabond traveling the country, and I related to that where I was at the time—thinking of being away from family and on the road."

Western Psych failed to "straighten" Boomer out. Today Boomer is happily Boomer—so happy he can laugh at the Dr. Phils and the Kimmels and the Fallons of the world, embracing and dissolving their condescension by putting their insults on his website. "I thought it was funny and people would get a kick out of it. Plus fans come to my site and they want to see stuff like that too. I want to be open-minded, letting people speak for themselves. I think it's something people like about my story, and it's good for me too, like a Triumph of the Pooch. Most Dogs are direct and open and I feel that way too."

Boomer, the human being once known as Gary, doesn't have a tail, but his inner self, Boomer the Pyrenean Shepherd does—and it's safe to say it's probably wagging right now.

Nature or Nurture

Are furs born or made?

Judging from the non-scientific, anecdotal information I've gathered (i.e., the furs I've asked, not to mention my own experience), definitely the former. In story after story, furs have described a fascination or identification with animals that preceded their discovery of furry fandom. They all experienced a similar sense of validation upon discovering the fandom: they weren't alone. Their personal interest in something their peers wouldn't understand or approve of didn't isolate them from the world after all—it connected them to one.

Eddie and Marty Lee were furry before they even got into kindergarten. Twin brothers from Central Illinois, they're now sixty and furrier than ever. I've seen them at a couple of conventions—they're hard to miss: identically dressed in shorts and matching T-shirts, pushing a shopping cart overflowing with small stuffed animals, wearing shaggy fox ears.

Marty created his first fursona when he was four years old: a fox named Foxxy. "I can remember, this is way before kindergarten," Eddie recalls before Marty jumps in to continue the story.[18] "Kids don't have to be trained to have their temper tantrums: fall on your belly, stomp the hands, kick the feet on the floor . . . I threw a tantrum fit because I didn't have a tail." (A handkerchief attached to the back of his pants served as a temporary substitute.)

Like many furs of their generation, the brothers credit exposure to the then continually screened-on-TV *Looney Tunes* as setting them on their furry path, along with a particular comic book superhero. "We had some comic books and one hero that turned out to our favorite was Beast Boy," a green-skinned DC Comics character able to transform himself into any animal he wished.

"We were into him when the animated Disney *Jungle Book* came out in 1967. We got the movie coloring book and the comic book and other *Jungle Book* stuff for Christmas. We wore the comic book out, and we when we colored Mowgli in the coloring book we always made him green with dark-green hair—Beast Boy colors instead of human colors. The Hulk was green too—the right color, but he was too muscular and didn't change shape." At least, not from human to animal as Beast Boy could.

"I looked off and on for that Beast Boy comic for years but never could find it—then the Teen Titans brought him back. They advertised the show: Robin, Starfire, Raven, Cyborg . . . and Beast Boy. Bingo!"

The brothers play-acted as animals for years, imagining being, or like Beast Boy, turning into foxes, horses and even centaurs, their discovery of fandom still decades away. It wasn't until they well into their forties, a few

---

18 At least I think it was Marty. The brothers sound so similar over the phone it was sometimes hard to tell their voices apart, and as twins are known to do, they occasionally completed each other's thoughts or took turns telling the story.

months into owning their first computer in 2001 when they finally had their "We're not the only ones!" moment.

"It was a Saturday night," Marty remembers. "I was watching *Inyuasha* and searching the Internet. I put in 'fantasy, wolf' on the computer. It took me to a site called Elfenwood and a picture of a Native American with a wolf head on him. I said, 'That looks cool,' and the people on the site said, 'Well, he's a furry.' There was all sorts of art on that website, but I said, 'Let's type that in and see what this "Furry" is—I hope there's more.'"

There was a lot more. Marty and Eddie had finally connected with furry fandom. "I said, 'Brother, you know the pictures we drew in high school? Those were furries! The head's like an animal's, they talk like humans, but they're animals.'"

The brothers found their way to Second Life, a popular online virtual world. They marveled at the anthropomorphic animal avatars with which they could represent themselves in the virtual realm. "I said 'I'd like to wake up tomorrow morning and look like that cute fox.'" A fox suit followed not long after and Marty's wish came true: he was now "Foxxy" for (more or less) real, while Eddie became a Texas Red Wolf with the easy to remember name "Wolfie."

Like me, Eddie and Marty are old enough to be fathers of most of the furs at a given convention, and grandfathers to quite a few as well. Do they ever get funny looks from the younger generation?

"Some of them are surprised. They say, 'You're that old and you're a furry?' But seems to us that at the conventions we're all on the same wavelength; age doesn't matter that much to furries."

In fact, being a couple of greymuzzles does have its advantages. "We are retired now and oh," the brothers exult, "that's the best thing in life that ever happened. It's even better than childhood because you got money to do stuff. When you're a kid, you got the time, then school slows you down, but you ain't got the money to get this and that and this, and parents ain't very reliable to do what you want.

"Once we started working in the real world we lived off my paycheck and Foxxy's went all into savings. We ended up putting too much money away and we got to retire three years early."

Some furs know from the day they were born that they're part of the animal kingdom. If there was ever someone who without a doubt was born furry, it's Chaston.

"When I was two or three, my mom told me I would act like a cat. I'd go around the house meowing, I'd curl up on family members' laps. One day in middle school a friend of mine said 'I drew something that made me think of you.'

"It was an anthropomorphic cat [and I thought it was really cool]. She just said it was anthropomorphic art—[art of] animals that are like humans. She never mentioned anything about it being furry. It's kind of funny that when I was smaller I always acted like a cat, then years later a friend drew me as one."

Not only was Chaston born furry, he gave off an unmistakable furry vibe that pulled other furs into his orbit.

"I finally learned about furry fandom when I was a freshman in college. I was talking with a guy I met when I noticed the background picture on his phone was an anthropomorphic animal; once again an anthro animal popped up in my life. He said it was his character, and I'm like, 'Character? Are you in a play or something?' He's like, 'No, I'm in the furry fandom.'

"We sat in a restaurant until the place closed talking all night about furry fandom. Two weeks later I had my fursona: Chaston [a lion/tiger hybrid]."

As it turned out, Chaston didn't have to tell his family he was furry; they found out on their own.

"I was having dinner at my mom's house when she said, 'Explain Furry to me.' And I'm like, 'How did you hear about Furry?' She said my dad repeated something he heard from my aunt, that I was worshipping Satan. My mom said it was a bunch of crap—my dad's side of the family are all bible thumpers."

Chaston's mom heard from his dad that an aunt had told him his son was worshipping Satan. (Who, let's not forget, is often depicted as half-human, half-goat, a blending of human and animal—in other words, *a furry!*). But how did this daisy chain of semi-hysterical gossip originate?

"I guess my aunt saw some furry artwork online or a mention of the convention I'd been to recently. Since it's not something she agrees with, it automatically goes to Satan." But still, how did she find out her nephew was a furry? "Ah, it was on my Facebook page. Everyone else in my life—friends, co-workers, my bosses, all those people—all of them know I'm a furry. Actually, I've gotten half of the people at work to start meowing at my bosses—it's hilarious. I'm slowly turning my entire workplace into a bunch of furries."

Either that or Satanists—including his mom.

"I was actually out to everyone else before my family found out, so I wasn't 100% sure how they'd take it. After my mom found out she's bugged me several times—in a good way! She wants to go to our local furry convention, IndyFurCon. She's like, 'I want to go and experience it. I want to see all the fursuits. I want to see everything.' My dad still hasn't come around. He just kind of looks the other way. . . . We'll discuss everything else we normally talk about, we just won't bring that part up."

Chaston isn't the only fur to talk about "coming out" as furry to friends and family. I've been there myself. It can be hard to talk about because it's "strange." It's something intimate and personal—not necessarily on a sexual level, but in terms of one's identity.

"My fiancée and I talked about it," Chaston continues. "I love the art, the literature, all of that, but one of the biggest things that drew me into the fandom happened at one of the first cons I went to. I didn't know anybody, yet everyone was so friendly, and the fact that every con is based around a charity shows how much people care. At Midwest FurFest last year, the charity was like $1,000 short of the goal. Everybody started going up to the stage, putting money on the stage and within ten minutes we had raised another, I think, $7,000.

"That's what I'm all about. I'm a very caring person, and to be in a place with so many people that are so caring and giving and loving—it makes the world go round."

Judging from its cover, *Fur Science!* looks like a furry comic, with a blue-and-white cat and a brown bunny, both in lab coats, gleefully leaping away from an explosion just behind them. If you read the subtitle, however, it's actually a scientific report: *A Summary of Five Years of Research from the International Anthropomorphic Research Project.* Its 165 pages are filled with facts and figures, charts and definitions of and about furry fandom, based on "the systematic study of more than 15,000 furries over the past decade."

Courtney N. Plante is one of the four authors of the report, along with Kathy Gerbasi, Stephen Reysen of Texas A&M University and Sharon E. Roberts from Canada's University of Waterloo. Courtney is also a fur who goes by the name of Nuka.

"As far as furries go, I'm a pretty boring one," he claims. "I grew up watching *Pokémon* and absolutely loved Mewtwo. I thought he looked so cool, especially in the movie when he had all those wires and technology on him.

I spent hours online looking for tutorials on how to draw Mewtwo, finding Mewtwo fan art and all sorts of fanfiction that featured Mewtwo. Eventually, I stumbled on an old webcomic called 'Scured' that featured anthropomorphic cat characters.[19] I liked them because, well, they sorta reminded me of Mewtwo. The main character's name in the comic was Nuka, a bratty and mischievous child who could shoot fire from his hands. I thought the name was cute, and I liked the character, so it became my nickname online."

Like so many furs, Nuka was fascinated by anthropomorphic characters before discovering a fandom existed for people like him.

"I didn't consider myself a furry then—I didn't even know what a furry was. In fact, for all of junior high, high school and undergrad, I admired fan art of anthro cat characters and Mewtwo characters and spent a lot of my time

---

19   The *Scrued* website's last update was in 2003.

in chat rooms full of people with anthro animal avatars, but had never heard the term 'furry.' It wasn't until my last year of undergrad when a classmate noticed the wallpaper on my laptop and said, 'Oh, you're a furry too!' I was like, 'What's a furry?' He dragged me out to a local furry meet. That's when I started calling myself a furry."

Fur Science! reveals furry fandom's astonishing growth has turned it into a largely young peoples' fandom: 75% of furs are under the age of twenty five, and 55% of those are between eighteen and twenty-five years old. By contrast, only 9% of furs are willing to call themselves "greymuzzles," their average age just over forty two. (Marty, Eddie and I have probably collectively upped that average by several years.)

Furry is, by its very nature, a gathering of people who have a strong identification or fascination with animals, an "alternative" to conventional attitudes, and as such, welcoming to folks whose attitudes and values differ from the population at large. Straight folk still make up the majority of furs, but they're a less of a pronounced majority. *Fur Science!* states that furs are "approximately seven times more likely to be predominantly or exclusively homosexual than the general population," with a much greater proportion of men than women exclusively gay. The percentages of gay, bisexual and transgender people in the fandom, while still in the minority, are significantly greater than in other fandoms. The report claims the gender split in the fandom is 72% male to 27% female (with 1% declaring themselves exclusively neither)—but judging from the crowds I see at the conventions I'd round it out to a 70/30 split.

Of course, when covering a topic as intriguing as Furry, one might just be swept up into the fandom like

Kathy Gerbasi, the furry researcher you met earlier

"I had to get a badge because everybody had badges. My husband and I had a rescue dog we loved—half Basset, half Springer—named Sparky, aka the Sparkster. He passed away on Easter in 2011; that year the Anthrocon theme was The Anthropomorphic Institute of Magic. I had my computer with me [at the con] and there was a picture of Sparky on it. I showed it to an artist who used it to make my first badge: Sparky coming out of a magician's hat. I loved it.

"Then a couple years later I had pictures of both my dogs with me. One is kind of a shaggy wire terrier, sort of orange and white, and another one is a Brussels griffon/pug mix. So I went to this lovely artist, showed her both of their pictures and asked if she could sort of mesh them into one face for me. That was my second badge.

"I think it was 2009 or maybe 2010. I was at the reception [the con has] for dealers in the art show when I saw a small flamingo sculpture. My husband, who's a pediatrician, collects flamingo things, so when the art show opened I bid on the flamingo.

"I'd been advised that if you want to be sure you don't get outbid you stand by your bid as they're closing the art show on Sunday. While I was standing there guarding my flamingo bid, I saw a fur suit on the table. The asking price was $300, but no one had bid on it yet. It was just a partial: a head, tail, front and back paws. But it was a dog. That's key.

"Remember, this is about 2010; I didn't know as much then as I do now. No one had bid on it, [so I started to wonder if] there was something wrong with it. People said no, there's nothing wrong with it, but nobody wants a fursuit unless it was made for them, so unless it looks exactly like what they want, they're not going to bid on it. I thought it would be a good idea to get a fur suit, just to see what it's like to wear one—scientifically speaking, of course.

"While I was protecting my flamingo bid, I bid the minimum $300 for the partial. Nobody outbid me, so I won the fursuit—and the flamingo for my husband who keeps it in his office. (When I go to Anthrocon he takes care of our four rescue dogs.)

"I didn't have a chance to make a body for [the suit] for a while because my middle kid was getting married the next summer, and there was a lot going on. But by 2012 I thought, 'This thing needs a body. I can sew, so I will make one,' which I did.

"If the partial hadn't had been a dog, I probably wouldn't have bothered. It was a couple years after Sparky had died, but he was just black and white; it would have been fairly easy to make a color palette like his basset/springer mix. Now, our rescue dogs are Dooley, who is mostly black and some silver; Curly, who is orange and white; Mon-T-Zoomer, kind of tan with black and white; and Huckleberry, the dog of many colors: brown, black, silver and tan with orange and black stripes on his belly. And they all have floppy ears; all of our dogs have been floppy-eared. The partial's head was a short-eared Corgi. [But I knew what it needed.] Floppy ears.

"I made new ears for it: big, black, floppy ears just like Sparky had had. Much better, but the orange head and the all-white body I made for it was not quite right. I got fabric paint and changed the color. I added black to the head, the feet and the body. It looked great—except for the tail. So I made a new tail.

"Now I had a suit, but it still needed a name. You see all these badges [at cons and meetups] with really clever fursona names—so it couldn't be any old name. It had to be something special.

"Then I remembered I'd seen a list on a website with the names of all of Pavlov's dogs. Oh my God, oh my goodness! I spent two or three days searching like heck until I found a cached copy.

"My dad was born in Italy. His middle name was Ralph and my family nickname is also Ralph, so I wanted some kind of Roman name, something with Italian flavor—but with some Pavlov-ey thing going on. So, instead of Ralph, I went with Raphael. But wordplay, gotta have wordplay! So instead of Augustus, which I think was the name of one of Pavlov's dogs, I made it Dogustus. Now my fursuit had a name: Raphael Dogustus.

"I was finally in business—I had a suit, it had a name. It was a guy's name, but it didn't matter. That was one of the first things my team told me when they returned from Anthrocon in 2006: You can be talking to someone in a fursuit and you think it's a guy inside, but it's a girl—or vice versa. That just blew everybody away.

"Now I had to actually go and wear [the fursuit] . . . I was going to be in the Anthrocon fursuit parade. Oh my God, I hate to be hot. I can't even tell you how much I hate to be hot, but I said, 'I'm going to do it,' and I did.

"Later I watched video of the parade, and there I was, there's Dogustus. That's me . . . and I was dancing! I am not a dancing person. But this creature is dancing. It's so cool; you can do something that you wouldn't normally do, and it's okay!

"Two years later, I wore [the fursuit] there when they

were going for the Guinness World Record for the most people in a fursuit parade. I said, "Oh, I've got to contribute to this." In 2015 the parade had moved outside and, oh my gosh, that looked like so much fun! So the next year Raphael returned for the parade.

"I made a bunch of prizes for him to distribute to kids and whomever along the parade route. I used the vending machine capsules we give our survey prizes in and put a ribbon in each one. I could hide one in my paw and when they thought I was shaking hands, I'd give them a prize instead. People of all ages loved it!

"I think 2016 was the biggest fursuit parade up to that point, and I was really busy with research responsibilities, so I arrived at the assembly area just in time to get in the back of the line—and we were still waiting in line when the people up front had completed the parade. Without the head and paws, and with the suit unzipped, I could keep fairly cool waiting to march, but when I finished the parade I was flaming red. I think it will be a couple years before poor Raphael gets into another parade!

Photograph courtesy of and © Dr. Gerbasi

CHAPTER FOUR

A Fandom Is Born

JUST OFF TRASK AVENUE in Garden Grove, California, there exists a large ranch house that looks, more or less, like any of the other large ranch houses lining the street. There is one difference, however: An enormous tree stump at least ten feet tall stands in the middle of its front lawn. A sign affixed to it depicts a weasel-like animal in a high-stepping Michigan J. Frog pose, sporting a top hat and diamond-tipped cane, with a pair of antennae sprouting from his head. He's framed above and below by the words "PRANCING SKILTAIRE."

"Skiltaires are an alien species I created, based on Earth weasels and other mustelids. They're semi-biped, have a natural electro-generative 'battery,' electrostatic range sensing and a kind of tele-empathy. I created them in 1969 when I was in high school because I was tired of all the aliens in science fiction that were just slightly different humans—and I happened to really like weasels.

Rod O'Riley, Mark Merlino and a Skiltaire
Photograph by the author

"When I was a kid one of our popular rainy day activities in school was to watch Disney's *In Beaver Valley* from their True Life Adventure series. The cool thing about the movie wasn't the beavers—it was the otters. I'd never seen animals that appeared to be playful on purpose. They seemed to just enjoy the heck out of living. You don't think of that with wild animals, you think there's always a struggle going on, they're always hunting or being hunted. Here's a big group of animals, several families, all sliding down slopes in mud or snow and just having an absolute *ball* with each other, just crazy fun."

The speaker is Mark Merlino who, together with his partner Rod O'Riley, owns the house known as The Prancing Skiltaire, their home for more than thirty years. It's the only house on the street (and most likely in all of Garden Grove) with its own name, inspired by a friend's fondness for English pubs and a nod to *The Lord of the Ring*'s Prancing Pony inn. Inside the sprawling five-bedroom house furry art and literature abound: on the walls, on the bookshelves and atop end tables while DVDs of animated features fill a shelf next to the TV.

Someday there may be an historical marker attached to a tree stump as well, an engraved brass plaque reading, "Home of Mark Merlino and Rod O'Riley, creators of Furry Fandom." An exaggeration perhaps—a blending of cartoon animal, anime and science-fiction fans with overlapping interests in anthropomorphic characters birthed our fandom. But Mark and Rod delivered—and named—the baby.

Just about every fur has an early memory of a cartoon, book or movie that activated their furry gene. For no small number of 1970s kids, it was Disney's all-animal *Robin Hood*.[20] For baby boomer Mark it was seeing *Bambi* at the tender age of four, transfixed by the talking animal inhabitants of its watercolor-painted forest. A childhood devouring animal-themed comics and cartoons followed, with Mark spending many a school lunch period discussing yesterday's *Kimba* episode with his fellow cartoon nerds.

It was inevitable that Mark would find his way into the world of sci-fi fandom and its numerous conventions, beginning with Equicon, a *Star Trek*-themed convention in 1971.

Every con has a "dealers' room," anywhere from hotel-suite to convention-hall size. The vibe is more like an exotic, sometimes ramshackle bazaar than twenty-first century shopping mall. Merchants stand behind tables loaded with action figures, prop weapons, bootleg videos, T-shirts and boxes of vintage comic books. Not just superhero comics, either, but boxes filled with the war, romance and "funny animal" comic books that long ago fell out of favor with readers.

It was over those last boxes Mark accumulated more friends who shared his interest in cartoons and anthropomorphic animals. In 1980, at the Loscon 7 sci-fi convention in Anaheim, California, Mark met a fellow sci-fi/animation/funny animal fan who became far more than a friend.

"I was a senior in high school when I met Mark," Rod

---

20 One of those kids might have been Byron Howard, who grew up to direct Disney's *Zootopia* and has repeatedly pointed to the film as a major influence on his life. The next generation of furs may likely credit his film as *their* gateway drug into the fandom.

O'Riley recalls. "Our science-fiction club went on a field trip to a sci-fi convention. I thought conventions were all about costuming; this was the first one I'd been to that had an art show.

"I was already a weasel fanatic when I saw Mark's skiltaire art in the show. When I met him I asked why his otters had antennae. He started explaining them to me, and when he mentioned he was running the video room at the convention I asked him if he had any *Kimba* episodes."

Mark did indeed have *Kimba* episodes on hand. Rod then asked if the same held true for *The Amazing 3*—a much more obscure series than the widely distributed show about the white lion cub. "I think I have some," Mark replied.

It was the beginning, as the expression goes, of a beautiful friendship, which eventually led to an even-more-beautiful partnership as Mark and Rob became furry's number-one power couple.

"All my life I'd been looking for something like [anime] fandom, but I didn't know what it was," Rod continues. "I wanted to be with someone who gets it. I started hanging out with him. We got together with other geeky kids and circled the wagons."

"Rod and I became partners when I went into college," Mark explains. "But we celebrate the day we met as our anniversary. We never really noticed until we were kind of into it that it had become more than [a friendship]. You had to hit me with a two-by-four before I realized what was going on."

"It definitely wasn't a 'hey, let's do this,'" Rod adds. "We just started cuddling and then started more, and then . . . there it was. We looked back and said, 'Oh, we're a thing now, aren't we?'" he adds with a chuckle. "I know very little about the human experience 'dating' because the first person I ever fell in love with I'm still with.

"We're kind of weirdoes on the outside to the LGBT community because of the [furry] fandom—both of us are geeks before anything else. We went to a couple of meetings of a sci-fi society for gays where everyone was watching *Star Trek: The Next Generation* episodes in cuddle piles." Mark adds, "We never felt like we fit in other than the [sci-fi] fandom connection. When we went to a gay sci-fi convention [and] we showed them gay furry art—they just didn't get it."

Things have changed since the 1980s. As Rod puts it, "Homophobia has kind of gone out of fashion. [Nowadays] people care more about your fan intensity than anything else, including your gender: 'I don't care who you are, we're both into *Adventure Time.*'"

In 1976, with an electronic engineering degree under his belt, Mark was part of a company designing and building hi-fi speakers. His network of cartoon-minded friends extended into the Hollywood animation community, many of whom had personal libraries of classic 'toons and movies on 16mm film and in early (and now long-obsolete) video formats.[21]

With a U-matic and two V-cord VCRs in his possession, Mark began cultivating his own collection, beginning with off-air recordings of Japanese giant-robot shows, *Kimba* episodes and trades with fellow collectors. He'd screen them (along with sci-fi movies and *Star Trek*

---

21 Half-inch open-reel portapak tapes, industrial-strength 3/4" U-matic cassettes the size of library books and Sanyo V-cord cartridges, all of which now reside in the Museum of Obsolete Recording Formats (aka The Junkyard).

episodes) at local sci-fi conventions and at the Los Angeles Science Fantasy Society's clubhouse.[22]

Fred Patten was a regular at the monthly screening. Fred's appreciation and participation in all things fannish goes back to the early 1960s when he cosplayed the Golden Age Flash at the 1962 Chicago Worldcon. (His costume was perfect, right down to the wings adorning Jay Garrick's boots and World War I helmet.)

Now in his seventies and hobbled by a stroke, Fred is still active in the fandom, reviewing furry publications and anime releases for the furry news website Flayrah, and editing furry fiction anthologies with titles like *An Anthropomorphic Century: Stories from 1909 to 2008* and *Cats and More Cats: Feline Fantasy Fiction.* His most recent accomplishment is *Furry Fandom Conventions, 1989-2015*, an exhaustively detailed cataloguing of every furry gathering held during that period. Tall and hefty still, Fred's natural fursona might be ursine; he preferred raccoon or coyote, but thanks to his bald pate, a fur dubbed him a bald eagle, and he remains one to this day.

Fred describes himself as "the biggest funny animal fan around" who learned to read when he was four from newspaper comic strips and *Walt Disney's Comics and Stories*,[23] but "got sidetracked when I discovered science fiction" and the LASFS in his college days.

---

22 Founded in 1934, the LASFS is the world's oldest ongoing fan association and boasts its very own clubhouse, a distinction few if any other fan groups can claim. Its alumni include science-fiction authors Ray Bradbury, Larry Niven and Jerry Pournelle, and *Famous Monsters of Filmland* editor Forrest J. Ackerman.

23 "When I was a kid I worked out an elaborate set of rules for funny-animal stories . . . [m]y first favorite comic book hero was Sheldon Mayer's Amster the Hamster; he could talk anybody into anything, a talent I considered highly desirable." From Fred's introductory essay in the first issue of *Rowrbrazzle*, a furry "amateur press association."

An exhibit at the 1970 Westercon introduced Fred to the Japanese comics known as manga. "Manga were paperback volumes 300 pages long, very thick. The art was more imaginative than American comics, and even though I couldn't read the stories, I could tell from the pictures they were a lot more dramatic and serious than American ones."

A few years later Fred discovered anime at Mark Merlino's animation screenings. Attendees at Mark's screenings were familiar with Ray Harryhausen movies and *Twilight Zone* episodes, but the giant-robot series was something completely new and different. Requests to include more Japanese animation grew until the screenings were all but entirely anime.

Fred, Mark and others considered organizing the screenings into an animation fan club. Finally, on Saturday, May 21, 1977, four days before the premiere of the original *Star Wars* movie, the first official meeting of the Cartoon/Fantasy Organization[24]—the C/FO—was held with a program consisting entirely of *Kimba* and giant-robot TV episodes, another anime specialty.

The C/FO screenings also attracted funny-animal[25] fans, there for anime series starring anthropomorphic characters like Kimba, *The Amazing 3*'s Bonnie Bunny and *Fables of the Green Forest*'s Johnny Woodchuck. Many hadn't met each other previously; the C/FO screenings were their first chance to link up and network with each other and anime fans who also enjoyed anthro

---

24 "Fantasy" was included in the club's name to cover the live-action movie or TV episode occasionally screened at the C/FO.

25 "Funny animals" were the stars of a now-extinct comic book genre featuring the humorous antics of anthropomorphic animals.

characters—people destined to become some of the earliest members of furry fandom.

In his fandom career Fred has always been the organization man, whether it was creating the Ursa Major awards honoring anthropomorphic achievements[26] or editing *Rowrbrazzle*, a highly influential furry publication for seventeen years. "You seem to wind up running a lot of things," I recently suggested to Fred. "Yeah, because nobody else would do it." Did he ever resent being the only person willing to do the heavy lifting? "I do sort of enjoy it, but at same time I get so annoyed that everybody is dumping all the work on me."

Enthused by the rapidly multiplying C/FO chapters, Fred rolled up his sleeves and with his standard "git 'er done" commitment to the task at hand, wrote newsletters and created a members' directory. According to Mark, "at one point [Fred] wanted to create a nation-wide club, with membership cards, dues and administration including a president, secretary and treasurer. He pushed for elections, and that caused a lot of drama about one area of the country dictating what everyone else could do."

"[Mark] Merlino has always been a pretty fervent anarchist," Fred counters. "When we set up the C/FO in 1977 Merlino said it should not have any officers, all the members should be equal. He wanted to just show episodes at random, [while] I insisted that we should have a planned and announced schedule and stick to it. He carried that [same] attitude over into furry fandom."[27]

---

26 "I was complaining furry fandom didn't have its own awards like science fiction had the Hugos and the Nebulas. Almost everybody I talked to said, 'If you feel so strongly about it why don't you do something yourself?'"

27 Or as Mark himself said at the time, "Let's never organize furry fandom as an overall club."

The C/FO as an international organization enjoyed a good ten-year run until internal dissension and conflict between various local chapters led to many going independent or simply shutting down. Fred's ambitious plan—all the chapters would report to a C/FO central that would publish their monthly activities—never came to pass. In 1989 the C/FO as an international club was officially disbanded, but the original Los Angeles chapter, as it has since May 21, 1977, still meets the third Saturday of every month at the LASFS clubhouse.

> *It's much easier to humanize an animal than it is to humanize a human.*
>
> —CHUCK JONES

Once upon a time, before steroid-powered superheroes muscled other comic book genres out of existence, before graphic novels made sequential image storytelling respectable, "funny animal" comic books abounded. Many featured A-List *Looney Tunes* and Disney superstars, but most starred long-forgotten Barney Roosters, Foxy Fagans and Dizzy Dogs. They cavorted in silly, colorful stories that (once you track them down online) have lost none of their charm. Sadly, these particular critters were doomed to extinction when after-school and Saturday morning cartoons came along to provide kids with their funny animal fix.

Even real animals couldn't compare to the incredible antics of TV anthros for the young mind of Ken Fletcher. Ken's dad was a zookeeper who worked for the Seattle Zoo for almost a decade. "[He] became one of the head animal keepers," Ken reminisces. "He would take me to work and I would watch him rescue baby animals their mothers refused to feed—tiger cubs, creatures like that. In Seattle he helped raise a baby gorilla to adolescence. I would watch him work through thick glass; babies could catch human colds and get sick.

"He worked a lot with primates, in the monkey house. In the zoo stories they call apes and monkeys 'mischievous'; you can put mischievous in quotes [because] that doesn't [even] begin to describe them. It's a little bit dangerous for an unsupervised kid to be close to animals—especially those.

"Besides, to be candid, it was too smelly in there for me."

The primates might not have been all that funny, but cartoon animals were. "My parents bought Little Golden Books and things like that before I was in kindergarten and read them to me. Funny animal comics too, like Bugs Bunny and Uncle Scrooge, and secondary comics like [those with] Andy Panda. When I was five or six they gave me a subscription to *Walt Disney's Comics and Stories*.

"I started to read before kindergarten. I recognized my first word in an Andy Panda comic: 'BOOM'—a very distinctive, large explosion filling a panel. Once the idea lit up in my brain, I was able to learn reading by phonetics pretty quickly."

Reed Waller's story is similar, but without the BOOM. "My parents read comics to me and [books] like *Treasure Island* and *Tom Sawyer*, whatever they thought might interest me. They kept reading me comics because I responded to them and seemed fascinated by the interaction of story and art; good judgment on their part. Their intent was to raise themselves a creative genius.

They continued to read to me constantly, until I was reading to them, and drawing comics of my own. As long as I [can] remember, I wanted to be a cartoonist when I grew up."

It was the day after Thanksgiving: November 25, 1966. The University of Minnesota campus was all but deserted, the school closed for the holiday. However, the office of *Minnesota Technolog*, the school's technology journal, was far from deserted. Ken and a handful of friends were there to found Minn-StF: the Minnesota Science Fiction Society.[28]

"It grew relatively fast, because it was the appropriate time for people to be interested—the original *Star Trek* series had premiered two months earlier and NASA's full-tilt effort to land a man on the moon by the decade's end was still going strong. Minn-StF was originally centered at the university but eventually grew into an open club for local sci-fi fans.

"Some of the members had experience in other cities' clubs and were familiar with all the cultural aspects of sci-fi fandom." Several others, he notes, were in the high-IQ society Mensa and received the Mensa newsletter that featured Reed Waller's articles and illustrations.

---

28 The Society's original and soon-abandoned name was The Minnesota Scientifiction Society. The lower-case "t" in Minn-StF was a nostalgic nod to Hugo Gernsback, one of the founders of modern science fiction and its attendant fandom. Gernsback introduced the contraction of "scientific fiction" in a 1916 issue of his *Electrical Experimenter* magazine. The clunky-sounding "scientifiction" never really caught on and was ultimately replaced by the more familiar "science fiction." ("Hugo Gernsback." Wikipedia. Retrieved August 23, 2016. [https://en.wikipedia.org/wiki/Hugo_Gernsback]) The 1950s craze for high-fidelity, or hi-fi, audio equipment inspired Forrest J Ackerman to nickname the genre the now universally accepted "sci-fi," much to the chagrin of certain science-fiction purists who insisted on pronouncing the neologism "skiffy." "Forrest J Ackerman." Wikipedia. (https://en.wikipedia.org/wiki/Forrest_J_Ackerman) Retrieved August 23, 2016.

Memories and the specific details of who contacted whom first can get a little fuzzy in a half century. Reed joined Mensa in 1971, five years after Minn-StF's birth. "I was bored. I didn't know about science fiction fandom, though I read heaps of science fiction. I heard about Mensa through the back pages of a science fiction magazine, wrote for info and discovered a local Twin Cities chapter. I was tested, admitted and met many interesting people."

Once ensconced, Reed began publishing *Motley,* his own personal "Mensazine," most likely the newsletter Ken recalls seeing. Reed explains: "Most Mensa fanzines were published by local chapters, but one renegade Mensan started his own zine and mailed them to people in exchange for theirs. I imitated him, sent my zine to everyone on his list. Among the stuff I got in return was a package from Ken, which included his zine, *Koyotl,* and [cartooning] jams he participated in—wild, improvisational adult comedy with funny animals in surrealistic settings."

Ken and Reed began a correspondence that led to regular get-togethers when Reed traveled from his small southern Minnesota town to attend local conventions and fan gatherings.

"I'd see him at least once a month or more," remembers Ken, "hanging out in people's apartments. He seemed like just another guy in person, but we both had the 'wiggle the eyebrows' persona hidden away until we trusted other people.

"I was impressed—he was just as weird or weirder [when it came to] cartooning ideas as I was. He seemed to have more natural ability to do the drawings than I did. We were certainly compatible in terms of what our general interests were. And one of the things we discovered [was that] we both liked animal comics—and enjoyed drawing them too."

Ken and Reed realized they were kindred spirits who appreciated each other's work and shared a fondness for funny animal comics, classic *Looney Tunes*, Fleischer animation, and underground comix artists like Robert Crumb[29] and Vaughn Bodē . "Soon," Reed recalls, "Ken and I were regular contributors of humorous art to science-fiction fanzines around the world. We jammed regularly with other sci-fi fan cartoonists, especially in Minn-StF's official organ, *RUNE*. The club also had its own 'APA,' *Minneapa*, which had 200 members and was very active."

While fanzines (a contraction of "fan" and "magazine") created by enthusiasts of just about every pop-culture manifestation are a well-known contemporary presence, not as many people are familiar with APA's— "amateur press associations." While similar to a fanzine, an APA differs in one significant way: it's a closed-membership, invitation-only affair. Members create a limited number of copies of their contribution (or "trib"), usually equal to the group's total membership. They go to the lucky individual who volunteered (or was drafted) to be the "Central Mailer" and has the fun job of compiling the tribs into finished issues to be mailed to each member.

The upside of an APA: no one person has to create an entire issue single-handedly, and each issue contains a multitude of voices and perspectives on the APA's subject. The downside: the only way to acquire a copy of a finished

---

29 There's no shortage of funny animals in Crumb's work, the best known of which is Fritz the Cat. Crumb was so upset by Ralph Bakshi's animated feature version he subsequently killed off the character.

APA publication is to be in it. (Actually, it's only a downside to a non-member; part of an APA's appeal is its "for your eyes only" exclusivity.)

Ken and Reed began to plan an APA of their own—a funny animal APA.

"We dedicated ours to funny animal cartoons," Reed explains, "because it was the main bond between us. We were both sad that funny animals and humorous comics in general had died a horrible death because of the new 'seriousness' of 1970s comics like Frank Miller's 'Dark Knight' Batman—we felt they were an endangered species. We were uninterested in swords and sorcery or dark fantasy. We were cutting our teeth on *Monty Python's Flying Circus*, the Firesign Theater[30] and underground comix—anarchist humor."

"We were kind of aware that we weren't alone," recalls Ken, "that there were people out there with the same interest in reconstructing, reusing funny animal tropes from the 1930s and forties who felt themselves as isolated as we did.

"We'd seen indications of this on the fringes of comic collecting and science-fiction fandom: in the 1950s some of the first EC Comics fans were also science-fiction fans. They would publish EC fanzines because they knew they could send it to fifty or one hundred similar fans. There were people doing this for *Pogo*, for example; some of the earliest *Pogo* fans that were recognized as part of a group and not isolated individuals were science-fiction fans who created serious *Pogo* fanzines.

---

30 The Firesign Theater was a troupe of four young L.A. comedians who created a series of surreal, countercultural and extremely funny LP comedy records in the style of 1940s radio dramas.

"We knew this probably continued to exist, that there were science-fiction and comics fans also interested in funny-animal-style drawings. It wasn't in a vacuum, either: the counterculture *Air Pirates*[31] underground comic came out in 1971. There were other things like Fritz the Cat, Robert Crumb doing underground comics in the 1960s with funny animals. There was even a *Fritz the Cat* movie in 1972, and Disney's animated *Robin Hood* in 1973. Ten years later we discovered there were a lot of kids and teenagers who didn't realize what could be done with funny animals as characters until they saw *Robin Hood*.

"We knew this wasn't an isolated thing, that there were other people like ourselves—[or even people we guessed were like us]—and there was a low-cost way to communicate with them if we knew someone in their city. Reed and I were both in APAs in the late sixties, early seventies. We knew how they worked; even in the 1970s it was a way of forming a community."

Ken and Reed created a one-page flyer and a sample "issue zero" promoting their planned APA. They distributed copies at the local comic con, made use of Ken's contact list ("I'd been an active fan since 1968; at that point I had accumulated eight years' worth of addresses"), reached out to artists in fanzines and APAs doing funny animals, and to ones they guessed were funny-animal-friendly. ("If they're doing science-fiction aliens but doing them funny-animal style, they're probably sympathetic; let's send them an issue and see if they respond to it.")

---

31 *Air Pirate Funnies*, published in 1971 by a handful of underground cartoonists, was sued by Disney for portraying Mickey and company having sex and using drugs. Other underground comics featuring funny animals included the deliberately misspelled *Funny Aminals, Quack!* and *No Ducks!*

The sample issue's cover, a joint effort by the pair, was inspired by the final panel of a 1950s *Mad* spoof of the *Today* show.[32] Their cover depicts a chimpanzee, but their chimp is a parody of *Mad*'s parody: dressed in a *Star Trek* tunic, the chimpanzee is (so to speak) aping Mr. Spock's split-fingered Vulcan salute. They adopt the *Mad* chimp's one word of dialog—"Vootie"—as their title. *Vootie*'s subtitle is "the apa of Funny Animal Fandom," and the Spock-chimp is warning potential readers "NO HUMANS ALLOWED!!" They gave their publication a tongue-in-cheek political edge, declaring it "the official organ of the Funny Animal Liberation Front."

 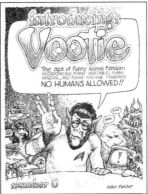

MAD # 26 © 1955 E.C. Publications, Inc.

Illustration courtesy of and © Reed Waller and Ken Fletcher

---

32 From 1953 to 1957, a chimpanzee named J. Fred Muggs was *Today*'s on-camera mascot. There was supposedly no love lost between host Dave Garroway and the chimp; the *Mad* parody concludes with "J. Fred Gluggs" usurping "Dave Garrowunway" as the show's host and appropriating his palm-in-the-air "peace" sign-off.

The response was a pleasant surprise for the pair: Ken remembers getting ten to twenty "enthusiastic responses" from their first mailing, drawing from, in Reed's words, "the Twin Cities' huge congregation of young, adventurous cartoonists who were looking for something fun and crazy to do."

"We were halfway surprised because we could make gestures", says Ken, "but we never knew in advance which were the right gestures, so we were very deliberate. We knew that we would have some effect, but we weren't really sure what the effect would be. If we spent two years sending out a publication like this every other month to fifty or one hundred people, based on what happens in fandom we knew at least thirty to forty people in the core community would respond."

The APA's first official issue in June of 1976 was essentially a home-grown effort, with nearly all of its contributors participants in the local cartooning scene mentioned by Reed.

"The hardest thing was knowing this wouldn't be a matter of putting out one or two issues," recalls Ken. "[It was knowing] that we'd have to do it for maybe a year or two before it started crystallizing. What was interesting was that some people who didn't respond [to what we sent them] put their sample copy [out in places like a] coffee table during a party, and five or ten years later we'd be hearing from people who discovered *Vootie* this way."

Fueled by Ken and Reed's enthusiasm the APA kept growing, as the pair sent spare copies or individual pages to potential future members. A year and a half later *Vootie* number nine was seventy pages long, filled with artwork from twenty-five contributors.

"We were really lucky," Ken reminisces. "We'd always have at least four or five people, sometimes as many as eight or nine when it was time to collate the issues. Not everyone was in *Vootie*; some were local comic collectors or science-fiction fans who enjoyed participating."

Participating, in the case of assembling an APA, involved circling the table, grabbing a copy of each contribution until you had a complete issue in your hands and then repeating the process until the table was cleared of separate contributions and replaced with collated copies—a form of musical chairs, only without the chairs. Dizziness and the possibility of incurring the occasional paper cut were considered acceptable risks, more than made up for by the inevitable pizza and soda pop.

"It was really good, a very refreshing social event," Ken continues. "Every two months for several years we had an excuse to get together and hang out—sometimes around a basement table, sometimes in somebody's living room if they had small apartment or house. It was very lively, and when we were done we could hold the newest *Vootie* in our hands. It wasn't a surprise to read; it was proof this was actually working."

Reed and Ken initially hoped to create a new issue of the APA every other month, but the relentless reality of soliciting, receiving and assembling a mountain of contributions from a slew of members soon butted in; the interval between *Vootie*s grew from two to three months. After the first ten issues the pair resigned as editors in favor of another APA member who shepherded the publication through its next twenty issues, until he too threw in the towel and was replaced by a succession of editors including a briefly returning Reed.

Five years and thirty-one issues into its existence, *Vootie* was beginning to run out of steam due to waning interest of many of its members (aka "fanzine fatigue") and the inevitable, personality-driven head-butting (endemic to any organization) between folks with different ideas of what *Vootie* should be.

"There were disagreements about the quality and professionalism of some members' work," Ken admits. "Some wanted to strive for excellence [and] more professional work in *Vootie*, others were not as strong on that." Reed's move to a small town ninety miles south of Minneapolis complicated the picture, making editing an issue that much more challenging. (And then there was Reed's side project, a comic about a feline exotic dancer that was beginning to occupy more and more of his time . . .)

Ken goes on to speculate perhaps *Vootie* was a bit too exclusive to cartoonists. "I was thinking very much that all the new funny animal cartoonists would get together and create a social community to support themselves, and communicate cartoonist to cartoonist.

"That was short-sighted. I forgot the community wasn't necessarily just the cartoonists. It seemed right at the time, but it put people off. We said, 'No writing. You can write things for *Vootie* but it won't be included in your page count—we want art.'

"We closed off a whole batch of people who were essayists and collectors and story writers because Reed and I both wrote and drew and had ambitions to writing our own stories. We didn't really think it through—there are people who can write marvelous stuff but can't draw so they [might be] writing scripts or text stories instead. In retrospect we probably ended up offending some people by not allowing them to play in our sandbox."

Vootie's last official issue was published in February of 1983—but one member was determined to keep the APA going.

Meet Tim Fay, or as he's known online, "Tim Kangaroo." Although nominally a marsupial, Tim is also a "brony," a fan of the supposedly for-little-girls-only cartoon series *My Little Pony: Friendship Is Magic*. When visiting the show's land of Equestria he's no longer a 'roo, but the librarian pony "Tympany." Like Mark Merlino, exposure to Disney's *Bambi* the week of his seventh birthday set Tim on his furry path ("I really identified with the characters, especially Bambi"), along with generous helpings of Hanna-Barbera funny cartoon animals.

But now *Vootie* was on life support. Tim had already put a funny-animal 'zine together at a 1981 sci-fi convention, Col. Pud's One Shot Much like Paul McCartney trying to keep the Beatles together, Tim tried his best to resuscitate the APA with another single-shot: *Revolutionary Vootie*. (Its slogan, of course: "*Viva la Revolución!*") "If you're waiting for *Vootie* no. 38," Tim's editorial read, "don't hold your breath. I'm putting together a single-shot apazine. *Vootie* is in danger of dying out; if you want to do something about it, please contribute."

A handful of *Vootie* artists participated. Sadly it wasn't enough to resurrect the funny animal APA that was *Vootie*, but it was enough to lay the groundwork for what was even then slouching towards Bethlehem, waiting to be born: a bigger and better APA, something with a name every bit as weird as "Vootie." Something called *Rowrbrazzle*.

EVER SINCE he was a kid, Steve Gallacci loved aviation. He loved the idea of flying, and he loved building plastic models of his favorite airplanes, from World War II-era bombers to Korean War jet fighters. Squeezing just enough Testor's Plastic Cement out of the tube to fit the pieces together while holding his breath (that stuff could get you high, which for certain kids was the point), adding the models' moist, sticky insignia decals without letting them wrinkle—his favorite pastime.

It was a welcome distraction from a childhood as the oldest of four sons in a single-parent household that seemed to relocate around Seattle and its environs fairly often. Thanks to his mom ("a fairly good portrait artist in her own right," he recalls) who wanted her kids to appreciate art and culture, Steve became an avid reader and a classical music enthusiast—and a bit of an artist too, able to express himself in drawings and watercolors.

Times were a bit tight in the northwest U.S. in the early 1970s. There weren't a lot of jobs to go around, especially for a kid who didn't take high school all that seriously. "Lazy on the day-to-day school work," he admits, "but I knew the material and could ace the tests" and managed to graduate.

Military service seemed like a practical alternative; the draft had recently ended and the Vietnam War was winding down. Steve enlisted in the U.S. Air Force, hoping to become a graphics specialist, but was tapped to become a Vietnamese translator instead. It was a career path that hit a dead end when it turned out his theoretical aptitude for the job was not matched by his ability to actually speak the language.

As luck would have it, a graphics specialist position became available at a Florida Air Force base. He created graphics and visual aids and did layouts for the various publications and documents the base generated. "I was working with sober professionals, all Vietnam veterans, no clowns or cowboys."

In Florida Steve finally tasted flight, finally took to the air— but only as a hang-gliding enthusiast. A slight case of color-blindness had rendered him ineligible for actual flight training.[33]

In 1977, his rendezvous with his furry destiny fast approaching, Steve was reassigned to the U.S. Air Force's European HQ in Ramstein, Germany. Cartooning was an almost non-existent part of his professional duties, with little more than the occasional call for a spot cartoon to liven up a publication.

A few months earlier the twenty-two-year-old Steve had caught a serious case of sci-fi-itis after seeing the then brand-new *Star Wars* "which turned a minor interest in science fiction into a major passion." He was also falling under the spell of the underground comix of the 1960s and the 1970s "ground-level" alternative comics.

If any one external force can be credited for helping to create furry fandom, it would be Communism. Steve's department was working on a presentation warning of the dangers of electronic warfare and asked him to create a cartoon bear to represent the Red Menace.

It was an "Aha!" moment for the young man. Why just read comics when he could create his own?! And in particular, why not create a sci-fi comic set in his own far-away galaxy—a galaxy inhabited by anthropomorphic animals?

---

33 "I know color theory well, I just can't see everything I'm doing. Every once in a while I'll goof and inadvertently do something in an odd mix. In an issue of *Albedo* I didn't notice one of my color pens was contaminated and did up a green coyote that I thought was brown."

Steve considered himself an unremarkable cartoonist, lacking the slick mainstream comic book style of the day. But "funny animals in space" had a particular hook to it. His initial efforts featured a very loose and simple style, but one he considered attractive and effective. He'd spent a lot of time analyzing what worked in others' cartooning, especially Charles Schulz's *Peanuts* where a circle and a couple of dots could evoke a range of emotion. Unleashing his sci-fi passion while cultivating his writing chops, Steve's funny animals rapidly evolved from simple cartoon characters to anthropomorphic genetic constructs with complex backstories set in a futuristic world.

Save for Bugs Bunny's first encounter with Marvin the Martian in 1948's *Haredevil Hare*, no one had ever put anthropomorphic characters in a sci-fi setting before. Thanks to Steve's Air Force training as a technical illustrator, his highly detailed, high-tech environments were far more believable than the cigar-shaped rocket that carried Bugs to the moon.

Steve brought a portfolio of his work to the 1980 Boston Worldcon. One piece in particular stood out: a painting of a flight-suit-wearing anthropomorphic cat climbing into a fighter spacecraft. With her flowing hair, anime-style oversized eyes and modest breasts she was no doubt anthropomorphic—but in no way was she a "funny" animal. Her name was Erma Felna, her first name borrowed from the World War II-era German arms manufacturer ERMA, her last a riff on "feline."

Erma started life as a background character in *Astro Duck*, a "somewhat absurd satire about heroics and military life," according to Steve. "She was a petty and officious foil to the titular Astro Duck, a trigger-happy slovenly slacker." But as the characters evolved out of their gag-cartoon origins and into a hard sci-fi[34] story, she became an idealistic young military member in an increasingly ugly and anything-but-idealistic world. Steve claims there was nothing autobiographical in Erma's background, although he admits many of his early characters were inspired by the careerism and office politics that soured him on military life.

Erma and her creator soon developed a following. Fans wanted to see more of her—they wanted Steve to put Erma in a comic book. Steve was uncertain but decided to give it a shot. After a few try-out appearances in anthology comics, Erma and company appeared in their own book (published by Steve himself and helpfully labeled "First Real Issue!"), *Albedo*[35]*Anthropomorphics*, in 1984. By Marvel/DC standards its sales were insignificant—a few thousand at most—but they were large enough to create a boom (and ultimately a glut followed by a bust) of independently published anthropomorphic comics; they all had their moment in the sun and all contributed to spreading the fandom.

Sometimes it just comes down to synchronicity. An idea floats around, waiting for a receptive brain resonating on the right frequency to tune in, amplify it and share it with the world. The public didn't know it yet, but they would soon make a quartet of anthropomorphic animals mainstream superstars.

---

34 "Hard sci-fi stories" as in stories based on actual science—not stories difficult to understand or enjoy.

35 An albedo is a planet's reflected sunlight, a reference to the real-world elements Steve wove into Erma's stories.

With its sophisticated political intrigues and introspective characters *Erma* never stood a chance of breaking out of its genre niche. But just a few months prior to *Albedo*'s 1984 debut, Kevin Eastman and Peter Laird—two young, ambitious comics fans—self-published their own anthro-centric comic. Their creation spoofed several popular comics genres at once (in particular, Frank Miller's gritty *Ronin* DC series) including funny animals. Its you-gotta-be-kidding title: *Teenage Mutant Ninja Turtles*.

It was an indie hit. More in spite of than because of its goofy premise, *Turtles* was an unusually popular independent comic, at one point outselling Marvel's *Avengers*. The eighth issue of *Turtles* sold 135,000 copies—astonishing sales for an independently published black-and-white comic.

Eastman and Laird *were* kidding when they started the series, but a licensing agent named Mark Freedman wasn't. Freedman saw gold in them thar shells.[36] The Turtles' skeptical creators gave Freedman a thirty-day window to come up with something and a first-printing copy of *TMNT* number one.[37] (A note inside read, "Go out and make us $1 million, or else.")

Freedman came back with a million-dollar offer for a line of Turtle action figures. With an ambitious agent on their side and the early issues' graphic violence toned down to make the characters more kid-friendly, a daily cartoon

---

36 "When I first heard the name 'Teenage Mutant Ninja Turtles' I jumped out of my skin," Freedman recalled in a 2014 documentary. "There was something about that name . . . "

37 A first-printing copy of that $1.50 comic goes for $4,000 today. (A second printing is a bargain at a mere $300.)

show soon followed.[38] Just as they had with comics fans, the four terrapins won over the after-school TV crowd. If *Albedo* put anthropomorphic characters into outer space, the Turtles proved anthros could be action heroes—and a mass audience success. (For more than a few of its preteen and tween viewers, it also instilled a fondness for anthropomorphic characters: in addition to the Turtles themselves the show featured their anthro rat mentor, a conflicted alligator, and bumbling rhino and warthog villains.) Other cartoonists tried to ape the Turtles' success with their own black-and-white titles, but none made anything close to the Turtles' impact.

At almost the same time *Erma* and the *Teenage Mutant Ninja Turtles* were taking off, *Vootie* was winding down. Finally, after thirty-seven issues, the "official organ of the funny animal liberation front" passed into extinction— but the following year two *Vootie* veterans created its successor. Just as *Vootie* appropriated a nonsensical word spoken by a comic book chimp as its title, the new APA named itself *Rowrbrazzle* after a pseudo-profanity often bellowed by Albert Alligator, *Pogo*'s cigar-chomping saurian.

Amateur artists, writers and enthusiasts were networking like never before. *Rowrbrazzle*, which began as a funny-animal-centric publication but eventually evolved into a furry-themed one, attracted an assortment of fellow former *Vootie* contributors, high-profile anthro fans, and because it was based in Los Angeles, animation

---

38 Down the road there would be a 1990s trio of live-action films, a '97 live-action TV series, 2003 and 2012 TV cartoon reboots, a 2007 computer-animated feature, 2014 and 2016 big-budget Michael Bay action flicks starring live actors and CGI turtles . . . (And then there were cartoon knock-offs on the order of *Biker Mice from Mars* and *Street Sharks*.)

Cover illustration, Rowrbrazzle no. 26; illustration courtesy of and © Taral Wayne

professionals and people who went on to become animation pros. (Cartoon historian Jerry Beck was a contributor to its earliest issues, as was *Lilo and Stitch* director Chris Sanders.) Even though its distribution, like *Vootie*'s, was limited to its membership, the publication soon achieved near-legendary status within furry fandom; if you were in *'Brazzle*, you had it made—you were an art god.[39] If you weren't, you wanted to see the work that was. (Members who were willing to let other furs xerox pages of their copy suddenly acquired lots of friends.)

Unlike *Vootie, Rowrbrazzle* welcomed non-artists, including Fred Patten. Fred's contributions to the quarterly publication included essays on past anthropomorphic creative efforts and sightings of contemporary ones. When the publication's original editor resigned in 1988 to focus on his animation career, Fred was once again there to save the day and keep *Rowrbrazzle* alive. At the peak of its popularity, a *Rowrbrazzle* issue could be as much as 600 pages long, stapled into four or five separate sections and stretching a padded mailing envelope to its limit.

Numerous other furry APAs and fanzines have come and gone, but *Rowrbrazzle* is still going strong even without Fred at the helm. It's been shepherded by a succession of shorter-term editors, none to date matching his endurance. Issues now average around one hundred pages from twenty members, versus sixty contributors (plus a waiting list) at the APA's peak.

The villain of course is the Internet and its ability to

---

39 A waiting list of artists (including me) eager to join *Rowrbrazzle* soon accumulated. I was finally accepted in 1990 when membership was increased from fifty to sixty contributors. I never considered myself an "art god," merely a mortal, halfway decent cartoonist lucky enough to see his scribbles in print alongside the work of vastly more talented artists.

provide instantaneous, real-time communication. (By comparison, a question/answer/response dialog carried across three issues would take six months to unfold.) Perhaps it's only a case of pre-Internet nostalgia for a print publication, but in spite of its shrinking size, *Rowrbrazzle* shows no signs of going away.

CHAPTER FIVE

Pretty as a Picture: Furry Art

ANTHROPOMORPHIC ART has always been part of civilization, as long as there's been civilization; just about every culture has at one time or another depicted animals acting as people.

In twelfth-century Japan the first of the "Animal Frolic" scrolls was created. Frogs and rabbits abound, standing on their hind legs wrestling in one image, and in another chasing after a hat-wearing monkey, branches in hand to swat the fleeing miscreant. The nightmarish rightmost panel of Hieronymous Bosch's *Garden of Earthly Delights* is filled with animals harrowing unfortunate humans, like the rabbit hunter who carries his captured human prey upside-down or the pig wearing a nun's headpiece smooching a guy who appears less than overjoyed about it.

You can find anthropomorphic representation in every aspect of modern society: in cartoons and kids' books, sports and advertising mascots, mainstream entertainment and fine art—and, absolutely, in the furry community.

Furry was birthed by cartoon and "funny animal" comics fans and artists. The majority of furry activity still takes place on paper, and increasingly on computer screens. Fursuiters standing outside the convention hotel are easy to spot, but the buying, selling and creation of furry art going on inside (or online) is where the real action takes place.

Furry artists are equally likely to draw for fun, for self-expression—or for bucks. (Those who can, draw; those who can't commission those who can.[40]) Provide a description of what you'd like to see and they'll gladly translate the anthro action in your head into reality. Not sure what floats your furry boat? Check out their "Your Character Here (YCH)" rough sketches of existing scenes with room for your fursona to become the center of attention.

How much does it cost? It depends. It depends on whether you want black and white or color, a pencil sketch or an inked one, single or multiple characters, background or no background . . . Prices may (and will) vary depending on the artist's skill, popularity and availability. Expect to pay anywhere from $10 to $30 for a single black-and-white sketch, and $50 to $60 or more for something in color. (Backgrounds and additional characters cost extra of course.)

Art styles can range from slick art school/commercial illustration to raw punk primitive, from generic anime-tinged characters to unmistakably unique creations from artists who have cultivated a look as personal as their signature. Content-wise, furry pictures can range from "Grandma would like this" to "Good Lord,

---

40   Non-artist furs who commission scads of art sometimes refer to themselves as "art whores."

I wonder what this person's childhood was like."

How much anthropomorphism do you want on your furry art? With thousands of furry artists on the scene, it's easy to find one happy to season your commission to taste.

Their creations tend to fall into one of five distinct, if occasionally overlapping, categories. Were one to invent a Morph-O-Meter (patent pending . . . someday) that covered a zero-to-one-hundred scale with zero representing a fully human human being and one hundred a real-world feral animal, how anthropomorphic any critter might be becomes a matter of degree.

Let's start climbing that ladder:

Nekomimi

A fixture of anime and manga, these Japanese catgirls' only animal attributes are a pair of cat ears[41] and a feline tail. They're usually organically attached although they can just as easily be add-on fashion accessories. **Morph-O-Meter rating: 5%**

Animal-headed people

The category encompassing the widest range of furry art; depending on their human-to-beast proportions, animal-headed people can be found anywhere along almost half of the Morph-O-Meter. They stand upright and possess human or semi-human bodies (occasionally sporting a tail and/or modified animal "jacklegs") topped by a realistic-looking animal head. You've seen these folks on *Bojack*

---

41 "Nekomimi" literally means "cat ears" in Japanese.

Horseman, or in the French graphic novel *Blacksad*. *Bojack* takes place in a world populated by both humans and anthros, while black cat private eye John Blacksad lives in a film-noir, all-anthro universe depicted in detail-packed, beautifully rendered panels.

When realism is thrown to the wind, animal headed people become cartoon characters who might walk upright or on all fours and wear as many or no clothes as they see fit. (Fortunately the unclothed ones have no visible genitalia to offend more sensitive viewers.[42])

Morph-O-Meter rating: 15–60%

SHENANIGAN! 2016

Illustration by Shenanigan, courtesy of and © Cooner

---

42 At least the ones starring in TV shows and animated features; the situation can be *quite* different when it comes to furry characters or fan art of cartoon celebrities.

Semi-realistic animals

An anthropomorphic animal based on actual animal anatomy but represented in a stylized manner. They're often dressed (if only from the waist up) and in spite of being quadrupeds in real life have no trouble standing upright if they feel like it. Even though they keep all four hooves on the ground, the angular animals of Disney's *Home on the Range* best represent this look. **Morph-O-Meter rating: 75–85%**

Ferals

Illustration courtesy of and © Heather Bruton

It's a designation accepted by the fandom at large but one I personally take issue with. In scientific terms (not to mention Disney's *Zootopia*, where anthros suddenly turning mindlessly savage are referred to as such) feral animals are untamed, "wild" beasts with absolutely nothing anthropomorphic about them. I prefer calling furry-drawn ones "naturalistic" because they're closely modeled on their real-world counterparts: if they have four legs in real life, their furry versions tend to stay on four legs. (Simba, Disney's *Lion King* is probably the best known example of a feral anthro.) Like the semi-realistic animals, they boast human emotions, intellect, facial expressions and most of all, speech; apart from their ability to accomplish tasks no actual animal might be capable of, they could easily be mistaken for the real thing.

Morph-O-Meter rating: 90–95%

Furry art and where to find it

One answer: any furry convention. A better answer: the Internet. Numerous websites (also known as "image boards") are chock full of the stuff; they exist for no other reason than to allow furry artists to share their art with the world and with each other.[43] Anybody who wants to display their work can open a no-cost account, create a page and upload their efforts (including non-furry photography, prose and musical compositions); even non-

---

43 DeviantArt (deviantart.com) is a semi-exception. The sprawling website hosts just about every genre and style of illustration, furry included, as well as photographs of artisanal creations from jewelry to dessert dishes. The site's profusion of categories, subcategories and sub-subcategories, however, can make it challenging for an artist to decide where their work belongs.

artists can build pages highlighting their favorite works from the rest of the site or beyond. Sophisticated browsing and search functions make it easy to locate specific artists, species or subject matter. Many of these sites include a journal with each account where users can document their musings, and a messaging system to communicate with others within the site. Numerous forums let members chime in on issues of particular interest to them.

The sites have names like SoFurry (sofurry.com), Inkbunny (inkbunny.net), Weasyl (weasyl.com), Transfur (transfur.com) and the like. Within the Furryverse, the best known and most popular is Fur Affinity (furaffinity. net). The other sites may each have hundreds of thousands of users and uploaded submissions, but in 2015, FA, as it's commonly referred to, had over eleven million submissions from some 1.2 million users.[44]

"I never expected Fur Affinity to reach the level it did. I don't think anyone did," says "Dragoneer," who started as a regular visitor to the site and eventually became a site administrator, then its director. "FA began as an answer to a popular furry art site that surprised the community by banning mature and adult content pretty much overnight."[45] That site no longer exists, while "FA grew, and grew fast, to the point nobody on staff was able to

---

44 "Fur Affinity." WikiFur. Retrieved December 4, 2016. (http://en.wikifur.com/wiki/Fur_Affinity)

45 Fur Affinity has no problem with adult art; in fact some of can be it quite eye scorching, Art uploaded to the site can be classified as General ("suitable for all ages"), Mature ("tasteful/artistic") or Adult ("sexually explicit"). Dragoneer estimates the site's content "is about 75% General, and the rest about half and half, Mature and Adult. The vast majority of content on Fur Affinity is squeaky-clean wholesomeness [even if] it doesn't always feel that way." (Choosing Fur Affinity's SFW ("Safe For Work") setting will keep one's eyeballs at room temperature.)

keep up with it for the longest time; every time you'd catch up the site had outgrown itself again.

"The speed at which FA grows is hard to quantify. I think we're almost up to about ten thousand new submissions a day. The last time I checked, the daily registration numbers for new accounts ranged between six hundred and a thousand; some days it spikes up to two or three thousand. In 2009, we were averaging about 864 gigabytes of data uploaded per day. Today we're doing well over two terrabytes of data on a daily basis.

"There's a point where you start to go, 'Okay, just how many furries are actually out there?' I think I stopped counting after we hit a million user accounts. The idea of it all just seemed staggering. We're projected to hit the two million account mark sometime in 2017."

With an entire menagerie to choose from, which species tops the list? "Foxes are the most popular animal on FA; you're never going to get away from foxes," Dragoneer says without a doubt. "They're sort of the de facto species, and for good reason. Foxes are the embodiment of fun. They have unique markings that set them apart and, visually, a raw sleekness and deviousness that just draws people to them.

"As for themes, anything that plays on the predator/prey dynamic are huge within the community, as are transformation and size differences. They tie into the heart and fantasy of the community. Oh, and anything game related. We're all a bunch of fun loving geeks at heart."

The thirty-six-year-old Dragoneer lives in Manassas, Virginia. His pre-Fur Affinity history includes employment spells with the Department of Defense and Amazon, along with a stint as an animator on the cable TV series

VH1 ILL-ustrated where he helped create pop-culture parodies on the order of "Spongebong Hemppants."

Dragoneer fell into the furry community in the mid-1990s. "It's hard to pinpoint the exact time," he says. "Trying to remember the nineties now is like trying to dig through ancient history. I remember a lot of neon and slap bracelets.

"I used to be a diehard *Werewolf: The Apocalypse* gamer," he shares. While searching for images of werewolves online, he took a wrong turn and came across Fur Affinity. "That wrong turn that turned out to be the best mistake of my life."

Fur Affinity is probably well on its way to hitting that two-million mark if it hasn't already, and as mentioned above, there are also hundreds of thousands of accounts on other furry art sites. It's likely that some of these users have accounts on more than one website (or multiple accounts on a single site), but their numbers are probably more than made up for by people without accounts who drop in to browse around. Which means, in all likelihood, there are over *two-and-a-half million people* who are either furry artists or interested enough in the stuff to sign on to these sites. (Why, you might be sitting next to a furry at this very moment!)

Just what is it about images of anthropomorphic animals that furs find attractive? For starters, it's the blending of human and animal forms to any of the degrees mentioned above. They have an exotic, otherworldly nature—a "best of both worlds" situation. As imaginary beings they're "perfect" because there's no reality for them to fall short of.

My personal theory applies more to furry femmes than

males but holds true for both sexes: if one of the things that makes the female form attractive are its curves—the curve of its hips, the flow of its breasts—then the addition of a curvaceous or flowing tail adds to that appeal. It's one reason skunks are much more popular in the furry community than in the real world, why curve-tailed huskies are one of the most fashionable canine breeds in furry art and why sinuous-tailed reptiles and dragons abound on the furry image boards.

The IARP (The International Anthropomorphic Research Project) has been researching just about every aspect of the furry community for years, including furry art and artists. They've uncovered one particularly interesting detail: the ratio of male to female artists is exactly the opposite of the male to female ratio in the fandom as a whole: women comprise over 70% of furry artists, but just under 28% of furry fans, while men are over 72% of the fandom and just under 30% of the artists.

One such artist is Heather Bruton. If you had to classify her art style, "romantic" wouldn't be a far-off term. She cites Art Nouveau painter Alphonse Mucha and J.W. Waterhouse, who favored mythological subjects and enigmatic women, as inspiration for her work.

Her lush watercolors and delicate forms conjure up a world of sensual fantasy where centaurs stride and dragons fly. Her command of anatomy—both human and animal—makes her anthropomorphic creations come to life impressively. It's no wonder her work is more in demand (and more expensive!) than that of your average furry artist. There aren't many who can support themselves strictly from their work, but Heather is one of them.

The fifty-five-year-old Canadian depicts herself as a golden-haired leopard, but in person her mane of curly white hair frames a smiling, almost jolly face. She's a regular on the convention circuit, where she can be found in the Dealers' Room working on the stack of commissions she quickly accumulates.

"I stumbled across furry fandom through a dear friend, Terrie Smith—one of the first great artists in furry fandom and a fellow centaur fan. I've had a life-long fascination with Egyptian mythology and demi-humans that combine human and animal traits like centaurs, satyrs, mer-folk and the like," Heather explains.

"I began doing furry art in 1995 and almost immediately started taking commissions. I depict a wide variety of subjects as well as Furry: fantasy and wildlife work including gaming art for collectible card games and playing manuals, book covers, T-shirts, tattoo designs and more. I do indeed make my living off my artwork.

"I love all kinds of art styles. I love well-done cartoony art, but have no ability to do that sort of work. I lean towards calling my art style realistic; I think my fascination with Alphonse Mucha shows strongly when I'm doing ink and watercolor work. I like to portray my subjects as if they are part of our world, and I strive to make them as real as possible.

"I enjoy doing furry art, and I feel very at home with furry fans who are wonderful, creative, enthusiastic people. They've treated me very well. I love the fandom's openness to different ideas, interests and sexual orientations, and the way they are welcoming to many; it's one of the strongest and most appealing aspects of the fandom.

"I [also] love how Furry is such a culture of creators; it seems like everyone is drawing, writing, fursuiting, making music, crafts—all kinds of creative endeavors. It's very inspiring."

Kjartan Arnórsson, the Icelandic artist known as "Karno," is six-feet, eight-inches tall. Naturally, his fursona is a giraffe. Unlike most furry artists, he rarely draws single-image illustrations. He's primarily a storyteller and works almost exclusively in creating multi-paged comic book stories.

The fifty-one-year-old cartoonist specializes in stories abounding in over-the-top violence, uninhibited sex and no small amount of goofy humor—and very often, any two of them simultaneously. While he takes on commissions

Illustration courtesy of and © Kjartan Arnorsson

from people looking to imbue their own stories with the same qualities, the majority of his work is done simply for its—and his—own sake, an outlet for his remarkable imagination.

Karno sometimes refers to himself as Iceland's foremost pornographer. He enjoys drawing preposterously over-endowed males and balloon-breasted females eagerly engaging in carnal athletics few would find actually arousing, and that fall more into the category of raunchy burlesque.

"I was drawing anthro characters long before I discovered furry fandom," Karno says. "I have some strips from my kidhood that are poorly disguised rip-offs of Donald Duck and Mickey Mouse.

"I came to the U.S. and studied at the Boston Art Institute, but that was after my comic strips "Peter and the Robot" and "Swinehard Smallsoul" were published in *Thjodviljinn*, an Icelandic newspaper.

"I also created a series of five-minute illustrated stories for TV before coming here: "Hannes and the Patts," "Captain Iceland," "The Explorer," and "The Time-Wilders." They taught me how to work fast: each episode needed about thirty full-color pictures in a very short amount of time. "Captain Iceland" was eventually collected in three books. I studied at the Art Institute because at the time that seemed like the best way to reach my dream of becoming a professional illustrator.

"The underground comix, particularly Robert Crumb's work, were a big influence on my style—but I'm also a huge fan of Carl Barks's Donald Duck stories. I actually got to meet Barks when Disney sent him on a European tour—his first stop was Iceland. I wasn't gonna miss my all-time artistic hero's one-and-only visit to my home turf, so I hung a camera around my neck and snuck into the reception with the reporters. I got to talk to the man. He was humble, friendly, a lovely fella. If I have half as much class as he did when I reach his age, I'll be doing damn well.[46]

"I discovered furry fandom in the late 1980s during the "small press" comics boom. Some furries came across Savage Squirrel, my parody of Marvel's Punisher character. His adventures were reprinted in *Karno's Klassics*, a collection of my stories that was advertised in one of the small press comics of the day. Savage resonated with them and they told me about the fandom."

Illustration courtesy of and © Lucius Appaloosius

"Lucius Appaloosius" is a centaur; Bill is a chameleon. "Lucius" is Bill's fursona, if a centaur can be called

---

46   Barks reached the age of ninety-nine before passing away in 2000.

such. Like Heather Bruton, a fascination with those human/equine hybrids was one of the lures that pulled Bill into furry fandom; another was a fascination with the idea of human-to-animal transformation.

But when I call Bill a chameleon it's not a fursona reference; his ability to exquisitely mimic any number of classic artists and art styles is a skill few if any other artists in the fandom can approach.

Bill's classic sensibilities extend to his sartorial choices (he enjoys dressing like a gentlemen circa 1900, in tweed garments and straw hats) and musical tastes. "I like early music, from Medieval to Renaissance, Baroque, Ragtime and other weirdo stuff like that," he explains. "I listen to wax cylinders much of the time.

"I was born in 1958 in Bristol, Connecticut, and started drawing at a very early age. My grandfather was an amateur painter, and my mother studied art in college (although she later went into medicine) so we had a good many art books in the house when I was growing up. I appreciated the works of the Old Masters and genre artists such as [William] Hogarth. I also read the usual comic books and enjoyed the cartoons in the *New Yorker* and *Punch*.

"As a career in art seemed like the best choice for me, I enrolled in the Hartford Art School and earned a BFA degree in 1981. One of my youthful ambitions was to be a cartoonist. When I first saw Robert Crumb's work I was naturally impressed and started reading the underground comix.

"My earliest exposure to anthropomorphism came from watching Saturday morning cartoons and Disney movies. When I was six years old the transformation scenes in *The Sword in the Stone* stirred my emotions—a combination of fear and fascination that stuck with me.

Perhaps the decisive moment in my journey to furry fandom came when I stumbled upon issue number ninety two of *Superman's Girlfriend, Lois Lane*. On the cover was a picture of Lois Lane as a centaur, galloping away from Superman with the title "The Unbreakable Spell!" This made such an impression on my pre-pubescent mind that it became, so to speak, "imprinted" with a fascination with centaurs.

"This was long before furry fandom [as we know it] existed. I felt very self-conscious about my predilections and kept them hidden from outside opinion. I followed anthropomorphism from a discreet distance, quietly sketching for myself and peeking at anything anthropomorphic that made its way into the media. I was secretly delighted when Disney's *Robin Hood* came out. Later I was fascinated—and slightly disturbed—when [Peter Shaffer's] *Equus*[47] appeared on the stage.

"I first heard of 'furries' in the late 1980s in a less-than-flattering 'News of the Weird' item in the local free paper. Not until I finally overcame my rather Luddite prejudices and went online in late 2002 did I dare search for fellow centaurophiles, animal transformation art, and the like. I found them in the furry fandom."

---

47 Peter Shaffer's 1973 play was inspired by the true-life story of a teenager who blinded six horses. In Shaffer's fictionalized version, a psychiatrist "attempts to treat a young man who has a pathological religious fascination with horses" after he commits the violent act. (*Equus (play)*, Wikipedia, retrieved December 3, 2016.)

Illustration courtesy of and © Vander

Many furs have more than one creative outlet--for example, "Vander." In addition to being an accomplished furry artist, he's a DJ who can be found at late night convention raves. The suited and non-suited alike dance the night away to his propulsive rythyms under flashing strobes and spinning lights--a high-tech watering hole where animals of all species participate in a common revelry.

But come morning, you'll find him at his "Artist Alley'"s table, an earnest, quiet young gentleman with a neatly trimmed beard.

"I first became interested in anthro characters in middle school, when I was exploring the idea of creating characters with animalistic traits, as a reflection of my own interests and my own personality.

"I started with fan art from [the video game] *Jak and Daxter*, creating different fursonas based on Daxter being an 'Ottsel'—an otter/weasel. It evolved into creating my first white tiger character. I was just personally interested in creating animal characters; I was drawing furry art without realizing there was a whole fandom based on it. Near the end of secondary school I discovered the fandom online via DeviantArt and Fur Affinity.

"I went to the Savannah College of Art and Design (SCAD) for a major in illustration and worked on developing my personal style and overall visual language; it's also where I met other furries for the first time. SCAD not only influenced my style, it was also my entrance into furry fandom. I attended my first con in 2015: Furry Weekend Atlanta.

"It's not easy for me to describe my own style because I feel I'm still lacking in that department—but then again, most artists probably feel this way. My visual language was heavily influenced by music and DJing, film, animation, and looking at [the work of] other anthro artists with technical skills I admired. This helped me develop my two main styles: realistic figurative work with a strong focus on anatomy, and a simplified graphic novel style creating very clean and visual pleasing compositions.

"Most of my furry work tends to be a combination of the two. People have told me they're drawn to my clean linework and figures, but they also appreciate my more rendered and painted environments and characters.

"I enjoy furry fandom. I've made many dear friends who share similar interests, and I'm part of a large group of creatives I can always count on for input and critique of my personal and furry work. Furry fandom is very inclusive; it's a safe space for people to express themselves in the ways they want. It's a wonderful environment to be creative in."

Illustration by Pickelle, courtesy of and © QtHusk

Of course, in any fan zone you're going to find artists with specialties. "Pickelle" is an artist whose main work comes from transformation scenes, or TF as they're called within the fandom. Her specialty commission is what's known as a "bust sequence"—a four-part image of a person turning into their fursona—and she gets a *lot* of orders for them.

"I was always fascinated by werewolf movies and all matter of folklore surrounding part-human part-animal creatures, but my first major introduction into TF art was the *Animorphs* books—I LOVED those as a kid. I always enjoyed drawing animals, sci-fi creatures and transformation art. I drew a lot of anthro creatures when I was younger, but didn't know there was a community for it until I was in high school, thanks to an IM [instant messaging] friend.

"They were sad because their friends had forgotten their birthday. I offered to draw something as a gift, and they asked for their fursona; cue to me asking what a 'fursona' was. I found Fur Affinity shortly thereafter and started taking commissions as soon as I set up my account. I had a lot of personal art in my gallery when I first started, and about 90% of it was TF-related, which is probably why so many TF commissions came my way!"

It seems that most furry artists work alone, like a tiger protecting its territory, but sometimes two artists are better together. LeeLee and Thadd are a young couple, both of whom were drawing anthropomorphic characters long before they discovered the fandom. They met in college and now travel the convention circuit together. The landing page of their website, bigblueraptor.com, shows their fursonas: LeeLee's furry velociraptor sitting atop Thadd's more traditional winged dragon.

LeeLee is the primary artist (although Thadd draws as well). His expressive characters are charming, bursting with personality: a happy rabbit (more rabbitty than anthro) strolling through a snowfall, his scarf trailing on the ground behind him; a big blue-furred critter leaping over a bar, his eyes on his competitor: a small lizard with an insanely eager smile and a prehensile tail wrapped around the bar; a surly blue-eyed raccoon with a finger raised as if to say "and another thing"; a muscular anthro rabbit in a bathing suit showing off his biceps to an awestruck child . . . LeeLee's sophisticated color sense, his use of thick lines for character outlines, and thin, supple line weights for detailing makes the drawings pop off the page—or screen.

"I can't remember not being interested in [anthropomorphic characters]," he says. "Like most kids I grew up watching cartoons and Disney; animated films were a huge staple in my life. I loved the Ninja Turtles, I always had my Curious George toy with me, I had the talking Teddy Ruxpin and Mother Goose dolls that read you bedtime stories. I loved Sonic the Hedgehog and King Koopa from the Mario Bros. cartoons—and just about any other talking-animal cartoon on TV.

"Watching *Beast Wars*[48] and *Gargoyles* is what really made me a furry. When I played with the neighborhood kids we were all Beast Wars bots. I was Dinobot because raptors are just awesome. In *Gargoyles* the villains turned humans turned into animal-spliced gargoyles called 'mutates.' One of them became a black-panther-gargoyle named Talon. It just blew me away how creative the producers were, and for many, many years I dreamed of being one of the animal-spliced gargoyles.

"I taught myself how to draw by watching cartoons and movies. I'd pause VHS tapes and draw the characters and even the box covers. I drew lots of furry characters before I knew about the fandom. I did a tiny comic about a turtle named Herman going to school; his best friend was this cool tiger named Tim.

---

48 *Beast Wars: Transformers* was a follow-up series to the original *Transformers* series, in which the robots' alternate forms were animals, not vehicles.

"Years later I found DeviantART, VCL[49] and eventually Fur Affinity. I learn from observation; I've watched hundreds upon hundreds of artists over my lifetime, and I gather everything up like a squirrel does nuts and apply it to my own work.

"For the most part the fandom is a very loving and understanding group, but like any fandom you have your weirdoes and such. The best way I'm able to explain what furry fandom is to outsiders is comparing Furry to Disney characters; it's a *lot* simpler now that we have *Zootopia* in the mix."

The word "visionary" is tossed around a lot these days, usually referring to sci-fi and fantasy movie directors (whether they deserve it or not), but LeeLee's fiancé, Thadd, has definitely earned the title. For starters, Thadd has a "post-gender" identity, a concept a lot of people are still having trouble wrapping their heads around.

"I don't care what pronouns people use. Most people think of me as female, while others may assume I'm male and apologize when my voice pitch changes mid-conversation. I never really think of myself as female or male. In a gender-fluid sense I may feel female today and male the next. I'm always just me.

"I started drawing anthro characters when I was in middle school. I didn't know what they were called but a friend eventually told me they were anthros. I didn't officially get into [Furry] until I met LeeLee and he went, 'You don't know about Fur Affinity, but you know about DeviantArt—HOW?'

"As a kid, I was very influenced by anime, and I actually (please don't tell LeeLee) hated the goofy art style of

---

49 "Velan Central Library" (often referred to as "Vixen Control Library")

Looney Tunes or *Mickey Mouse* cartoons, but going to art school beat a snotty attitude out of me and made me appreciate all art styles for what they are: creative and beautiful."

Thadd's "department" is the still relatively young field of 3D printing. When I ask her what piqued her interest in the technology, she tells me, "In a way I've *always* been interested in the technology. Sculpting with clay seemed so painfully slow, and many, many times I wished for the literal invention of 3D printing."

When her wish came true she was ecstatic. Using Sculptris software she created a virtual copy of an Alola Vulpix Pokémon as a demonstration of the medium's possibilities. (Her software file was sent to a 3D-printing company to be turned into a physical object.) The wonderfully detailed sculpture sports a smoothly flowing mane and tail; even subtle details like the extruded paw pads under the Vulpix's feet are beautifully rendered.

Merely a beginning, Thadd says. "I plan to do a lot of work in the field. 3D printing will become incorporated into our badges and item creation."

If predicting the creation of 3D-printing technology doesn't qualify Thadd as a visionary, her embrace of VR technology certainly does. "We plan to expand into VR production for the furry market when we have the technology to manage complex sculpting. Will it be fun-time stuff or something for more 'exotic' tastes? Probably both; that's yet to be seen. I'm opening commissions to 3D print people's custom characters, and all sorts of things along the line. But I plan to go way beyond simple figurine printing—the horizon of possibility is massive, and I hope to reach as much of it as possible."

CHAPTER SIX

Together Is Just What We've Got to Get: The Convention Age Begins

THE WEATHER WAS MILD in Boston the Friday before Labor Day, 1980, the temperature in the mid-seventies. Over the course of the weekend it gradually warmed up, finally topping ninety degrees on the holiday.

The sci-fi fans in town for the Noreascon-hosted Worldcon[50] didn't mind or even notice the heat. In fact, they hardly left the Hynes Auditorium on Boylston Street or the adjoining Sheraton Boston hotel except to pick up a quick slice of pizza or a fast-food burger nearby.

Funny-animal fans attending the convention had another reason to stay indoors; they had come across Steve Gallacci's Erma Felna portrait in the convention's art show—and they'd never seen anything like it before. They might've seen high-tech, hardware-heavy environments in outer-space anime, but never one inhabited by an anthropomorphic animal.

---

50 Local sci-fi conventions bid for the right to host the annual Worldcon, much like cities bidding to host the Olympics.

Cartoon/Fantasy Organization members, *Vootie* contributors and miscellaneous animation fans at the convention were drawn to the painting—and its creator. They discovered it wasn't a one-off; Steve had bought several other paintings and a briefcase full of sketches and notes for an anthropomorphic deep-space epic, something he'd been doodling and noodling with for years. "For whatever reason," Steve later wrote in the third person, "his plopping in their midst as an unknown with all that material in hand was some kind of gosh-wow."

Steve invited the crowd to his hotel room to look over his goodies and chat about their mutual interest in all things anthro. It was the first meeting of what would come to be known as a "Gallacci Group." For the next several years, whenever a convention brought them together, a Gallacci Group would spontaneously form. Almost all of those who attended were artists who brought their sketchbooks along, brimming with their own animal creations. They'd talk about Erma, trade sketches and share opinions on their favorite sci-fi movies and cartoon characters. They'd discuss their own ideas for anthropomorphic epics late into the evening until Steve had to toss them out to get some rest before the convention festivities would resume in the morning.

When *Rowrbrazzle* launched in 1984, the artists gathered around Steve—and Steve himself—were an immediate talent pool for the new APA. Thanks to *Rowrbrazzle* they didn't have to wait six months or a year until the next convention; they could share their thoughts and opinions with everyone at once, every three months via the APA. That same year Steve shared Erma with the world at large via his newly published anthology comic *Albedo*

Anthropomorphics. As with *Rowrbrazzle*, Erma fans didn't have to wait until the next convention to catch up with her adventures. The Gallacci Groups were coming to an end, but the energy they created would continue.

The Gallacci Group's convention gatherings had been traditional room parties, a place where folks could continue to socialize after the con's official events were done for the day. They were open to everyone with a fondness for funny animals. On the other hand, *Rowrbrazzle*'s room parties were like the APA itself: a members-only affair, a Mount Olympus to which only the art gods could ascend; mere mortals could do little but gnash their teeth at the unfairness of life—until an alternative arrived.

The alternative was born at the 1985 Westercon in Sacramento, California. Mark Merlino and Rod O'Riley were hanging with a pair of friends, one of whom suggested they throw an open-to-all funny-animal room party[51]. They needed a name for it, something to put on the flyers publicizing the event. It didn't take them long to come up with something: the gathering would be a "Prancing Skiltaire" party, in honor of Mark and Rod's Garden Grove residence.

It was a low-key affair, with Mark screening videos from his voluminous cartoon collection, including the funny-animal fan favorite *Animalympics*. New faces joined the regulars, people who'd been drawing or imag-

---

51 As mentioned before, people's memories of decades-ago events tend to diverge over time. According to John Cawley, one of *Rowrbrazzle*'s founders, artists-only furry parties existed before the APA's birth. (Email to the author, December 4, 2016.)

ining their own anthros but never had a crowd to hang with before. They perused each other's sketchbooks and traded opinions on all things anthropomorphic between occasional glances at the *Looney Tunes* episodes currently onscreen.

Mark and Rod kept it up, hosting funny-animal-themed parties at other conventions the following months. They attracted more fans, almost all of whom had never dreamed others were into the things they were into. When it was time for the next Westercon, Mark and Rod decided to call their party by a different name: the 1986 iteration would officially be known as a "furry party."

Why "furry?" What was wrong with "funny animals"? For one thing, not all of them were "funny," Erma case in point. Adjectives had been floating around, "fluffy" and "fuzzy" among them. Mark credits a former Skilt-aire resident and self-proclaimed non-furry known as "Dr. Pepper" (no relation to the soft drink) for pouncing on the adjective.[52] (Meanwhile, an Australian fur and an American one who are friends have each told me the *other* first used "furry" in a 1983 fanzine!)

Thirty-plus years later it really doesn't matter who said it first. (Maybe Dr. Pepper had read that fanzine, or perhaps it was just a case of furry minds thinking alike.) Mark and friends blanketed Westercon and subsequent conventions with flyers featuring attractively drawn anthro characters

---

52 Dr. Pepper authored an early, semi-accurate description of the fandom in an essay titled "Furry Fandom Observed": "Furries are those who get into the concept so much that they deliberately develop alternate personas that actually have those animal traits. Each persona takes on a life of its own in a sort of controlled schizophrenia such as ventriloquists and fantasy gamers practice," went a passage written before the word "fursona" came into use. Most furs would agree "controlled schizophrenia" is an interesting but not particularly accurate way of describing one's fursona.

Example of a furry party flyer
Illustration courtesy of and © Mark Freid

promoting furry parties.[53] The fans who attended started calling both themselves and their anthropomorphic characters "furries" and their shared interest was inevitably dubbed "furry fandom," thus cementing the adjective to the noun forevermore. As Rod O'Riley put it years later, "We didn't start furry fandom, we just introduced it to itself."

The premiere furry party was a success and a tradition was born; furry parties (and the illustrated flyers promoting them) became a mainstream con tradition. In 1987, Mark suggested the San Francisco area's BayCon become the unofficial gathering place for West Coast furries. The suggestion spread via word of mouth and pre-Internet electronic bulletin boards. A sizeable crowd of furs turned up—but as it turned out some of the convention's mainstream sci-fi fans were less than overjoyed by their presence.

Why? For some, giving cartoon animals a human-like attractiveness seemed to be highly discomforting. Furry-party flyers were torn down from bulletin boards and convention hall corridors, and, in a memorable bit of snark, some were doctored to promote a "skunk fuckers" party.

Indeed, BayCon and the furries never quite hit it off. In a "did they jump or were they pushed" clash of memory, the common perception is that furs were asked to leave

---

53 Ray Rooney travelled to the 1988 San Diego Comic-Con and convinced Warner Bros. to support the planned Batman event at the Philadelphia museum. He also met the artists at the furry party whose work he'd been admiring from the other side of the continent, his real reason for traveling west. Mark and Rod gave Ray the okay to host an "official" furry party at Philcon later that year—the one I received an out-of-the-blue invitation to attend. "They had originators' rights [to the name]," remembers Ray. "I didn't want to appropriate it. We held the party at Philcon in November; they called afterwards to congratulate us for holding the first one on the east coast." Thanks to Ray, the furry virus now had a foothold in the east—and would continue to spread.

BayCon.[54] In one of our conversations, however, Mark claimed the furry crowd decided to abandon the convention, following in the footsteps of anime fans who started their own convention after *they* were invited to leave.[55]

It was time to kick Furry up a notch. Encouraged by the growing attendance at their sci-fi convention room parties Mark, Rod and a few others organized a furries-only convention dubbed "ConFurence"[56] to be held in January 1989 in Costa Mesa, California, not far from the Skiltaire. Its official title was "ConFurence 0"; it wasn't so much a real convention as a dry run for an *actual* ConFurence they hoped to throw a year later.

Sixty-five furs from all over North America (and one from Australia) showed up to mostly lounge around the lobby of the Costa Mesa Holiday Inn. The program book (more a pamphlet, actually) featured essays from Mark:

> *"Some people criticize Furries as 'wish-fulfillment' or a mask we wear to hide ourselves. My experience leads me to believe the opposite is true. Your Furry is the face that lies behind the mask [you] wear in everyday life."*

---

54 As Fred Patten recalls, a non-fur "took some phony flyers to the convention committee and tried to get the furry fans thrown out of the convention. The committee was aware they were done by an anti-furry group, but it did create a very bad situation. The organizers' attitude was more or less that the furry fans were innocent and shouldn't be thrown out, but since the majority of BayCon attendees were anti-fur 'we'd appreciate if you keep a lower profile or maybe [went] away next year.'"

55 In a later fanzine essay, Fred described a 1991 BayCon panel, *Furry Fandom— Threat or Menace?* "where the moderator kept interrupting the panelists to ask why they weren't doing something constructive such as joining protest marches against vivisection if they really loved animals, instead of just putting all their efforts into drawing disgustingly sexist, adolescent fantasy-pornography."

56 Mark credits the mysterious Dr. Pepper with inventing this name as well.

—and from Rod:

> *"We are not, as it turns out, a new fandom.*
> *We are an old, very basic fandom that has been*
> *waiting its turn to proudly shout its name in*
> *public"*

—as well as a few others, along with an assortment of furry art and a "Make Your Own Tail" tutorial.

For those sixty-five furries the lure was irresistible. What could be better than a furry party that lasted the entire weekend? In 1990, the first "official" ConFurence attracted 130 furs, a crowd exactly twice as large as the year before.

Year by year the numbers kept rising as word spread: 250 for ConFurence 2 in 1991, four hundred for ConFurence 3 . . . At ConFurence 9 in 1998, attendance peaked at 1,250 furs—an increase of over *1800%* in the course of a decade. Furry fandom had arrived—and it wasn't going away.

But for ConFurence itself, it was all downhill from there.

From early on, stories circulated about less than family-friendly behavior at the convention. There was indeed a more adult vibe to ConFurence than later furry conventions would have. Regular ConFurence attractions included a "slave auction" (later renamed a "pet auction") and the "Fur Le Dance" cabaret, both described by Mark as "super-sexy fun events" held to raise money for animal-related charities.

Rumors, and rumors of rumors—the "out of control" stories peaked at ConFurence 8 in 1997 with legends of "jizz" found in an hotel elevator and an attendee cavorting with nothing more than a Dixie cup covering his genitals.

Some people began pointing accusatory fingers at Mark, claiming he had been promoting the convention as an "anything goes" weekend to the party-hardy contingent of the Los Angeles gay community.

"They very, very deliberately billed the convention as a sex party. They advertised it heavily in the fetish community," claims Sam Conway, CEO of Anthrocon, the world's largest and most successful furry convention, before adding, "I wish I could give [evidence of the advertising] to you." He continues, "All I saw was the outcome. By ConFurence 6 it looked like PrideFest."

"Nothing happened at ConFurence that hasn't happened at other conventions," Mark counters. He goes onto explain it was actually a smear of pool-water chlorine in the elevator; the alleged Dixie cup was a leather thong worn by the creator of a gay furry comic book series imitating one of his own characters.

"I question bits of the elevator story," says a fur who attended ConFurence 8. "As I recall, the elevator was relatively fast, so if someone 'did it' in the elevator, they had to be pretty ballsy to do it [when] someone could walk in on them at any time. I heard from a few people who (supposedly) saw the 'evidence' that 'it looked more like mayonnaise,' which would be quick and easy to [leave behind if] someone wanted to make Mark look bad.

"There was much talk about Mark advertising ConFurence as nothing but a sexfest, but I've never seen anything corroborating it."

Did Mark promote ConFurence to the Los Angeles gay community, inviting kinksters to crash the con? In 2014 I visited the LGBT Resource Center on the UCLA campus in Los Angeles in search of any mention of ConFurence 8 in their collection of local gay magazines, newspapers and newsletters for the period leading up to the January 1997 convention—and found nothing. The case was closed . . .

Or was it? More recently on the lulz.net website—one of those wretched hives of scum and villainy that infest the Internet—scans of an undated issue of *Black Sheets*, an artsy-fartsy sex magazine appeared. (Its subhead: "kinky – queer – intelligent – irreverent.") The issue's theme: "Bestiality and Glamour."

Before we go any further I want you to know bestiality, aka "zoophilia," is an absolute and 100% no-no in furry fandom. Furry fandom is about the *idea* of animals—not their reality, but what they represent in our minds. It's a stereotype based on the assumption that people so fascinated by animals must be sexually attracted to actual ones—and the fandom has been fighting this assumption since it began.

Believe it or not, the *Black Sheets* issue was quite classy, with short stories, a poem or two, several pages of thoughtful book reviews, a bit of erotica, ads and an assortment of BDSM-sounding pet-food labels (including "Beg-More" cat food and "Yes, Sir" dog food)—and not a single photograph of a girl (or guy) making it with a donkey or anything even approaching that sort of subject matter. The closest it came was a rather sweet drawing of a woman in a red dress happily dancing with a smiling, top-hatted, tuxedo-wearing lion and two pages of Tom of Finland-style art of super-endowed, animal-head-on-human-body male anthros from a furry artist.

However, page twenty-four listed information sources

for "zoos" looking to pursue their four-legged interests, addresses of several creators of adult anthropomorphic comics, a mail-order house specializing in anthro titles—and a one-sentence mention of "an annual convention for creators and fans of anthropomorphic comics. For information write to: ConFurence . . . " The convention's post office box address followed, and that was it: a completely neutral, essentially accurate description that could've appeared on any publication's events listing page, but ran in the "kinky – queer – intelligent – irreverent" *Black Sheets*. It's interesting to wonder whether the people who inquired were intrigued or disappointed by what they were told.

1998's ConFurence 9 was a much more sedate affair with the convention hitting its 1,250-fur peak. Interestingly, it wasn't the presence (or rumors) of untoward behavior that started ConFurence on its slide towards oblivion—it was a move a year later ninety miles south to San Diego and a date change from its traditional January slot to a mid-April weekend that happened to include Easter Sunday. Attendance plummeted to 850 and kept dropping. A move back north to Irvine didn't help matters, and in the meantime, a new California anthro convention—the San Diego-based Further Confusion (later known short-handedly as FurCon)—had usurped ConFurence's traditional January timeslot.

The final three ConFurences, overseen by a fur who had taken over from an exhausted Mark, were held at a Burbank hotel, each to a smaller crowd until only 470 attended the last ConFurence in 2003.

Among the attendees that year were a camera crew from ABC's *Jimmy Kimmel Show* and one from the series

Kimmel had just left months earlier, Comedy Central's *The Man Show*. Unaware of the tabloid-y bent of the Kimmel show and promised a respectful piece, ConFurence's new head okayed their visit.[57]

The Man Show segment never aired; those who saw the finished *Kimmel* piece said it was anything *but* respectful.

As of 6:00 p.m. on April 27, 2003, ConFurence, the original furry convention, ceased to exist, leaving no shortage of hard feelings behind. The unlucky fur who had taken over from Mark and Rod found himself barraged by accusations from disgruntled furs—and $60,000 in debt after signing a three-year hotel contract based on ConFurence attendance that never materialized.

ConFurence was no more, but the following year a team of furs that included Mark and Rod created CaliFur, a new L.A.-area furry convention to join the others springing up around the country.

The convention age was just beginning.

---

57   The hotel—not Confurence—gave *The Man Show* the okay to record the convention for a segment that never aired. In the wake of ConFurence's collapse, angry furs accused the convention's head of—among other things—pocketing a fee from *The Man Show*. That fee, however, was actually paid directly to the hotel by *The Man Show*, in order to access the convention.

CHAPTER SEVEN

Walk a Mile in My Fursuit

IT DIDN'T BEGIN with today's furries; people have been dressing as animals for tens of thousands of years, beginning with the earliest indigenous cultures. Native Americans donned bison hides and performed the Buffalo Dance in hopes of a successful hunt; they wore eagle feathers and danced in honor of the sacred animal whose domain extended beyond the clouds.[58] The shamans of the Pacific Northwest Nootka tribes dressed in bear skins and bear masks to "abduct" children in a ceremony bestowing adult privileges.[59] Mesoamerican and African tribes created and wore animal masks and masks of human/animal hybrids as part of their religious ceremonies.

These rites are still taking place. In some parts of the world it's a living tradition; in others, a way of entertaining visiting tourists. At year's end in Romania's Trotus Valley

---

58　*The Spirit World*, Time-Life Books, 1992.

59　Hall of Northwest Coast Indians, American Museum of Natural History.

region the "dancing bears"—people dressed in actual bear skins—travel between towns dispelling evil spirits. It's a ritual that originated with the country's Roma minority in the 1930s and was adopted (some would say appropriated) by ethnic Romanians—but now local governments and cultural groups are struggling to preserve the tradition in the face of economic downturns and the lure of westernization threatening the "bears" with extinction.[60]

Today's modern "tribes" are sports teams, the animal spirits their cartoon mascots. They're brought to life by performers garbed not in animal skins, but in suits of polyester, foam and fake fur. The practice may no longer carry the spiritual weight it once did but it's the identical instinct—to mingle the human and animal—taking contemporary form.

As residents of contemporary times, furs express their animal identities using the same materials to create fursuits—the head-to-toe animal costumes that have come to represent the fandom. ("Furries—those people who dress up as animals? Yeah, I saw them on TV.") It's a natural if inaccurate assumption; fursuiters always get the lion's share of attention when the furry circus comes to town. If you work for the local paper or TV station you'd be crazy—or fired—to not put them on camera.

Many furs opposed fursuits at the start. Furry fandom was birthed by artists and writers whose anthropomorphic creations existed on paper, and later on the Internet. Back in the day there wouldn't have been room for a fursuiter in a crowded hotel-room furry party. (There was at least one fursuiter on hand at ConFurence

60   Alhindawi, Diana Zeyneb. "Bear Dance." 2014. (https://www. dianazeynebalhindawi.com/bear-dance-romania/) Retrieved May 5, 2016.

0 though—a professional Disneyland mascot performer who showed up not as one of Walt's creations, but as a "Bambioid," a sexy outer-space deer partial to knee-high leather boots.) It was a bit of surprise to cartoonists when 'suiters started showing up in growing numbers at the conventions; they were interlopers invading "our" art-centric fandom.

It really shouldn't have been a surprise that fursuits became a popular form of anthro expression. Costume contests and masquerades have been part of sci-fi and comic conventions since their inception. Cosplay is a huge aspect of anime fandom, and if you go to a Renaissance Faire you're guaranteed to run into more than your share of knights, wizards, damsels in distress and possibly a unicorn or two. There's simply no reason that a goodly number of fans of anthropomorphic characters wouldn't want to express themselves the same way—it just took a while for them to get up to speed.

Despite the aforementioned contention, fursuiters continued showing up at conventions in gradually increasing numbers. Lance Ikegawa, an accomplished costume builder with decades of experience under his belt, was one of them. While not a fur himself, he shares that "furry fandom is where a lot of creature-costuming grew up, so I gravitated towards those conventions. Furry cons are fun. It's easier to be one of many creature-costumes at a furry con than the only monster at any other convention.

"This predates furry fandom by quite a few years: when I saw a science-fiction masquerade at the 1978 Worldcon I was blown away. I had no idea ordinary people could make elaborate costumes like I'd see in the movies.

"There were hardly any costumers at the early furry

conventions; very few people had the skills to build their own or the money to buy a costume from a mascot company. Over time though, through convention workshops and panels, more and more costumes began appearing. The number of costumes exploded when tutorials started showing up on YouTube. Now anyone could see how these costumes were made without having to attend a convention, and they began doing it themselves. With this burst of makers, some began to take commissions.

"Furry fans were already commissioning artists to draw their furry character: the idea of having a costume made that would allow them to 'become' their character was irresistible. Suddenly there were dozens, then hundreds of costumes showing up at conventions, festivals, parades and gatherings.

"Mass media was the conduit that cemented the association and made furry costumes the face of the fandom. Ordinary, non-costume-wearing attendees, nerds and sketchbooks are boring . . . but someone wearing a technicolor lion costume? Media gold. Just as everyone back in the day believed all *Star Trek* fans dressed up as Spock, the public thinks everyone in furry fandom wears costumes."

As a youngster, Lance was fascinated by *kaiju* TV shows, series like *Ultraman, Kikaider* and *Kamen Rider* starring gigantic monsters—actually actors in rubber suits—stomping on scale-model cities. "Their ability to disguise the human form had me wide-eyed from a young age. To me, animal costuming is just a subset of creature costuming. People are most familiar with my furry costumes, but I am keenly interested in any challenge that involves hiding the human form. My masquerade costumes are quite varied—from a ten-foot-tall snow creature to the Beatles' Blue Meanie Boss to a black unicorn puppet from *Adventure Time*."

Lance may not name himself a furry, but he's made his fair share of extraordinary fursuits. "I've made full suits, partials, puppets and prop-costumes. Going through my photos, I'm coming up with eighty-eight, more or less." Half of those suits are in his personal collection. It's not an inexpensive hobby, though. "As commissions go, the most expensive thing my partner and I made was in the low five figures. It was a manticore, with a detailed muscle suit, NFT fur,[61] wings, etc. The materials alone made up more than half the cost. NFT fur is pricey—a whole suit can use $4,000–8,000 worth of fur. It was a fun challenge, and I'm still proud of the results.

"For the most part, other builders' suits come in at the low thousands of dollars, but more complicated ones can run into the low five figures. The irony is, if you add up the hours spent and subtract the materials, shipping, etc., these costumers would be making well under minimum wage."

Like many niche art styles, the fursuit name rose out of a play on words, this time from a once-upon-a-time Indiana farm boy who grew up to be a computer engineer—and on occasion, a busty female skunk.

"In 1994 I started a mailing list dedicated to sharing furry costume construction and performance tips, and I needed a name for it," explains Robert King. "This is a

---

61 National Fiber Technology (nftech.com) manufactures natural-looking synthetic hair and fur many suitmakers swear by. (Incorporating actual fur into a suit is a major no-no among suitmakers; apart from the ethics involved, real fur is expensive and much heavier than the fake stuff.)

hobby—and another word for hobby is 'pursuit.' I decided to make a pun on 'pursuit' and named it the 'fursuit list.' Soon there were one hundred people on it. Everyone thought the list was named after the costumes and began calling the costumes 'fursuits.'[62] I didn't push the idea; the fandom just took it and ran with it.

"There were lots of people who wished for a suit but were too intimidated by the difficulty of creating one. I acted as a catalyst to help them create their own. I gave panels on how to make fursuits back in the mid nineties. I pushed a 'just do it!' philosophy and said, 'It's better to do a bad suit than to never do anything.'"

Robert started meeting and networking with other fursuiters at ConFurence 2 in 1991 (though it wasn't until 1996 at ConFurence 7 that he arrived in a suit of his own creation). Out of that early convention's two hundred attendees he estimates perhaps ten 'suiters were present—a minuscule 5% versus the 20–25% at today's largest furcons.

He adds that he was more relieved than surprised to find other fursuiters in the fandom. "I hung out with costumers [at mainstream sci-fi conventions] from the early eighties on, but I really wasn't that interested in costumes that weren't of furry characters."

Robert describes himself as only a little bit surprised people assume all furs wear them. "It makes sense; the fursuits upstage everything else just by being there."

Like so many other furs, cartoon animals introduced

---

62 According to Lance Ikegawa the term "fursuit" was already in use in special effects world: "Wardrobe and the special-effects techs would refer to hairy costumes as 'fursuits' as opposed to latex creatures or make-up effects." The fursuit/pursuit pun is irresistible, judging from the numerous newspapers and magazines headlining their furry fandom story "The Fursuit of Happiness."

Robert to the pleasures of anthropomorphism.[63] In particular he liked the sultry feline M'Ress, an Enterprise crewmember in the Saturday morning version of the original *Star Trek*, whose tail had the painful habit of getting caught in the ship's turbolift doors. "I was also very impressed by [1968's] *Planet of the Apes*' beautifully realistic ape appliances."[64]

Robert's passion for science took him from the heart of the Hoosier State to a pair of electrical engineering degrees and a career in computers. But it was an appreciation of "the beauty possible in blending the human and the animal form" that attracted him to Furry.

Before discovering furry fandom Robert was active in sci-fi fandom. That's how he came across *Centaurs Gatherum*, the same newsletter that ultimately led me to the furry world. In his case, another *Gatherum* reader read and recognized Robert's furry interests from his printed comments and sent Robert a copy of *Furversion*, an early furry fanzine, for which Robert says he is "forever grateful."

"I was already immersed in sci-fi fandom, so Furry was just an offshoot that focused on things more aligned to my interests. The *Gatherum* helped me develop an interest in costuming as an expression of what I liked; I've done multiple satyr costumes for example.

"My early costumes were barely above Halloween-

---

63 Robert demolishes my assumption that his farm-boy upbringing sparked his interest in anthropomorphism. "Actually it tended to oppose it. As a small boy I witnessed numerous veterinary procedures, performed pig castrations and had to haul pig manure by the thousand-gallon load. To this day, I find pig anthros more difficult to enjoy than other species."

64 Robert is referring not to what might be found in a simian kitchen, but to the face-altering prostheses used to transform actors into animals, aliens or monsters for the camera.

costume grade. I made matching unicorn costumes for my wife and myself that we took on our honeymoon cruise in the Caribbean. I also had a black cat costume, but those early costumes don't really count as fursuits because they didn't fully hide the human face. I created other sexy-looking animal costumes for my wife that highlighted the female figure." Robert and his spouse ultimately found this approach unsatisfying: "The attention she was getting in my costumes didn't interest her, and her efforts to credit me for them weren't that effective." An understandable situation, since the furs were likely far more fascinated by the attractive anthropomorphic female than the puny human alongside her who'd actually made the suit.

There was only one way to deflect attention from his wife and get the ego boost his work deserved: "I had to make a female furry costume for myself. I started researching female body padding and how to construct a proper full face mask.

"My first real fursuit was a costume of Samantha Kemple, a character created by artist Ken Sample. I started working on her in 1994 and first wore her in 1996 at ConFurence 7. She turned out very well, and she still gets lots of compliments."

As well she should. Robert's mephitic alter ego is a *zoftig* skunk gal, dressed in a low-cut red-and-purple miniskirt and sporting a plush tail that begins where a tail should and rises to the top of her head. (You'll never see them, but there's a pair of nipples under that miniskirt added for the sake of realism; beyond that, Robert wants everyone to know the costume is *not* anatomically correct. And as for his own "equipment"—add wink emoji here—he adds "it's very compressible—don't worry.")

Mister Rogers once said "there's more than a smell to a skunk." In Samantha's case, that "more" includes Robert's character description: "Samantha is contemporary and suburban. She is an athletic tomboy, a little shy and very good looking." And in case you or Mr. Rogers were wondering: "She can't spray and does not smell like a skunk."

No small amount of work went into translating a two-dimensional drawing of Samantha into a sophisticated full-body fursuit. Samantha's character description is only the beginning of a lengthy document detailing (in great detail) the work that went into creating her. Robert's shopping list included fake fur, polyurethane sealer, oil-based clay, liquid latex, polyfoam, Plexiglass, zippers, hot rolled steel, a corset, a bra fastener, foam packing peanuts to fill out Samantha's tail . . . and water-filled "ice bag" breasts to give her bosom a pleasing jiggle.[65]

Robert estimates about $500 worth of materials went into Samantha's fursuit, icebags and all—and were he to commission a big-name vendor to create Samantha today, she would probably cost between four and five thousand dollars—"but she would look better due to more advanced techniques that have been developed."

It's not enough just to suit up though; if you really want to adopt an anthropomorphic alter ego (and in particular, one of the opposite gender) you've got to walk the walk and, although it's not always possible, talk the talk. "I can't do a good feminine voice, and I can't be easily heard,

---

65 "When people ask how big are Samantha's breasts I tell them 'four pounds each,' which usually isn't the kind of answer they expect."

so I avoid talking. I also have trouble hearing with the mask on. I've practiced a variety of feminine walks and Marilyn Monroe moves; lots of people have given me advice, but I still don't have it quite right." At the bottom of it all Robert admits "her personality when I perform her is really a feminized version of myself."

Robert experienced a *Tootsie* phenomenon not unlike Dustin Hoffman's: "I must admit it was really fun having drooling men competing to open doors for me; I could practically see their IQs dropping."

Out of costume though, "people start inferring all kinds of things about my gender identity, sexual preferences and such . . . that's when I have to remind them, 'it's just a costume!'"

For some fursuiters the costume is more of a reflection of their true selves than their human bodies could ever be. "Charleston Rat," or Clayton as he's known in the real world, is a twenty-two-year-old British graphic designer whose fascination with anthro characters began with *The Wild Thornberrys* and *Animorphs* TV series.

"I loved Eliza Thornberry because she could talk to animals. I thought, 'That seems like the most awesome superpower ever—that's something I want to do!' *Animorphs* captivated me with images of kids morphing into other creatures. I was fascinated by the idea and created stories in my head where I'd morph into animal, usually a dog or a tiger. I'd wander out of the house, play with my animal buddies then come back home and morph back into a human without my parents knowing where I'd been. Doesn't that sound awesome to you?"

In his early teens Charleston discovered the Internet and along with it, the "liberation of finding out [about]

Charleston Rat
Photograph courtesy of and © Charleston Rat

nearly anything." That liberation included coming across *Animorphs*-style pictures of humans transforming into animals both naturalistic and anthropomorphic.

"Out of curiosity I compared dressing up as an animal to actually transforming into one, which made me wonder if people made costumes of these animals. That's when I did an Internet search and discovered the word 'fursuit'—instantly I wanted one. I adored the idea of jumping into a fluffy costume and becoming a whole new character in both body and mind."

Charleston continued researching fursuits, but his "passion became less about the dressing up itself and more about performing as the character I wanted to become. I knew from the start I was going to be a rat. Rats and I have a lot in common: they're small and I often feel small, rats are curious and I'm curious, and so on.

"But I didn't just want to be any old rat; I wanted to be one with an identity of his own."

Charleston was a regular viewer of the British TV series *Strictly Come Dancing*. (It's been franchised all over the world; in the U.S. it's known as *Dancing with the Stars*.) One night he caught an episode where a performer wore a snazzy outfit festooned with shiny buttons and danced the Charleston. "I already loved that style of dance—and that kind of music even more—but I'd never seen an outfit like that before. I loved how different it was, but I had no idea what it was about."

Charleston did his homework and discovered the dancer was dressed as a "Pearly King," saluting a tradition dating back to the nineteenth century when Henry Croft, a Cockney London street sweeper, decorated his clothes with attention-getting mother-of-pearl buttons to help fund local hospitals and orphanages for the poor. "Pearly Kings and Queens are a lot like fursuiters: they both create elaborate, one-of-a-kind costumes to attend local events, make people happy and raise money for charities."

Charleston named his rat fursona after the dance; in his mind he could see the animal's wardrobe down to the last detail. Now there was just the slight matter of learning how to create a fursuit. As a young man starting out in the world, commissioning a suit builder was out of the financial question. Once again he turned to the Internet and discovered an abundance of helpful tutorials and forums.

"I never found [a single] tutorial that gave me all the information I needed, but I learned what I needed from a variety of them and from online forums. One tutorial had really good advice on how to build my head, whilst another had tips about foot paw construction, and a forum helped me choose my padding."

Something else helped Charleston, something you might not expect: his autism.

"My autism has helped me be part of the furry community. What autistic people lack in social skills they tend to make up for in practical skills, very often visual ones. I think autism has given me a deeper understanding of shapes and colors than most people. I was more confident using that padding to give me short stubby legs than I would have otherwise, and more optimistic to sew by hand even though I'd never sewn before.

"I'll never forget the moment when I showed my completed head to a friend. His first reaction was 'where did you get that?!' He honestly thought a professional made it for me. That really made me smile—although to be fair, my fursuit head is always smiling!

"I have mixed feelings about people knowing I'm autistic. If they don't know I get treated like a regular guy and not talked to as if I'm a toddler. On the other paw, if I do something weird like walk on my toes, not make eye contact whilst talking or react badly to something intended as a joke (autistic people tend to take things literally) things can get awkward and uncomfortable. When someone does know I'm autistic they understand some of the unusual things I do—but I tend to get treated overly nicely and wrapped up in cotton wool. It's a hard balance for people to get right.

"Most furs seem to understand and find that balance, especially since the percentage of autistic folk in the fandom seems much higher than among people in general. And, because we already have that ice-breaker of being into cartoon animals, we already have something to talk about and build a friendship on."

In the fall of 2016, Charleston the human completed Charleston's fursuit. His final task was sewing several hundred shiny buttons onto his waistcoat, in swirling patterns up the coat's front, across its back and along its bottom, where they frame his name, spelled out in buttons as well: CHARLESTON THE PEARLY RAT.

The suit's "short, stubby" legs look perfect; rat Charleston's crotch is just above human Charleston's knees. The combined effect of Charleston's stubby legs and the small waistcoat sitting high on his chest creates a very convincing effect of a long and slender body—a ratty silhouette for sure.

"I'm impressed with how my fursuit has come out,

especially since this is my first ever attempt at something like this," he reflects. "There are things I'd like to improve, of course. His cheeks aren't puffy enough, and I probably made his teeth too long. On top of that, I made the arms too long, meaning I now have wrinkly arms when in suit.

"It's unlikely I'll make a full suit again in the near future, but if I ever were to do so, I now know where I'd change things and try to make things better. For now, I'll just have fun being a plush, wrinkly-armed ratty. There's something quite remarkable about seeing your character form before your very eyes," concludes the self-taught fursuit builder. "It's almost like bringing your animalistic alter ego to life."

My own experience inside a mascot suit started the year I marched in the Macy's Thanksgiving Day Parade as "Baxter," a magical clown from a now all-but-forgotten 1980s kids' TV series: *The Great Space Coaster.* It was hot and sweaty inside the costume. (Even though it was a cold morning I probably shouldn't have worn a sweater.) My view from the character head was the equivalent of peering out of a narrow slot in a World War II-era pillbox waiting for enemy soldiers to storm the beach; all I could see was a peripheral-vision-free slice of the world through the mesh fabric disguising an eye-level opening in the brim of Baxter's cap. In spite of the discomfort, the experience was fun, seeing kids cheering for someone they thought only existed on TV. For the length of the parade I was that someone. The two-mile walk from New York City's Upper West Side to Herald Square seemed to fly by in no time at all.

Still, I'd never felt a yen to repeat the experience, even

when fursuiters started showing up at the cons in ever-increasing numbers. But as they say, if at first you don't succeed . . . maybe another look at the world from inside a fursuit would change your point of view.

It was a late Sunday afternoon, that sad time when conventions wind down and fursuits are packed up. I was in a friend's hotel room—he was a middle-aged guy with a husky build not unlike my own—helping him put away his suits from Anthrocon 2011. There was a fursuit lying on the bed, and out of curiosity I asked if I could try it on; he invited me to go for it.

I suited up and looked in the full-length mirror. A blue-furred female rabbit was staring back at me.

I look pretty cute, I thought.

I had a white chest (sporting slender but definitely visible breasts) and abdomen, and a slight swell to my hips. I turned and looked over my shoulder for a glimpse of my bunny tail; there it was, just above my bunny behind. I shook my rear end and watched my tail give a saucy wiggle.

I smiled inside my suit. I didn't feel like I was in a pillbox; I wasn't peeking out of a mesh-covered peephole. (The suit's eyes lined up with my own, giving me a much more natural field of vision.) I didn't even feel like I was in a fursuit.

I felt like a bunny rabbit. I *was* a bunny rabbit—a cute, blue-furred, anthropomorphic lady rabbit. I realized I'd been looking at the fursuit situation entirely wrong.

A fursuit isn't a costume—it's *a skin*, an other self made visible. To borrow some dialog from *Donnie Darko*, you're as much taking off "that stupid man suit" as putting on a "stupid bunny suit." The suit isn't housing the person wearing it—it's the wearer's alternate personality (and species) manifesting itself. I'd been rejecting fursuits because I thought they were a failed attempt to make an imaginary animal "real," when the animal standing in front of me already *was* real.

Two years later I was in Portland, Oregon, visiting a furry couple I'd known quite a while. They were a couple of cool guys—funny, warm and friendly—and had full-sized *Ms. Pac-Man* and *Dig Dug* arcade machines in their living room. My kind of people.

They also had quite a few suits between them, and they asked if I'd like to try one on.

A few minutes later, a grey rat with a big black nose and long pink tail is hiding in the kitchen, spying on a meerkat in their living room. The meerkat, a big-footed fellow who might be mistaken for *The Lion King*'s Timon is marching up and down in place, his pumping arms energetically matching his footsteps.

When the meerkat realizes he's being watched he chases the rodent out of the kitchen. The frightened rat loops around the hallway and returns to the kitchen via its other entrance, narrowly avoiding the irritated meerkat who's now looking for him in the hallway.

The meerkat expresses his frustration at the rat's elusiveness with a fist-thrusting "dammit" gesture; he motions to the observer watching their encounter to stay close with a "follow me" finger waggle, then shushes him with a finger against his lips gesture. After a few loops around the kitchen the meerkat finally corners the rat, extending both arms towards him as if to say "all is forgiven." The rat meekly steps into the meerkat's tender embrace—which immediately turns into a headlock as the 'kat pummels the hoodwinked rodent's skull and the observer slowly backs away.

I crack up every time I watch the "observer's" video of the pair's pantomimed encounter. When I play it for a friend he guesses—incorrectly—that I'm in the rat suit when I'm actually the meerkat. It was my first attempt at fursuit roleplay and I'm not half bad at it; in fact I enjoyed it a damn lot.

A fursuit isn't a generic animal of any particular species, and it doesn't just represent a furry animal. It turns its wearer *into* that furry, into a real person whose species and personality just happens to be different from the one the wearer was born with. (One could say the furry is the fur's secret identity, but the reverse might equally be true.) A fursuit has to bring that personality to life. It has to be there on its face, in its eyes, its mouth, even the shape of its tail; it might be as subtle as the tilt of an eyebrow or the angle of an ear. It's a process with a steep learning curve, from cultivating an eye for materials and fabrics and learning the ins and outs of sewing to sculpting a face that captures an elusive personality.

"Denali" is an Atlanta-based fursuit builder who's mastered those subtleties. Her Fur Affinity profile picture depicts the beaming suitbuilder in a denim jacket, multicolored dress and high-topped purple-laced sneakers. She's posing on a staircase in front of a quintet of her creations: a stern-faced blue-and-yellow "Manectric" Pokémon; a hesitant-looking lavender-haired, cyan-muzzled "chibi shyena," a hyena sporting a ringed nose and a very threatening expression; and behind him another hyena,[66] this one mauve-colored and slit-eyed evil. Behind the hyenas stands an extremely worried-looking tan-and-brown rabbit. (I'd be nervous too if I were anywhere near those predators!)

Apart from a very successful sideline in scented sanitizing fursuit sprays[67] and three separate online shops, Denali's a full-time fursuit builder via her LobitaWorks company and has a months-long waiting list for commissions. Her "furry before discovering the fandom" story is identical to that of so many others furs. "I've loved animals, cartoons and mythology since I was a kid. I was the kind of person that would go over to someone's house and make instant friends with their pets but was kind of awkward with the other kids. I was one of the first in my area to have Internet access in the mid nineties; I found furry fandom looking online for werewolf art and *Lion King* fan sites."

Denali was a furry cartoonist before branching into fursuit construction, which explains her creations' cartoony aspect. "My goal with my fursuits is to have them look like my drawings come to life. My artwork tends to have expressive faces, so I carry that aesthetic into my fursuit work."

Denali enumerates the signifiers of cartoony facial expressions: "The brows, cheeks, mouth, eyes and—to a lesser degree—ears are all important. Happy, confident-

---

66 With their striped and spotted fur and leering expressions, hyena fursuits are quite popular—even multicolored ones.

67 Vanillazilla, Puppy Colada, Pawberry and Appleocalypse are among her offerings. Denali explains the original inspiration for her product line was misting her skunk suit, "Zero" (named for a caramel candy bar), with a caramel-scented spray; unlike real-world skunks, a sniff of furry skunk scent can be quite pleasing to the nose.

type characters usually have big pushed-up cheeks, lifted brows, upturned mouth corners and relaxed-looking eyes.

"A deviously smiling character's construction is similar, except the brows become furrowed and the eyelids may be heavier over the eyes. Sharp teeth (if applicable to the species) help sell a mischievous look. A mopey, sad character may have ears down, heavily lidded eyes and a mouth that's more closed. A crazy character can have wide-staring eyes with small irises and pupils and a big manic grin. A fun touch with those sorts of characters is a floppy tongue that lolls out of the mouth. It helps to know some basic facial anatomy for both humans and the actual animal you're making a suit of. Cartoons are also a good reference for stylizing a character's expression."

While most clients come to Denali with their character's personality already in mind, not all do. "If someone doesn't have a preference, the classic 'polite smile' is always a good bet. Most of my costume heads have that look as do most 'toon fursuits. A head that's not expressing an extreme emotion allows for a versatile performance [if its wearer is performing during a convention]. It looks good on most characters." She continues: "Another popular expression is the 'ne'er do well' grin with angry eyes and a smiling mouth."

Denali's suits fall on the toony end of the furry spectrum. "A cartoony style allows for a wider range of expressions, into the extreme and absurd, but realistic costumes can be expressive too. It's true a wolf can't have the same facial expressions as a human, but anthro characters are a blend of human and animal forms. A realistic fursuit can have a smile on its face or a sullen glare or a nervous grimace, because it's part human too.[68]

"Realistic suits are really, really hard [to make] and I respect the people who make them. I've tried realistic costumes several times—[they] usually end up being mocked on someone's snarky blog because I'm not that good at it. So I mostly stick to what I'm best at."

Denali credits a post-college stint with a company that made commercial mascot costumes with drastically improving her skills and efficiency at costume-making. It was only a matter of time before she quit her low-paying job to create costumes full time. "The risks were relatively minor. My job had no benefits or room for advancement. I wasn't leaving anything great, but it was still the scariest thing I'd ever done.

"I came up with a business plan and got to work. It's been four years now and I've never looked back; I am so happy getting to be creative all day, turning people into cute animals! This is my sole source of income and it's been a rocky ride but I love my job. My husband was in a similar situation with a dead-end job; he left his and now we work together full-time making fursuits."

If my bunny-suit revelation was the beginning of my transformation from skeptic to believer, my meerkat moment turned me into an enthusiast. The idea of embodying, of *becoming* an anthropomorphic animal for "real," not just imagining or drawing or enjoying pictures

---

68 In one respect, beaked and billed avian costumes (I'm tempted to call them "feathersuits") are a degree more realistic than frozen-faced fursuits: mammals possess flexible facial musculature impossible to reproduce on a fursuit, while bird faces are naturally immobile. (Though a hinged jaw that moves up and down when the 'suiter speaks adds a lifelike element to any suit.) Face painting is almost non-existent in the fandom, as is movie-style prosthetic animal makeup; while their flexibility and the wearer's exposed eyes vividly convey emotion and personality, thin, lightweight prosthetics are too fragile to survive repeated application and removal.

of them, was growing more and more tantalizing by the day. It had taken a decade or two, but I had evolved from an anti-fursuit purist to someone who couldn't wait to have a suit of his own, to become . . . something else, though I didn't know what yet.

My fursona, my gator self, had no personality apart from my own—he was just me made scaly, a generic, anthropomorphic *Alligator mississipiensis*. My suit had to do more than change my outside; it had to change who I was *inside*, liberating someone definitely not Joe Strike.

Over the years I'd dreamt up no small number of furry characters to populate my comics and stories. Among my mental menagerie was a character very different from my default personality. Someone I envied a great deal:

Illustration by Kjartan Arnorsson, courtesy of and © the author

arrogant rather than easygoing, not giving a shit what other people thought about him . . . and unlike Joe the Friendly Human, possessing and relishing power over others. He was "Komos," a shape-shifting anthropomorphic Komodo dragon.[69]

Komos commands powerful hypnotic and mind-reading skills—and the ability to temporarily turn people into animals, gifts given to him by Circe, the legendary enchantress who transformed Ulysses' slovenly crew into swine.

There's no shortage of modern-day reinterpretations of Circe, from classical ballet to comic books. In my version she lives in a timeless, extra-dimensional realm she can only leave at the cost of her immortality. In order to continue enjoying her hobby and keep up with modern times she created her own theme park, Circe's Funhouse, wherein the various attractions and pavilions transform visitors into the animal most appropriate to their personality. In need of someone to oversee her earthly interests, she turned a willing volunteer (me of course) into her reptilian servant, endowed him with powers and returned him to the real world to send people deserving or in need of a new species her way via a trans-dimensional portal.

A friend and I are working on a comic book starring Komos and his character "Goldie," a golden, reincarnated, super-strong Celtic sex goddess with a "statufying" Midas touch. Komos and Goldie have teamed up, combining their unique talents to battle a crime ring and

---

69 Although reptile characters are technically "scalies," as anthropomorphic animals they're every bit a part of the furry universe. And even though Komos is a shape-shifting humanoid reptile, he is definitely not an alien Reptilian, one of the "Lizard People" secretly controlling the planet.

take down its mysterious mastermind "Mr. Big." Fighting bad guys is a pleasant diversion for the reptile, especially alongside a goddess he admires and respects as much as his mistress. (Like my friend and I, Goldie and Komos's friendship is strictly platonic. However they're both exceptionally successful with the opposite sex, due in no small part to their supernatural abilities.)

Komos is possessed of infinite self-regard and bottomless condescension towards the foolish, inept or just plain evil humans who cross his path. He's both a shameless power fantasy and an escape valve for my ever-present but carefully repressed desire to pass judgment on other people. But boy, it would be great to be him, even for a little while . . .

A scaly green lightbulb clicked on above my head. It was time to find a real-world Circe, someone who can, just as in my homemade mythology, transform me into Komos.

In the fall of 2015, I began looking for a fursuit builder to bring Komos to life, someone capable of capturing his unique arrogance. I wrote a character description to help that person along:

> *Komos is an amoral character (a "chaotic neutral" in roleplay parlance) who has embarked on his adventure with Goldie for the sheer fun of giving the bad guys grief. He is cool as hell and he knows it. His expression is not so much a sneer as an accurate reflection of his innate superiority to, and amusement about, the antics of foolish, incapable or evil humans.*

My Komos suit couldn't be a "fur" suit either. Other 'suiters might not care, but for my money (of which I was prepared to spend quite a bit) a furry reptile is about as oxymoronic as you can get. Actual Komodos look like they're cloaked in chain mail, their scales small and pebbly. I didn't want a fursuit; I wanted a "scalesuit."

My fursuit builder had to be one with a knack for creating reptiles. Starting in fall left plenty of time (or so I thought) for someone to finish a suit in time for Anthrocon the following summer. After a bit of research, I decided to reach out to two potential artists: one who goes by the name Temperance and one who uses the racier name Artslave.

"Drawing comics may be hazardous to your health" isn't a warning sign you're likely to see anywhere, but the fursuit builder known as Temperance would probably agree with the sentiment.

"I've been a big comic nerd most of my life. I always thought one day I'd draw comic books for a living—but as it turns out that wasn't in the cards," says the thirty-five-year-old Canadian gal. "I've contributed to lots of anthologies, some comic-strip books and self-published stories, and one graphic novel. While making the novel I discovered sitting for twelve-to-fourteen-hour days over a drawing table was causing me extreme hip pain. The mind was willing, but the body was weak."

Fortunately, Temperance had a creative fallback. "I was a cosplayer as well as a comic artist, so I loved making and wearing things. My mother taught me to sew back in the day, but it was a bit of a failure: it took us two days to make a pair of shorts with one of those "easy sew in one hour" projects. I was so frustrated with it that I didn't attempt to sew anything [else] for years.

"I eventually got back into sewing when I made my first Halloween costume, Harley Quinn from *Batman*. Using what I remembered from my mom's sewing lessons I frankensteined some red and black clothes into a really awful costume. I wore it proudly and proceeded to make more and more awful costumes. I'm almost entirely self-taught; I learned a lot as I sewed and experimented."

In 2008 Temperance was at the Calgary Comic and Entertainment Expo when she saw a fierce-looking feline warrior—the auburn colored Red XIII, a *Final Fantasy* character come to life in a suit created and worn by an extremely talented (and as it happened, fellow Canadian) suitmaker named Beetlecat.

Red XIII is a four-legged, razor-clawed feral animal, with "an intelligence surpassing that of any human's under his fierce exterior," according to the *Final Fantasy* website. Beetlecat's two-legged version boasted bulging muscular pectorals, a narrow waist, realistic-looking digitgrade legs and a thick tasseled tail—a creation impressive enough to inspire Temperance to try her own hand at fursuit building.

"I made an Amaterasu costume and a generic minotaur suit with all the basic features one expects of a minotaur: horns, hooves, loincloth, bone necklace and some earrings. I loved the process so much I started making more animal costumes. I discovered furry fandom while researching how to make them; eventually a vast amount of my costumes were furry in nature.

"It led to my first commissions when friends who had seen my work wanted me to make suits of their own characters. At some point I realized the business opportunity of being a fursuit maker...and slowly, over the years, costume making dominated my life until it became an actual career I could make a real living at.

"I tried drawing a comic book last year and found the whole process more of a slog than I remembered. I was no longer excited or eager to sit and draw."

Temperance has been making fursuits since that 2008 encounter with Red XIII. She's lost count of her creations to date but estimates she's made "a couple of hundred at least, turning out two or three a month depending on their complexity," via her company Komickrazi Studios. She still gets the occasional, though increasingly rare, non-fursuit cosplay commission for an anime, comic or video game character. "The largest issue with fursuits versus other types of costumes and cosplay is cost expectation. Furries know how much costumes cost; with a little research they know how much an average fursuit will set them back.

"But thanks to China's mass production and sources like eBay and Alibaba.com, people can purchase relatively inexpensive cosplay costume at a fraction of what a normal seamstress would charge. Those $40 costumes are often made of inferior materials, mass produced in limited sizes and might last one or two conventions before falling apart. The prices I charge are too high for the average cosplayer who just wants a cheap and easy costume for a weekend. I get very few commissions for non-furry costume work."

There are currently thirty-four people in Temperance's queue waiting for custom-made fursuits. "I never close for commissions. I add people to my queue after I receive their deposit and work on their suits in order. Right now it's about a year between getting on the queue and finishing their suit, which is pretty average for me.

"Lots of makers open their commission list, fill X number of slots and work on those. I can see the appeal of working on a finite number of suits at a time, but I like my system and so do a lot of people. There's comfort in knowing they can put down money and be guaranteed a place in a line. Even if the line is long, it beats the alternative of trying and trying to commission an artist whose queue opens and closes sporadically and often fills before they can get on the list."

Temperance's favorite client however, might be herself. She proudly describes her three personal fursuits, each of which let her assume a personality to match the suit.

"Summer," a cheerfully smiling, multi-colored red panda "is one of a set of four I created to be worn as a group representing the four seasons. Spring is sultry and sweet, Summer is full of joy and fun, Autumn—or Otto—is a grumpy guy, and Winter is always ready for a nap."

Her second favorite is a rodent—but a loveable one. "Momo Mouse is just a basic grey mouse with glasses and a bow on her bum, but she's very outgoing and has a cute squeaky voice. She's got small feet and is easy to move around in, I made her for when I enter dance competitions, but she's so popular she comes to every con with me now. I think she's more popular than regular old me."

Her basic fursona bears the name she's known by in the fandom: "Temperance" is a duck-billed dinosaur. "She's pretty much me in dinosaur form. She wears hoodies and jeans, she's pretty casual and friendly. Although I mostly wear Momo, Temperance is nice to have when I want to suit but don't want to really perform.

"Some of my personal suits are quite expensive and complex. The nice thing with personal costumes is the freedom to experiment with materials and techniques and styles. I don't like to make costumes for customers until I have taken the time to research and experiment first. I don't want to provide a product that does not meet my quality standards. Failing at a costume I'm making for myself is perfectly fine, so I can be bolder and try new things."

Some of Temperance's more ambitious creations were a trio of *Game of Thrones* dragons ("the green dragon was made from upholstery fabric; expensive and difficult to work with"), a "charr," which is a multi-horned feline character from the MMORPG[70] *Guild Wars 2* ("a lot of padding and lot of leatherwork—he probably has about $600 of real cowhide on him") and a cosplay suit based on a "maggot marauder" villain from the Japanese TV series *Kamen Rider* ("the customer only had one request: 'make him look cute.'").

"I love cosplay and making furry and non-furry costumes for myself. Every now and again I make a non-furry costume for other people; it usually gives me a nice challenge to overcome. Yes, I'm a furry, but a rather laid-back one. A majority of my friends are furries. Furry is a hobby and a job for me, not a lifestyle."

"Artslave's" mom was a tailor.

"When I was two my mother said, 'Oh, you can read? Great, let's go learn how to use the sewing machine!'

---

70 "Massively Multiplayer Online Role-Playing Game"

'Mom, I don't think I'm comfortable using the toilet yet, [I'm not sure] I should be using heavy machinery . . . '"

Artslave, who has asked that her real name not be used, came highly recommended by several folks as someone accomplished at reptile suits. She's made two for herself: her giant lizardman, "Brokentail," and her personal character, "Monster."

"When I started working in fleece I wanted to make a lizard/dragon-type thing. Brokentail's not a representation of me so much, but he's my primary *Dungeons & Dragons* character. I like the idea of a noble knight on a white horse being a hideous monster but secretly a good guy. Where does the cultural acceptance line start and stop for being a really good person? It's a fun idea to play with. In a lot of accepted *D&D* canon, lizard folk are cannibals and [they] herd humans as a primary food source; can Brokentail eat people and still be one of the good guys?

"I don't know, but he wears a full set of paladin armor I made for him. Paladins are your standard warrior with a holy cause in *D&D* and other fantasy worlds. They're notoriously bigoted and stuffy, so a paladin meeting a lizard man on the road would likely lead to conflict. And hey, traveling is hungry work; who's Brokentail to turn down a free meal—or a set of armor the paladin won't be needing anymore? He's a lot of fun to portray, but I don't wear [that suit] to many furry conventions because it gets *hot*.

"'Monster' is [an] ambiguous demon who's a terrible beast but has a soft spot for children and animals. She'll go around doing her satanic duty—reaping souls, causing havoc and the like—but her favorite pastime is living under the beds of troubled children and helping them figure out how to cope with divorce, abuse, hunger, whatever bad situation they're in. Sometimes she ends up with a free meal at the end of it—parents are delicious! Obviously I have a real place in my heart for bad guy/good guy misunderstood monsters."

She talks as she works, salting her language with a profanity-rich vocabulary. I ask if her mom wanted her to share her love of sewing or if she was just looking for some free labor. "I think it was both. I didn't like using the sewing machine—what the fuck is a two year old going to do on a goddamn sewing machine? I never messed up or hurt myself, but I certainly couldn't sew a straight line.

"[My mother] kept telling me 'rip open the seam and do it again.' I got tired of that and started hand stitching instead. 'You can't hand-stitch everything,' she said. 'You're not going to make it if you don't use a sewing machine.'" The adult Artslave gives voice to her younger self's thought at the time: "'You know what mom? Fuck you.'"

Mother/daughter disagreements aside, Artslave had begun cultivating the skills (starting with hand stitching) that would serve as the foundation of her future career. It began with an acquaintance who wanted a cheap suit and didn't know who else to go to.

Over the past sixteen years she estimates she's produced about 150 full suits, one hundred partials[71] and more heads than she can remember. Fursuits are her full-time occupation—but it's a labor of love, not a quest for big bucks.

---

71   A "partial" consists of the head, paws and tail of the wearer's fursona, worn by a fur with their street clothes (lazy) or a wardrobe reflecting their character's personality (creative, like a Dalmatian firefighter, or a top-hatted and tuxedo-wearing canine). Furs on a limited budget often create or commission a partial as their first step towards a full fursuit to come later.

"It's not a lucrative line of work. A lot of kids think it is because they see suits going for two thousand, three thousand dollars. Even if you're booked year round [you might not make that much money]: a $3,000 suit takes me two months to make. That's $1,500 a month, minus materials; you wind up earning $750 a month.

"You get into it because it's fun, not to make money.[72] Most of the people who are in it for the long haul have been making suits for five, six, eight, ten years. We all sort of know each other. Whenever there's a run on fabric, the barking chain goes out: 'Guys, there's a run on Monterey Mills long-pile white—you gotta grab it if you need it!' If there's a sale going on, it's super beneficial because the more money you save, the more money you make."

It still seems unlikely: two months, day in, day out on a single suit?

"It depends on the suit," Artslave explains. "A muscle suit [one padded with ersatz abs, pecs and biceps beneath its beastly exterior] can take me forty-five to sixty days. It also depends on the client; a lot of them request a shitload of changes. It's understandable because it's their character and it has to be perfect. Some people just want a really cool suit to run around in—I can bang that shit out in a week and a half. That's why you see a lot of professional suitmakers selling pre-mades[73] because it's easier to produce three things a month for $1,500 each and make

---

72 It may be a fun lifestyle, but one does have to pay the bills. To avoid client misunderstandings, Artslave's website features a four-page "Terms of Service" document covering details like payments, deadlines, design changes, shipping, etc.

73 Artslave later explains pre-mades are quickly built, uncomissioned fursuits destined to be sold on eBay or elsewhere for far less than a time-consuming made-to-order suit.

$4,500 that month—'Oh look, I'm an adult mom! I'm earning a living!'

"I had client who asked for 102 changes on a head. It took me three months of building something that cost them $600, and I made $350 for three months' work. If it were just, 'Here's what I want,' 'Here, I have produced what you want the way I have perceived it,' 'Fantastic, thank you, here is your money"; if it was all that simple I'd probably be walking with twenty-five grand a year, maybe thirty if we're really good doing high-end stuff like Clockwork Creature (another well-known fursuiter group); their stuff is super awesome. Her suits are expensive, but she and her husband work on them full time with an assistant. Even though it seems like they're going for a lot, that's three people you have to pay at the end of day."

Like most furs, Artslave was born with the furry gene. "When I was little I would wrap a towel up and wear it in the back of my pants and be like, 'I'm a cat now.' My mom just let me do it: 'She'll grow out of it.'"

Artslave's furry tendencies temporarily subsided as she matured. She cashed in her Get Out of Reality Free card on genre entertainment, Halloween costumes and *Dungeons and Dragons*-type roleplaying games.

Like any hobby that requires unique stuff in order to participate, businesses opened up to provide said stuff to its participants. Shops offering miniature *D&D* characters who meet in battle (according to their accompanying rulebooks and guidebooks), miscellaneous paraphernalia and plenty of space for fans to meet and play began dotting the landscape. It was an encounter in a Games Workshop store that opened Artslave's door to the Furryverse.

"I got into Furry when I was around sixteen, or maybe

eighteen. I'm a huge nerd, and I played Workshop games built around miniatures like the old tin soldiers except they're fantasy creatures, space Marines type stuff. I really liked the modeling and painting. I was like, 'I can make a whole army of space werewolves! Sweet, lemme do that.'

"There was a guy at the store who was pretty cool. We played together a bunch of times, but he always wore a tail, this big fucking grey wolf tail. I was like, 'Man that's so weird . . . wait . . . why . . . where'd you get that tail man, why are you wearing that?' And he's like 'Oh, I'm a furry,' and I'm like, 'What's a furry?'

"He shrugs. 'Google it.' So I did. The first thing that popped up was the Maryland Fur Group. I didn't even look at Google Images—which is probably why I'm still in Furry. They were having a meet-up that weekend about ten miles from where I lived; 'shit, I'm going to go meet these guys.'

"They were all super nice, super nerdy—not super normal, but pretty normal for nerds and furs; weird in a good way, not weird in a creepy way. Nobody was wearing a suit or anything. I hung out with these guys because I liked them, but by the third meetup I was like, 'Will someone please fucking explain Furry to me?'

"[Someone] held out a picture and said, 'Here, this is my tiger.' I'm like, 'You own a tiger?' 'No, look.' It was a picture a big-time comic artist had done of him as a muscly comic-book–style cat-man. It looked a little like him. 'Oh, you're a tiger guy like in *Dungeons & Dragons*.' Basically, sweet, I finally got it—and I could get behind this 100%.

"Then they kept talking about this convention, Anthrocon. This was 2005; I went [to the con] and was like, 'Holy shit, look at all these people in costume! They just walk around in them—'" her voice rises several octaves to a squeaky, delighted "'— *all weekend?!*'

"I made my first fursuit for a Halloween party that year, a gryphon; it was an abomination, God, it was the worst. I made it out of papier-mâché with a five-pound clay beak and real feathers. It looked awful, but I had such a great time wearing it. I [decided I was] gonna make more of these."

Artslave went to Anthrocon the following year, in 2006, in a "proto Wound" partial, "equally subpar by my current standards, but I wore that thing until the fabric wore out and the seams disintegrated. I was addicted!

"I got into it for the opposite reason than you did," Artslave says, referring to my slow-motion embrace of fursuiting. "Halloween has always been my favorite holiday; now I can enjoy Halloween all the time. I live in Furry all year long—this is my home."

Artslave's advice to first-time fursuit builders: "Don't try to do your personal character first. You're going to be super, super picky about everything, you're never going to be happy with it. You're going to be working on it for three fucking years, and you're going to waste three years you could've spent getting better and then ultimately being happy with what you made. Make a bland generic one-color fox instead; you'll learn so much more making something you don't give a shit about.[74]

"Just to give you an idea of how long it takes, I've been making suits for sixteen years. I've made my personal character four times, and I've finally gotten to the point where I *think* I'm happy with how she looks."

---

74 At last report, though, Charleston Rat was quite pleased with his finished personal character suit, his first attempt at fursuit building.

I was awestruck by both Temperance and Artslave's work, but they were both backed up with existing commissions. In fact, winding up on the end of Temperance's never-ending queue means she wouldn't have been able to *start* work on Komos until the following July, after Anthrocon had wrapped for the year.

And Artslave? Like the majority of fursuit builders, Artslave opens for commissions at unpredictable intervals, and then for only two at a time. My only option: advanced begging mode. I began bombarding her with increasingly desperate inquiries as to when she would be accepting commissions again. Her not-so-reassuring responses ranged from "reasonably certain" to "very certain" she could create Komos in time for Anthrocon— as long as some non-furry, real-life issues didn't get out of hand. She suggested I email her a reminder January 1.

At 11:24 a.m. on January 1, 2015, I emailed Artslave a picture of Komos wearing a party hat, holding an air horn and wishing her a Happy New Year. Twelve hours later she responded with her own New Year's greetings along with some extremely comforting news: Komos had officially joined her queue!

On February 1, Artslave began detailing her plans for Komos's creation and shared some disconcerting news: she didn't know how to construct an *extremely* important feature of Komos's suit.

"No articulated tail!?" I emailed. "I want that *really* bad . . . there's just no magic to a completely stationary tail." An articulated tail, or anything articulated for that matter, is built in sections that are hinged or otherwise connected so as to allow flexibility of movement. In other words, I'd have a tail that moved to my liking.

Unlike most vertebrates, reptilian tails are an extension of the animal's torso, not an appendage to it; there really isn't a definitive point where the body ends and the tail begins. In fursuit form, they're generally sculpted from a single piece of foam attached to the back of the suit. They create an appropriate profile but they're fixed in place, incapable of moving independently from the wearer's body. As far as I was concerned you might as well have a sofa cushion attached to your butt.

That wouldn't do for Komos. Komos is a proud beast; he needed, no he *deserved*, an articulated tail, one capable of generating a commanding, curving, side-to-side sway as he walked—a tail to take pride in.

Fortunately, there's no shortage of help to be had online, courtesy of experienced furs eager to share their knowledge and give advice to aspiring fursuit builders. (Trade secrets and competitiveness don't exist among people who aren't in it for the money.) A YouTube search for "fursuit tutorials" brings up 5,370 results, from big-picture tutorials covering head and body construction to videos offering specialized advice in foam sculpting; fur shaving; ear, hand and footpaw creation; tongues and tails and digitigrade legs (the style used to portray a four-legged creature standing upright).

I sent Artslave links to several articulated tail tutorials that looked particularly informative, and *voilà*—Komos had a plan for his lively tail! In the weeks that followed, Artslave sent me the occasional in-progress photo of Komos's body, hands and feet. Thanks to the miracle of streaming video, I could watch over her shoulder as she created his head, taking large pieces of white foam she'd carved to precise shapes and gluing them to the cushion foam serving as Komos's skull. She added sliver-sized pieces to form his lips, eyelids and his circular nostrils' extruded borders. Above his yellow eyes with their black-slit pupils an enormous set of furrowed brows that rose to the top of his head; they added an extra touch of menace to his already intimidating expression while simultaneously disguising my human forehead.

The next day Artslave shaped, sewed and glued Komos's green-felt skin to his head. Under her skilled hands the material hugged the curves and angles of his face as if it were a coat of paint. Rows of pointy teeth and a forked tongue were visible inside his leering, open mouth. She sewed a patch of artificial hair to his chin to serve as his goatee, with a second patch soon to adorn his head.

A few weeks later my partner Marc and I were on our way to Artslave's apartment in rural Maryland (she's since moved) before she was to apply the finishing touches to Komos.

Her workshop is a work of art in itself. There's fabric everywhere: rolls of felt, piles of fake fur, a wall chart of "Cubby Bear Fur Fabrics" with swatches of "Pooh Short," "Honey Beige" and the like. Below a shelf holding a pair of massive cloven-hoof-shoes, a line of imposing character heads hang from a row of hooks: a dark-grey furred wolf head with a set of scary-as-all-fuck teeth; an unfurred, muzzled head with evil, hooded eyes and lengthy horns resembling the skull of some satanic beast; next to it a similar head with lengthy ears in place of horns. More heads overflow a bookcase in the bedroom next door.

Artslave sat atop her folded legs in a weathered office chair that let her spin in a 270-degree arc when not facing her desk. Just about anything she needs—whether from a hefty toolbox on the floor to her left or a fabric scrap on her right—is within easy reach. Next to the scrap pile a thin sheet of foam rubber folded many times over serves as a chair for visitors.

Spray cans and bottles of paint and coffee tins filled with tools, brushes and glue sticks crowd her desk, surrounding a computer keyboard that looks like it was salvaged from the remains of an exploded paint factory. A shelf atop the room's crowded closet groans under the weight of multi-gallon plastic pails and jugs of rubber compound, liquid plastic (parts A and B), silicone rubber, epoxy dough and cartons of "FlexFoam-iT!® 'Tuff Stuff' #4 Flexible Urethane Foam." On the floor in front of the closet were a pile of headless silver mannequins—one of which had my name written across its chest.

He was my "duct-tape dummy," although "mummy" might be an equally accurate description. If someone hundreds of miles away is going to custom build a suit to fit your body they need to know your exact—and I do mean *exact*—dimensions. Even though Artslave's webpage has a detailed guide to measuring one's body (eight separate measurements for the wearer's arm alone, including thumb length and circumference) she recommends creating the silver suit.

Earlier in the year, my furry pal Peter arrived at my apartment to wrap me neck to ankle in duct tape. (Obviously it's not a one-person job.) I was wearing an old pair of sleep pants and a long sleeve t-shirt which, apart from keeping the tape out of contact with my skin, eventually served as the dummy's interior after I was scissored free of my silver bondage. Once in her possession, and

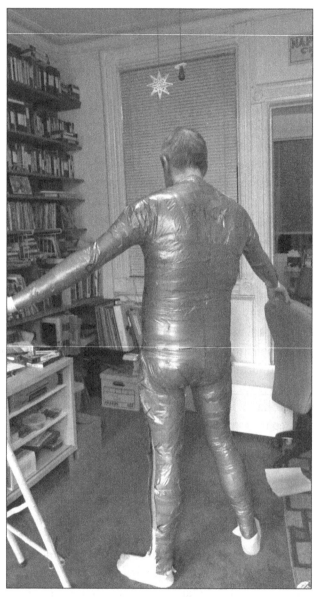

Photograph courtesy of the author

well before my visit, Artslave sealed up the cuts, stuffed its interior with newspaper and used it as her guide to construct Komos's body. I'm glad I went with the duct-tape dummy. The suit's intricacies might not have been as impressive if the suit had been ill-fitting.

Starring at Komos for the first time was a revelation. He was complete. And he was a thing of beauty.

Working from a few drawings of the comic book Komos and my character description, Artslave brought him to three-dimensional life, his unrelenting, hypnotic stare even more fearsome in person. Artslave revealed his massive hands and feet, their curved claws sharp and nasty-looking . . . and his magnificent, lengthy tail.

I was in awe. I was in love.

After several minutes of gaping at the marvel that is

A most sophisticated Komodo
Komos © the author; photograph courtesy of and © Dragonscales

the Komos suit, I finally got the nerve to wear my second skin for the first time. Puny human Joe Strike was going to forsake the mammalian world and let his scaly alter ego take over.

I started by replacing my shirt and jeans with a pair of Under Armour skin-tight leggings and an equally snug long-sleeve top. The undergarments were to wick the perspiration off my body, keeping me relatively cool and stopping my sweat from drenching the suit's innards. (Artslave still recommended Komos get a generous post-wearing spritz of antimicrobial spray.)

Komos's body is one piece, from cuffs to collar like a pair of coveralls—if coveralls had a full-sized reptile tail attached. I sat on the edge of a chair, slipped my legs into the suit and donned Komos's oversized feet.

I rose to my feet and pulled the suit up to my waist. It was just like putting on a pair of pants—until I felt my tail pulling against the suit. The tail's articulation, achieved by creating a flexible PVC spine supporting a series of circular vertebrae that diminish in size towards its end, had added more weight to it than the costume can support on its own.

Artslave's artful solution: rivet the tail to a four-inch-wide, heavy-duty weightlifting belt she'd sewn inside the costume. I pulled the belt around my waist and sealed its Velcro strap; now the tail's five-pound weight was spread across my entire body. I had no trouble problem bearing my new appendage or maintaining my balance (although sitting down was going to take a bit of maneuvering).

I slipped my arms into the suit's sleeves then pulled them up and over my shoulders. Even though he's a full-body suit and not a partial, Komos wears a silky dinner jacket adorned with a red carnation boutonnière and a silver-and-red medallion hanging from a chain around his neck. (This most stylish reptile would be at home on the cover of *Fursuiters' Quarterly*, if such a publication existed.)

The jacket was there for more than just looks though; it hides the neck-to-tail zipper running down the back of the suit—which means I was going to need help getting in and out of the thing. (The thought crossed my mind that an assistant who prefers me as Komos could simply refuse to unzip me.)

With the body suit on, it was finally time to get into Komos's head—literally and figuratively. It was trickier than I thought: pulling it straight down over my head didn't work, I could barely get it past my nose and it refused to let my chin in at all.[75]

I tried a different tack, holding its open bottom against my face and bringing my chin in contact with the inside of Komos's. Holding onto both chins as if they were a hinge connecting us, I pulled the rest of his head over mine. It was a snug fit, but I was in.

My eyes lined up with the black mesh patches nestled between each of Komos's piercing eyes and his muzzle; it's a standard fur- and mascot-suiting technique for providing the wearer with a view of the outside world. I can see through the thin, sheer fabric, but only dimly. (Later the fabric would be replaced by patches of thicker but more porous screen-door mesh, brightening my view considerably.)

My eyes are also recessed from the inside of the mesh;

---

75 The tight fit was by design; while an oversized head would have been easier to wear, I wanted Komos's head to be as human-proportioned as possible to avoid a mascot-suit-style appearance and to make him seem as "real" as could be.

the darkness of the head's interior framed my view of the outside world. It was a bit on the pillbox-y side, not quite the unobstructed vantage point I'd hoped for, but one I'd eventually adjust to.

I rose to my oversized, clawed feet and admired my new self in a full-length mirror: I was handsome, powerful . . . *dangerous.* My open-mouthed smile was exuberant yet commanding. I folded my arms across my chest, resting my big hands against my elbows. I brought a hand up to my mouth, as if thinking *what gloriously evil deed should I attempt next?* I pointed a clawed finger directly at the camera lens recording the event; the resulting picture shows a forceful being letting the observer know, without a doubt, who's in charge.

It was time for a bit of a walkabout. I tried a casual pace, somewhat clumsy at first, then sped up a touch, feeling my tail (*my tail—my nearly three-foot-long reptilian tail!*) swoosh and sway behind me. I broke into an energetic strut, exaggerating my hip motion until my tail was whiplashing side to side. I was imagining myself taking out a couple of bad guys with it when it collided with an end-table lamp, sending it crashing to the floor.

Giving Komos that articulated tail was *totally* worth it.

I couldn't wait to bring my alter ego to Anthrocon, my debut goal met perfectly by Artslave's timeliness. My partner Marc (or as he's known in the furry world, "Furio") and I, along with two of our mutual furfriends, shared a room in Pittsburgh's Omni William Penn Hotel, though it was exciting to think that there were actually, counting all our fursuits, eight of us in that room. (Luckily, I didn't have to pay for Komos' stay in addition to my own).

The first day, I suited up and walked down William Penn Place towards the convention, facing the world for the first time as Komos. Anthrocon's been in Pittsburgh for a decade by now. The residents have come to appreciate and welcome their annual multi-species visitors; they enjoy the sight of fantastical animals roaming the streets of their fair city. Parents even bring their kids downtown to pose for pictures alongside the fursuiters who are more than happy to oblige. Komos isn't quite as friendly or cuddly looking at as most of the other 'suiters; I only got one request from a parent to pose with their kid, who refused to get anywhere near me.

The adults were much more fascinated by my Komodo façade. Across Tenth Street from the convention center-adjacent the Westin Hotel, ground zero for fursuit sightings stands the Tonic Bar and Grill, whose outdoor tables are a popular spot for the locals to observe, photograph, and pose with the fursuiters for their friends' camera phones.[76] I was in heaven when one of them told me mine was the best suit they'd seen all weekend, although I couldn't help but hiss in response *"Sssorry, but I'm not wearing a sssuit."*[77] Komos speaks truth as much as possible. A very attractive woman embraced me; in all likelihood it was the alcohol talking, but neither of us minded one bit when my clawed hands came to rest on her hips. My fellow furs were impressed too; compliments of "cool suit" abounded

---

76 Sadly gone, Tonic *totally* embraced Anthrocon, offering "Roaring Refreshments" with names like "Yiff Me Berry Hard!" and "Paw Off."

77 I'm having a far better time than *Fight Club* author Chuck Palahniuk, who in his essay "My Life as a Dog" in *Stranger than Fiction* (2005) described a disastrous expedition through downtown Seattle as a "spotted, smiling Dalmatian" enduring young men throwing punches, rocks and homophobic slurs, leavened by the occasional, "You guys rock!"

and several people recognized Komos as Artslave's work.

There's a key aspect of Komos Artslave wasn't responsible for, a post-factory modification as it were: the visual representation of his powerful hypnotic and mind-reading abilities. Peter used his electronics know-how to install a pair of tiny yellow LEDs behind Komos's slitted eyes. Connected to an electronic doo-dad, they slowly cycle from dim to fully aglow and back again.

My glowing eyes snared a woman's attention. I gently rested my claws against her face and whispered, *"You are under my ssspell . . . you will make a mossst ssplendid ssservant."* "You're *frightening* me," she protested with a nervous giggle, sounding more than a little thrilled at the prospect.

They love that bad boy thing, they can't help themselves. Inside the convention center, Komos had the same effect on a guy wearing a spike-studded leather chin strap who made it clear he was ready to do it with the reptile right there on the floor in front of everyone. I was thrilled, though not interested at the time; Komos was having fun, but Joe was sweating up a storm inside Komos' body.

I made my way to the "headless lounge"—a standard fixture of furry conventions. Like I said, it gets *hot* inside those suits, and the lounge is the perfect place for 'suiter to take his or her head off and cool down without revealing his human identity to the convention as a whole. (A T-shirt often seen at cons depicts a 'suiter with his human face exposed and holding his costume's head, with the caption "I RUIN THE MAGIC.")

The lounge was a large room chilled by an excess of air conditioners and oversized fans. A tangle of vinyl tubes, each connected to a cold air blower, hung from a rack in the center of the room. The tubes are just the right diameter to dry out your head's damp interior or insert into your suit's open neck to cool your sweaty body.

It's important to keep yourself hydrated while suiting; cupfuls of water are on hand for that purpose. It's a challenge to strike a balance between dehydration and urination. Deprive yourself of water and you run the risk of heat stroke; overindulge and your bladder will start whining, "I gotta pee, I gotta pee!" If you exercise enough willpower your bladder will eventually say, "Ah, the hell with it," and give up until you unsuit, at which point both you and it will make up for lost time.

Back in the Omni for the night I sadly de-Komos-ized. Once outside the suit I discovered my Under Armour was over-soaked in sweat. I removed the tights and hung them in the room to dry for the next day's suiting. My roommates returned and did likewise until our room smelled like a gym locker whose contents had been festering since the beginning of the school year.

The next day brought the Fursuit Parade, another furry convention staple. Every year Anthrocon attendance and the parade size set a new record. In 2015, precisely 2,100 'suiters out of the convention's 7,310 furs took part in the march, including yours truly. (Without me, the total would have fallen short of that impressive round number.) It was the largest ratio of fursuiters to total con attendance ever—29%, as opposed to the usual 20–25% of the average furcon's attendees, further underwriting the misassumption that being a fur means wearing a fursuit.

Reptiles like Komos along with dragons and dinosaurs (and a tiny contingent of avians) made up a small percentage of that 29%. Truth be told, there is a certain sameness, a generic, big-eyed friendly toonieness to many fursuits—the classic "polite smile" Denali spoke of. The quickly made "pre-mades" and self-built suits rarely convey as much personality as the efforts of more experienced suitmakers working for clients who know exactly what their character should look like.

We lined up in the convention center's largest exhibition hall for the requisite group photograph, in rows spaced far enough apart for every one of us to be visible. (When the picture went online the following week it took several minutes and some serious magnification to locate myself in the crowd, a "Where's Komos?" moment.)

And then the parade began. We left the hall a row at a time until we were snaking through the convention center's corridors, down its escalators and in a recent alteration to the parade route, out of the building so that the fair citizens of Pittsburgh could delight in our creativity (and we could delight in their appreciation). I strutted imperiously, pointing an accusatory clawed finger at random onlookers, and pausing to give high-fives to children waiting with arms outstretched, being very careful not to scratch them.

"Look at the lizard guy!" someone shouted. I was also mistaken for *Star Trek*'s James Tiberius Kirk-wrestling Gorn, although I was much better dressed than that sadly

I'm in there somewhere (Photograph © Andy Oxenreider)

tailless alien. We were photographed and videotaped every inch of our route in and out of the David Lawrence Convention Center; within days dozens of parade videos were posted online. If I wanted to create a video following me the entire route my only problem would be which recording to use when several cameras capture me at the same time.

That evening I posed behind a mock newscaster's desk inside the convention center. *"Sssoon I will command all!"* I cried. *"I will control the horizssontal, the vertical—*and *the diagonal!"* I ended the night standing on a balcony overlooking downtown Pittsburgh, surveying my domain in arms-outstretched triumph—this reptile ruled!

CHAPTER EIGHT

Plugged In:
The Electronic Age

FURRY FANDOM and the Internet are siblings, nearly contemporaries. The fandom was born in the mid-1980s, and from its very beginning, electronic boards and Usenet platforms, the Internet's predecessors, helped it grow. When the Internet burst into full bloom in the 1990s, so did furry fandom. Aided and abetted by Google and its ilk, many a future fur's curiosity about cartoons, animal art or werewolves would ultimately lead them to the fandom—an experience that would in time be shared by thousands.

Electronic, online bulletin boards, or "BBSs", were in the forefront of turning Furry digital. These electronic communication systems ran on the earliest personal computers. In that pre-broadband era people had no way to reach the boards except via slow-speed telephone modems. For the most part the boards resided on private home computers, usually with a dedicated phone line connecting them to the outside world. (If the person running the board couldn't afford a dedicated line, people trying to reach the board had to wait until the phone was free for the evening.)[78]

The first of them was the Tiger's Den BBS. Originally a sci-fi board when it went online in 1982, it turned furry the following year when its founder moved to Mark Merlino and Rod O'Riley's Prancing Skiltaire.

The Den had areas set aside for users to upload and download images, exchange private messages or chew over various topics and several furry "storyboards." In spite of their name these boards weren't the kind used in movie or animation production, but places where visitors could add new chapters to ongoing, group-created stories—an exquisite-corpse–style exercise. The BBSs were the first opportunity for furs to present themselves as their fursonas to others.

It took a little longer for the East Coast to produce its own furry BBS, but in 1987 the Electric Holt was born. Based in Philadelphia, the Holt was administered by two local furs, one of whom we've already met—Mitch Marmel of the Cartoon/Fantasy Organization.

Mitch was one of the Holt's sysops—its system operators. "I was sysop on a couple of interesting BBSs in the Philadelphia area," recalls Mitch. "The Electric Holt was the most furry of the bunch, but I also worked on the Institute of Artificial Insanity and KAOS, the BBS named after the *Get Smart* bad guys."

"This was just about the time of the AT&T break-up.

---

78 A drawback of the early BBSs: with only a single phone line in, the boards were strictly one-at-a-time affairs. If someone was already connected the next user would have to wait until the phone line was free again before they would be able to sign in.

SprintNet, one of the first alternative telephone companies, was letting people make calls on their dedicated phone lines that were physically separate from AT&T's at a competitive rate, but only after business hours. That was one of the main problems with the early BBSs: long-distance calls were a pain in the rear.

"One way around this was a computer network called FidoNet that would daisy chain computers across the country. FidoNet relayed all sorts of boards from city to city; a subset called FurNet linked the furry boards together. For example, I could phone into a Philadelphia BBS, log in, type a message and hang up, then the next user would log in and repeat the process, etc.

"Now say you had a couple of hundred people running BBSs in Philadelphia. They in turn would call ten to fifteen hub computers. The hub computers would call a back-bone computer connected to FidoNet. That one would be making long-distance calls after peak hours; it would call one in Reading, Pennsylvania, which would call one in Pittsburgh, which would call one [somewhere in] Ohio and so on. The messages would work their way across the country in a series of local calls or low-cost toll calls. You could talk to a California BBS for next to nothing. It wouldn't get there instantaneously like nowadays; it might be overnight or maybe two or three hops before it reached the west coast, but it would get there eventually."

Usenet kicked things up a notch or two. Instead of single-line bulletin boards, Usenet (a contraction of "users' network") was a decentralized two-way system, at the heart of which numerous servers shared information with each other and with people logging on from their home or work computers.

Any number of newsgroups could be accessed, from academic ones dedicated to science and the humanities, to alternative, anything-goes ones collectively identified by the prefix "alt."

Alt.fan.furry in its day was the singular meeting and online communication hub for furs—a mega-BBS that required no registration or password to access. Discussion threads would be started, continue forever and split off into subthreads that likewise never seemed to end. As discussed elsewhere, alt.fan.furry also became home to heated arguments and flamewars, and eventually spun off alt.lifestyle.furry for furs wanting to explore a broader range of what Furry meant to them beyond alt.fan.furry's more constricted view of the fandom.

Alt.fan.furry and alt.lifestyle.furry were eventually joined by FurryMUCK, the first online gathering place to make a major impact on the still young fandom.

MUCK supposedly stood for "Multi-User Construction Kit," but in reality was merely a pun on "MUD," another messy-sounding online acronym which itself stood for "Multi-User Dungeon." As that D-word suggests, MUDs were places where people could roleplay as *Dungeons & Dragons*-type fantasy characters.

Many furs credit FurryMUCK, which was born in 1990, with introducing them to the fandom; one calls it "the single unifying trigger that blew up the fandom into what it is today." Here furs could gather to chat and roleplay as their fursonas without necessarily going on quests or fighting monsters.

FurryMUCK was a "MOO," a MUD using object-oriented software. In other words, all text, no pictures. Users had to learn to type in commands to go places, pick up virtual objects or do just about anything. FurryMUCK was an extension of the old text-adventure games like *Zork*, which were invented for the very first generation of personal computers, the TRS-80s and the Apple IIs. Unlike those primitive computers, FurryMUCK is still around, but nowhere near the essential site it was at its peak.

Mentally projecting ourselves into cyberspace in order to take on a new form is still a way off, but if Furry-MUCK was one small step, Second Life was the great leap forward.

Second Life might be called an MMORPG—a Massively Multiplayer Online Role-Playing Game— except its creator, Linden Labs, takes pains to point out it's anything but. It's a shared world where the main goal is to socialize (although one can make quite good money, both virtual *and* real in Second Life).

Created in 2003, SL (as it's usually abbreviated) had 1.1 million Residents (as they're referred to within SL) at its peak and still retains about 900 thousand regular users, 30 to 60 thousand of whom might be online at any one time. SL is a visual realm where everyone has an on-screen stand-in, an avatar representing who—or what—they prefer to be seen as, an attraction irresistible to furs. On the BBSs and in FurryMUCK visitors can only describe themselves as their fursonas, but in Second Life they can be *seen* as their idealized anthropomorphic selves.[79] I'm tempted to say the difference between FurryMUCK and Second Life is akin to listening to the

---

79 Second Life isn't the only online MMORPG virtual realm; people can also create an alternate self in IMVU (imvu.com) and *Minecraft* (minecraft.net). *World of Warcraft* (worldofwarcraft.com) is a D&D-style questing/combat world; several anthropomorphic communities exist within *WoW* including the panda-populated Pandari and Northrend, home to the walrus-like Tuskarr.

radio and watching TV, but a more accurate comparison might be the difference between reading a book and taking part in an enormous theme park cosplay.

In SL furs can enjoy an entire life as their fursona, living in furry virtual communities, partying in furry nightclubs, socializing in furry coffee houses and shopping in furry malls. Every environment in SL, furry and otherwise, is constructed by its users out of basic computer graphic shapes that can be manipulated and combined into amazingly detailed constructions. By design this means there are a ton of worlds to explore (many of them most definitely "NSFW"—Not Safe For Work).

To truly illustrate the measure of digital authenticity Second Life gives to furs, let's tour some of these furry environments, known as "sims." First, you need to select an avatar to represent yourself. Fortunately there's a bunch of generic avatars to choose from on SL's opening page. I opted for one resembling a Hogwarts graduate: a tall white-haired gent in a long coat, a wand in his hand and an owl on his shoulder.

You also need a viewer to enter and explore SL, a piece of software provided by SL (or third parties who offer their own variations), easily downloaded and installed. Once you've squared that away, you can begin your Second Life.

BigZtehwuff, a fur familiar with SL, offers to show me around the first time I'm there—and thank goodness, because there's a lot of take in. It's a bit overwhelming at first, but Big Z's avatar is so cool looking that it definitely calms the nerves. He's a heavily accessorized anthro wolf, dressed in black slacks and a short-sleeved shirt. He's wearing a set of headphones, has a panda on his shoulder, a cookie in his mouth, and he carries two glow sticks that leave a trail of colorful flashes of light as he walks. It's easy to find him if he gets out of sight, which he often does while I try to keep up with him.

The first thing Big Z does is take me to the SL Marketplace where he customizes my avatar with wolf head and tail "mods," turning me suitably furry.

The head and tail are free, as are a lot of goodies in the Marketplace. But plenty are not; you can spend quite a few Linden Dollars, SL's in-world currency, on any accessory or decoration you can think of. Just as between real-world nations, there's an exchange rate between Lindens and U.S. dollars. And like the real world, the rate fluctuates depending on conditions of the moment. (As of this writing, one U.S. dollar will get you 253 Lindens.)

I'd prefer an avatar resembling Komos, but building one from scratch is expensive. Zortech, a furry Resident who fluctuates between feline, canine and various dog/cat hybrids, tells me he has over thirty avatars to choose from and has spent over 35,000 Lindens ("L$" for short) or $143 USD.

Several in-world stores sell ready-made avatars. I visit one Second Life Marketplace page where I can choose from several hundred of them: male and female tigers in colors ranging from electric blue to hot pink (and one done up in candy-cane stripes), cheetahs, skunks, wolves, kangaroos and just about every other animal that sailed with Noah, all for a reasonable L$950. When I learn I can buy mods or clothing to augment or transform an avatar's original appearance, I realize rather than paying a pile of Lindens to create Komos from scratch, I can buy a premade lizard avatar, a dinner jacket, even a rose for his lapel, and create a reasonable facsimile for a lot less.

The Marketplace also offers over 150 thousand animations and motion packages to add to an avatar's basic mobility—everything from hand gestures to karate kicks. All told, SL's Marketplace has almost five million items available for sale, everything from a L$1 landscape painting to a L$17,000 beachfront residence to keep it in—and all of it is the work of SL Residents.[80] Those Lindens can add up to some serious real-world dollars too; Zortech was able to buy a real-world car with the pile of Lindens he made playing the SL real-estate market. (Since they're selling imaginary territory, Linden Labs regularly creates and puts new land up for sale to Residents who want to start an in-world business or just own some space to call their own.)

Guided by Big Z, I visit a few of SL's furry haunts. One can fly (it's one of your motion options) or teleport between them. It's fascinating to arrive in a new location and see it construct before your eyes. (These environments are data-heavy; depending on one's computer speed and which SL viewer is being used it may take a while for the various components of a locale to display.) We travel to GYC, an expansive disco/nightclub.

It's October in the real world, and here as well; autumn leaves are scattered in front of the club's entrance. I suspect were I to return in the winter I'd see snowy patches in their place. Inside, the club is all deep purples, dark blues

---

80 Second Life's CEO recently claimed SL entrepreneurs earned *sixty million* real-world dollars in in 2015. (*Inside Sansar, the VR successor to Second Life.* The Verge, November 18, 2016. [http://www.theverge.com/2016/11/18/13501492/linden-lab-project-sansar-vr-second-life-hands-on]) Retrieved December 27, 2016.

and bright-green accents. In the center is a big dance floor and lots of secluded spots where people can chat and get intimate with one another. Attractive anthro gals—a tiger, a skunk and a big-breasted bird with a peacock tail and angel wings on her back—are dancing in well-choreographed moves to a techno track. There's also a centaur hanging out at the bar.

Still, as a newbie I'm having trouble dealing with SL navigation. (A Resident tells me the motion controls are more akin to a CGI animation program than a game controller—I'm not particularly familiar with either.) I'm finding it difficult to keep up with Big Z as he maneuvers through furry SL locales or travels from one to the next; several times he has to rescue me by sending a teleport invitation to meet him up ahead.

We travel to the Furry Den, a cozy place set in a white-frosted landscape where snowflakes are floating to the ground. We land on the Den's outdoor deck. Pillows surround a fire pit, and nearby there's a hot tub, which at the moment is empty of both water and furry avatars. A snowman stands just outside the door to the Den's building. He consists of three white spheres, slightly squashed and atop one another with the usual coal eyes and tree-branch arms. Since spheres are one of the eight basic shapes, aka "primitives," everything in SL is made of (along with boxes, cylinders and the like) he's likely one of the simplest objects to be found within this virtual world.

There's bar and dance club inside the building, complete with an onstage DJ setup. A poster on the wall shows a grinning cartoony furry with the words FURRIES: WE KNOW DRAMA. According to the price list above the bar a lemonade can be had for L$1, a glass of Merlot costs L$6 and the most expensive drink on the menu, a "Blue Orgy," goes for L$11. On the way out I notice a cute, big-hipped tabby-cat babe by the door. She's looking demurely towards the floor, moving her head slightly, her default stationary position. The label floating above her head (every avatar in SL has one) gives her name as Marble Sodis. She's purple-haired with a green glow ring around her left ear; purple stripes decorate her lavender body—and every now and then she gives out with a random hiccup.

Big Z teleports us to GYC's open-air mall. According to SL's index GYC is "your SL resource for all things Furry since 2006. 18+" -An onscreen click brings up a window listing the attractions to be enjoyed there, including the bar/nightclub, a swimming pool and a movie theater. Wandering around, we enter a blocky-looking structure and find ourselves in an interior courtyard decorated with X-rated posters for adult businesses and products. Next door is an office building with a spacious lobby and an elevator that instantly shoots you up to the second floor when you press its call button; no need to wait for it to arrive and actually transport you there.

We're now in Furocity Media LLC's offices.[81] The place is deserted; all the workers have evidently gone home for the night. Big Z marvels at the desktop computers; they're still using Microsoft's way-outdated XP operating system. (Apparently not everything in SL is up to date.)

---

81 Just for the heck of it I check online to see if Furocity Media LLC actually exists in the real world. A business website tells me it does indeed; it's based in Ponchatoula, Louisiana, and reported $37,298 in revenue during its most recent fiscal year, an amount in all likelihood completely generated within Second Life.

There's an interactive schedule board on the wall where people who work for GYC can select their jobs (club DJ, bartender manager, security, etc.) and shifts for the week. "People take their work very seriously," Big Z tells me. They might work for tips or an hourly salary, but people who create SL content, avatars and the like can earn enough money to make it their full-time job and successfully live on a SL-generated income.

Big Z teleports to the GYC Cinema, an old-fashioned movie palace where, according to the marquee, *What Does the Fox Say?* is playing. (*Zootopia*'s Nick Wilde, evidently moonlighting from Disney to make a few Lindens of his own, is manning the ticket booth.) Next we visit a gallery where we can commission furry art from the artists whose X-rated work is on display, an alternative to Fur Affinity if one has more Lindens than real-world money.

Big Z's tour is interrupted by a Skype call: It's from "Pandemonium," a shape-shifting SL friend he hasn't talked to in a while. Pandemonium has a few avatars of her own and shifts between fennec fox, husky, dragon and cat, but, fittingly, Pandemonium—a red panda—is her favorite. "She's a very outspoken character with a big heart, but she doesn't hesitate to put her foot down when she has to."

In real life Pandemonium is Emma and lives in Galesburg, Illinois. "I've known Z for years," she tells me. "We were instantly friends. He's an amazing, kind-hearted wolf. When nobody else was there for me, he was. Even though we haven't talked for a long time our bond is still as vibrant, positive and goofy as when we last spoke."

Pandemonium sends Big Z a teleport invitation and suddenly we're in the same room with her. In real life we're almost a thousand miles apart—but here in Second Life she and Big Z are standing side by side. Her avatar is human-shaped with a red panda head, clawed feet that look more like boots and a long bushy tail that peeks out from under a black miniskirt. "I don't care if you're human, furry or anything like that," Big Z tells her supportively, "you're beautiful and you should know that." The bond, the care and concern Big Z and Pandemonium have for each other is palpable, the thousand miles between them meaningless. Without Second Life, their paths would never have crossed. Perhaps someday they will meet in the real world, say at a furry convention, or perhaps not. But as the second decade of the third millennium draws to a close, it no longer matters as much as digital detractors would have us believe.

We're joined by Pandemonium's SL twin sister and real-life best friend, Trina. Her avatar is currently human; the "sisters" are saving up to buy her a furry one. Trina's accompanied by her fiancé, "XIronBloodDragonX," who in spite of his name is there in human form as well. Even though they're onscreen together, he's not with her in Galesburg. She opens up a Skype video channel on a separate computer and there he is onscreen. His real name is Trevor, and not only is he not in Galesburg, he's not even in the U.S. As it turns out he's Skypeing and Second Lifeing from Belgium. Long-distance fur love. One day, XIronBloodDragonX may fly to his panda love on scaly wings, but until then, Second Life is a very acceptable alternative.

The connection provided to furries in Second Life is second to none. It's an accessible haven that provides the safety of anonymity and the chance to experience life in the way one truly feels.

Of course, the desktop version of Second Life is only the beginning. Virtual reality—VR—is rapidly becoming The Next Big Thing; headsets are coming down in price while the amount and variety of immersive VR material increases.

One would think combining Second Life and virtual reality is a no-brainer; it surely wouldn't take that much extra computing power to turn Second Life's navigable world into 3D. In fact, Linden Labs gave it a shot in 2014 with a limited testing of a Second Life Oculus Rift Developers Kit.

An SL blogger was unable to contain her enthusiasm after trying out the headset:

> The experience is mind blowing, truly amazing. Obviously I spend most of my VR time in the 1920s Berlin project, the sim[ulation] I build and live in, my baby. It felt and looked all so real and *so* good. I must confess that when I saw the Graf Zeppelin fly over I cried. It was so beautiful and a sight I've wanted to see ever since I was a little girl. But also jumping on a tram and being driven around the city is so exciting, I couldn't stop giggling. The details, the sounds, the textures, all great, but the general feeling of being inside something real, and proper 3D surroundings, is just impossible to describe. You experience depth, height, scale, all those things that get lost on a regular computer screen . . . There is nothing like it and it may sound rude but I have to repeat myself: Until you've actually tried the Oculus Rift,

you can't judge it. [It] truly transports you to another reality.[82]

Despite such enthusiasm Linden Labs pulled the plug on trying to bring Second Life into the VR world. Instead it began developing a *second* Second Life—Sansar, a new virtual world specifically designed to be explored with fully immersive VR headsets. Linden announced Sansar in 2016 and began inviting VR content creators to check out its brave new world, which the company plans to launch in 2017. If successful, Sansar will bring the virtual furry world that much closer to reality.

---

82 Yardley, Jo. "My First Oculus Rift experience in Second Life." joyardley. wordpress.com, April 1, 2014. (https://joyardley.wordpress.com/2014/04/01/ oculussl/) Retrieved November 28, 2016.

CHAPTER NINE

The Naughty Bits

TO PARAPHRASE MONTY PYTHON, there's absolutely nothing sexual whatsoever about furry fandom, and when I say nothing, I mean . . . well, maybe there is, just a little bit. It's a topic most furs shy away from; talking about it might seem to confirm the stereotype of furry fandom as a non-stop kinkfest. However it would be equally dishonest to pretend it doesn't exist, or that for a segment of the fandom it doesn't have its charms. That reputation, as unfair as it is, did not materialize out of thin air.

When Disney turned Mae West into the buxom bird Jenny Wren, strutting saucily into view[83] ("my little chickadee," indeed!) or presented a leggy mouse chanteuse wiggling her derriere while crooning "let me be

83 *Who Killed Cock Robin*, 1935.

good to you" (sung by Miss Kitty Mouse from *The Great Mouse Detective*)[84] fifty years later, most people saw nothing more than a cute spoof of female beauty. But a certain percentage of the furry population got more than a chuckle out of it. For these folks, a deft combination of realistic human and stylized animal attributes carries a certain heat with it. (The neologism "furvert" has been coined to describe us.)

Along with everything else, animals represent our physical selves—and that includes our sexual selves. But largely, anthropomorphic animals have been banished to the land of family-friendly children's entertainment. Any critters trying to escape that particular jail (or zoo) are going to make a lot of people uncomfortable.

It's a double whammy: to some, furs exploring (or inventing) the sexuality of supposedly for-the-kiddies cartoon animals seems a few inches away from pedophilia; giving them a human-appearing sensuality carries a vague whiff of bestiality to boot. But as an astute mainstream author once observed, "Once a dog is wearing pants, it can get undressed."[85]

Yes, there is indeed a sexual component to furry fandom[86] (one that doesn't include either of the above,

---

84 *The Great Mouse Detective*, 1986. An online mock "motivational" poster captioned a frame from this scene "Disney: Turning kids into furries for over ninety years." In the DVD's "Making Of" feature, Melissa Manchester, the song's performer, said "I think I'm very attractive as a mouse. I guess [the animators] used some of my body language while I was singing because I see some of my attitude—[the mouse's] shoulders are just jumping around. Of course she shakes her fanny a little bit too, which I must've been doing."

85 Stern, Stephen. "Bright Eyes." *Frieze Magazine*, March/April 1999. (http://www.frieze.com/issue/article/bright_eyes) Retrieved January 16, 2016.

86 Furs even have an all-purpose euphemism: "yiff." Depending on who you

thank you very much); how could there not be? Sex is a primal part of who we are, an irrepressible expression of our fundamental animal selves. It manifests itself in almost every facet of society—culture, entertainment, advertising and, of course, human and furry relationships alike.

Many a kid's first crush was on a cartoon character. The legendary underground cartoonist Robert Crumb admitted having a thing for Bugs Bunny.[87] On a British TV chat show Eddie Redmayne embarrassedly confessed he had "a weird obsession" with *The Lion King*'s Nala as a youngster. Host Graham Norton referred to it as Redmayne's "two-dimensional sexual awakening" and displayed a film still of Nala as a lion cub. "Look at that face, she's so sweet," the flustered Redmayne said, to which Norton responded with an emphatic "that's *wrong!*" Norton might have been more understanding had it been the adult Nala pictured, the one who gave Simba that sultry "do me" look later in the film.

Norton pressed on. "Isn't it true you liked [Disney's] Maid Marian as well?" "That is true," Redmayne answered. "She's a fox though," he added, speaking metaphorically as well as literally. Trying to suppress her giggles, fellow guest Anna Kendrick pointed out the

---

ask, yiff was originally either the cry of mating foxes (which would answer the musical question "what does the fox say?") or a greeting invented by foxy furs. It somehow evolved into a word encompassing everything from full-tilt lovemaking ("yiffing") to simple cuddling. Something sexy or arousing is "yiffy" . . . to which a fur might respond with an appreciative "murr . . . "

87 "When I was five or six I was sexually attracted to Bugs Bunny. I cut him off the cover of a comic book and carried it around in my pocket and took it out and looked at it periodically. It got wrinkled up from being handled so much, so I asked my mother to iron it. I was deeply disappointed because when she did it got all brown and brittle and crumbled apart." From the movie Crumb, quoted on imdb.com. Retrieved August 8, 2016.

obvious: "In Eddie's defense they draw them really sexy. Robin Hood was quite sexy."[88]

A picture of Disney's cartoon Robin Hood, his arms outstretched in a gallant pose appeared onscreen: the fox that launched a thousand furries. The audience's laughter somehow sounded a touch more appreciative than it had before. "That tunic is worn very low, I noticed," said Norton. "He's packing."[89]

Then there's the night Rob Corddry, subbing for Jon Stewart on *The Daily Show*, reported on a U.S. government FEMA website for kids featuring an anthropomorphic mountain lion family. A picture of "Purrcilla," the family's quite-fetching mom appeared onscreen wearing a strapless dress.

Corddry leered at the camera: "I don't usually go mountain cat, but I would *totally* pet that."

Folks who think furry fandom is nothing more than one big fetishy furpile, people in fursuits getting it on 24/7, should think again. It's furry *art* where the hot stuff can be found. Spicy portfolios and CDs can be purchased at any furry convention, and there's plenty more to be had online for free.

---

88 Cartoon maven Jerry Beck begs to differ: "I find it all a little too much for me . . . a fox portraying Robin Hood is a funny idea—not something to fall in love with." Email to the author, November 30, 2016.

89 Like Robert Crumb or Eddie Redmayne, I too had a pre-adolescent crush on a cartoon character, only in my case it was on Warner Bros.' romantic skunk Pepé Le Pew, not Bugs Bunny or Nala. I was a lonely kid with poor social skills who spent a lot of time watching cartoons and living in his imagination. I guess I identified with Pepé; I knew what it felt like not to have friends. I admired his self-confidence and wished I could be like him—and frankly I thought he looked beautiful, with his bouffant, fully animated tail that moved when he walked. It made him seem alive and not a flat cartoon drawing. And I knew he didn't smell bad, people just weren't willing to give him a chance, but I would. In my imagination he would use a magic scent to turn me into a skunk so we could play together. That way we would both have a friend—each other.

Don't ask what's in those particular portfolios and pictures. There's far more "G" and "PG"-rated furry art in existence than the naughty stuff—but of course the most provocative material always gets the most attention. You might have heard of "Rule 34: If it exists, there's porn of it on the Internet," Rule 34F isn't as well known (probably because I just made it up): "If a kink exists, there's a furry version of it on the Internet."

Furry pornography is nothing new; before the first furry artist drew the first spicy picture of an anthro animal, long before Disney busted the Air Pirates for their randy underground comix version of Mickey & company in 1971, an anonymous cartoonist drew the Tijuana bible *Donald Duck Has a Universal Desire!*[90] And when asked if Walt had a secret stash of naughty pictures, long-time Disney animator Floyd Norman admitted "Walt didn't—but a lot of the animators did."[91]

So do a lot of furs. Either drawn for a paying customer or for the artist's own enjoyment, the artwork ranges in quality from professional-illustrator level to "needs work"; the content ranges from tasteful "furotica" to hardcore porn,[92] from PG-13 to O-rated. (O as in "Oh my God, I wish I hadn't seen that.") They're almost always single, full-page illustrations, rarely comic-strip narratives like

---

90 Tijuana bibles were tiny eight-page comic booklets popular in the 1920s and thirties featuring comic-strip characters or celebrities in salacious action. (Unable to find a female with whom to indulge his universal desire, Donald reluctantly turns to a willing "fairy" as a substitute.)

91 My question to Mr. Norman during his Q&A session at Anthrocon 2008.

92 Also known as "spooge" art. The sheer sound of the word probably conveys its meaning better than a dictionary definition; it may have been borrowed from the manufacturing world where it's described as "any sealant or lubricant applied during the assembly of electronic equipment." Wiktionary.com. (https://en.wiktionary.org/wiki/spooge) Retrieved January 14, 2016.

the bibles. They might feature the artists' original characters or well-known 'toon stars in provocative pinup poses (even Roger Rabbit can look sexy in the right hands) or indulging their universal desire every bit as eagerly as Tijuana Donald.

Well-drawn furry pin-up babes are a staple of the fandom, their curvaceous human form enhanced with the extra curves of a tail behind and ears above. They're typically fairly tame, no more salacious than any human pin-up you might see, but every now an NC-17 comes along that is both particularly hot and ridiculously *funny*. Some examples I've found: a helpless character in the grip of a bunch of squirming tentacles is pretty standard *hentai*,[93] but one such image has tentacles violating a particular fox with those skinny balloons normally tied into animal shapes at the zoo or a birthday party—and the look on the fox's face isn't one of horror but more a nonplussed "oh dear, what kind of predicament have I gotten myself into this time?" And then there's a gray wolf happily slamming it to a white rabbit who's grinning the goofiest, eyes-closed, tongue-hanging-out-of-his-mouth-in-unadulterated-pleasure smile imaginable.

As fantasy art with fantasy beings as its subject matter, well-drawn furotica is perfect in its own way: unlike "filthy" photos of less-than-flawless human beings, anthropomorphic animals don't exist in real life; there's simply no reality for them to fall short of. They depict a reality all their own; taken to an extreme, furotica turns into plain-old furry porn: enormously endowed males,

---

93 Anime or manga porn, usually of the kinky variety.

maxi-boobed females and best-of-both-worlds hermaph-rodites, all of which exist in human porn, if not to the fantasy extremes possible in furry art.

Not every fur finds furry porn to their liking. "There is a lot of furry pornography in the fandom and for a while I found it tempting," says "Matthias Rat." "I want nothing to do with it now; I realized how attractive it can be and how it can consume people."

While not a porn fan himself, Lucius Appaloosius is more philosophical on the subject. "I personally stay away from the over-sexualized material, but those who enjoy it are none of my concern. Certainly furry art is allowed to explore the complete range of life's experiences, and I admire those artists who can handle their subjects with grace and skill."

Others feel differently—quite differently. "People ask me if there's any particular reason why there's so much sex and violence in my work. I just think it's funny, that's all," the Icelandic furry artist Karno explains. "Only the works people enjoy viewing/hearing/reading survive the ages; only beauty is immortal. That, and fart jokes. Ignore whatever political correctness the drones of your time try to impose on you. PC-rote work will be forgotten in a week. Write and draw what you want. You'll be long-time dead [while your work is standing the test of time], so have some fun during your all-too-brief hitch among the living, all right?"

Heather Bruton enjoys "the challenge of painting adult work. For many people, sexuality is a big part of who they are, and I think it would be no different for anthros. I don't think that all artists should be doing adult work, but if they want to do it, they should feel free to do so."

"I've recently started a *yaoi*[94] comic surrounding mer-furs because, well, I love merpeople!" enthuses fursuiter Thadd. "Also, my soul is free of any shame, so I will openly admit: I like porn. I would love to be paid to draw porn, but I'm terrible at advertising myself for this kind of work."

Furry porn can show up in the strangest places, too—like a mainstream feature film. Michel Gondry's *Eternal Sunshine of the Spotless Mind* may be one of the best movies to capture the uncanny dream logic of sudden shifts of locale and weird juxtapositions that don't seem the least unusual (or even noticeable) while you're in the midst of dreaming them. In Charlie Kaufman's script, Jim Carrey's character discovers his ex-girlfriend had her memories of their relationship erased, and he decides to do likewise via a procedure administered while he sleeps. Halfway through the procedure, asleep but dreaming, he realizes he still loves her. With no way to stop the process he tries to "hide" her inside other memories of his past, including one particularly embarrassing moment where his mother discovers him masturbating in bed to some very unusual comics—of animal-headed people having sex.[95]

Those anthros were drawn by Paul Proch, an underground artist/cartoonist and lifelong friend to Charlie Kaufman. The pair, who met at NYU's film school, shared an offbeat sensibility and hit it off immediately. (A 1987 photo shows Charlie in an ape suit and Paul wearing a clown mask.) They began collaborating on a variety of

---

94 *Yaoi* is a manga genre focusing on gay male relationships.

95 The comics are viewable on the artist's website at http://www.freewebs.com/blemph-o/7eternalsunshinezero.htm. (Retrieved October 26, 2016.)

projects—including Charlie's wedding, where Paul served as best man.

Charlie became a celebrated Hollywood scriptwriter, responsible for quirky films like *Being John Malkovich* and the even quirkier *Anomalisa*. When he began writing *Eternal Sunshine* he asked Paul to come up with some drawings for the masturbation scene.

Paul's website[96] includes scans of some notes from the production, including one from Charlie reading, "Michel asked for a comic-like sketch of an erotic scene... We will need more detail for this from Michel." So, did the idea originate with Charlie or Michel? "Michel never gave any further details," Paul told me.[97] "He just said he wanted an 'erotic funny-animal comic,' and I took it from there."[98]

Had Michel procured a slightly larger production budget, Paul's erotic funny-animal comic would have been a funny-animal *cartoon*. Judging from the storyboard pages on Paul's website,[99] the animated sequence would have been every bit as porny as any X-rated furry art found online.

It sounds like Michel first suggested the comic, but his request was probably triggered by Charlie's script. In fact, several of Paul's friends have commented that Carrey's character resembles Paul an *awful* lot; it's intriguing

---

96   http://webzoom.freewebs.com/blemph-o/

97   Email to the author, February 16, 2016.

98   On his own website a friend of Paul's adds, "Paul designed and drew the sketchbook for the movie . . . All those creepy sketches of Kate Winslet with bat wings and skeletons that you saw Jim Carrey laboring over," a scene which never made it into the movie. (http://grimshaw.jeff.tripod.com/journeyintomadness.html. Retrieved October 26, 2016.)

99   http://www.freewebs.com/blemph-o/storyboards.htm. Retrieved October 26, 2016.

to think a lifelong friend might have inspired Charlie Kaufman's furry-porn–loving hero.

Even earlier than that, in 1978, a for-real erotic funny-animal comic book story saw the light of day. Reed Waller and Ken Fletcher's funny-animal APA, *Vootie*, was chugging along nicely, laying the groundwork for the furry fandom yet to come. As a sideline Reed played guitar in a pick-up band that made the rounds of the local strip clubs, of which there were quite a few in Minneapolis at the time. Between sets Reed would sketch the strippers, just to keep his cartooning chops sharp. Jim Schumeister, a fellow cartoonist, quipped, "Why don't you do your own funny-animal comic about strippers? You could call it *Charlie's Bimbos*."

Just a passing quip, or so Reed thought—until a postcard from Taral Wayne, a Canadian *Vootie* contributor, arrived just around the same time. All it said was "There's not enough sex in funny-animal comics."

In his online journal Taral explained his suggestion:

> *Considering how much sex there was in underground comics, I thought it rather odd that there was so little of it in* Vootie. *What could I do but write to Reed Waller and complain?*[100]

Taral's reference to the underground was spot-on; Robert Crumb's *Fritz the Cat* was another outlet for Crumb's bottomless libido. But as much as Crumb was influenced by the funny-animal comics of his youth, Fritz was at heart a creature of the underground comix scene, not part of the funny-animal orbit *Vootie* occupied.

---

100 *It's True—It's All My Fault*, May 2010; journal excerpt Emailed to the author November 20, 2015.

One does not ignore synchronicity in matters such as this. "That was a red flag to me," Reed recalled in a convention video;[101] Taral and Jim's near-simultaneous suggestions had fired up his imagination.

> *Rather to my surprise,* [Taral continued in his journal,] *Reed used my critique as the basis of a story in the next* [Vootie]. *My remarks are read out loud by naked furry babes while they danced, posed, cavorted, balled, screwed and fucked (literally) like mink in every panel.*

Indeed. In the first page of Reed's mini-porno comic, a fox gal challenges a slavering wolf guy. "The trouble with you FOOLS is you been here so long you think you're PEOPLE! Well you're NOT! You're ANIMALS! SO ACT LIKE IT!"

The wolf rises to the challenge, ripping off the fox's dress and exposing a lovely pair of breasts. "NOW you're GETTIN' somewhere!" she cheers as carnality ensues— until "HEY!" They're interrupted by the owner of the bar they've been hanging out in. "GET OUTA HERE!" he tells them "This is a PUBLIC PLACE! Want me BUSTED?"

The public place of course wasn't just the imaginary one of the comic. It was the comic book medium itself, and to be more specific, the comic book world of walking, talking (and previously squeaky-clean) funny animals.[102]

---

101 "Sex in Funny Animal Comics," presented at Furry Migration II, August 29, 2015.

102 The hardcore story's appearance in the previously staid *Vootie* helped create a schism between (according to Reed) "a small group of radicals like myself" who wanted to explore funny-animal sexuality in their work and those "who were hoping for a future in the rigidly regulated kids' entertainment and children's book market." ["Sex in Funny Animal Comics" presentation, August 29, 2015.] The split was one of the factors contributing to Vootie's ultimate demise.

Illustration courtesy of Reed Waller, © Reed Waller and Kate Wor

A narrative, written by Reed's collaborator Kate Worley, began manifesting itself out of that raunchy jaunt. A background cat in the funny-animal orgy became Omaha, an exotic dancer. The story began as a takedown of Minneapolis[103] bluenoses out to shut down the city's strip clubs; as stories tend to do, however, it took on a life of its own as Omaha and her feline boyfriend, Chuck, find themselves caught up in deadly political intrigue.

Not that the sex fell by the wayside; Reed's deft pen created no shortage of beautifully drawn panels featuring Omaha and Chuck (among other characters) engaged in full-frontal, open-labia and erect-penis copulation, among other sex acts. Omaha was a real cutie with a shapely body, a sweetly coy face and a beautiful head of curly red hair. Other than her ears, tail and pussycat nose, Omaha was as human and sexy as any woman ever drawn.

In a strange, counter-intuitive way, the funny-animal cast made Omaha's adventures seem more realistic, exciting and believable—this might really happen. The same story told with human characters might seem far-fetched or clichéd by comparison, but *Omaha the Cat Dancer* was something new and different.[104]

In 1981 the first official Omaha story was published in the ninth issue of the uniquely titled anthology comic *Bizarre Sex*. As it turned out, the bar owner in that early story was right to worry about getting busted: in 1986, a Chicago comic book shop owner was arrested for selling

---

103 Or "Mipple City," as it was called in the comic.

104 The full story of *Omaha the Cat Dancer* and its creators can be found at www.omahathecatdancer.com/

Omaha among other "obscene" books.[105] The conviction was overturned, but the damage had been done. In 1990 New Zealand authorities seized copies of the comic; the country's Obscene Publications Tribunal declared *Omaha* innocent of indecency. The same year Toronto's police did likewise, claiming the comic was a hotbed of bestiality; later, the case was dismissed.

"It certainly proved how confused people were about funny animals," Reed observed in his convention presentation. "Since the characters were all animals and no humans were involved, it couldn't be bestiality.

"No matter how much we try to deny it, we're part of the animal kingdom and share most of our behavior with many other creatures," he added. "Sex is a big part of every animal's life. Funny animals are the symbols of peoplehood that we grew up with and love, the magic link between our [childhood and adult] selves, the link we have to cross to find happiness."

While there's no shortage of sexy furry art online, the percentage of people who actually *act out* their sexuality in animal drag is quite tiny. Since (judging from convention attendance) only 20–25% of furs wear fursuits, my best guesstimate is perhaps 5–10% of them are willing to put their fursuits at sticky risk, a total of, at most, perhaps 2.5% of the entire fandom—*way* too few to tar every fur with the same brush, not that it's ever prevented anyone from doing so. (I certainly wouldn't abuse Komos that way; he'd never stand for it. It's far sexier simply *being* him and tapping into his commanding personality—and a lot of people he meets feel the same way.)

---

105 The successful battle to have the conviction overturned led to the creation of the Comic Book Legal Defense Fund (www.cbldf.org), a free-speech advocacy group.

For one thing, it's *hot* inside a fursuit—temperature hot, not sexy hot. (And then there's the humidity.) You have to have a real commitment to doing the deed to be able to endure all that. Still, there's something to be said for the experience, if only to a certain degree.

New York City's Greenwich Village Halloween Parade is internationally famous. Every October 31, thousands of revelers march up Manhattan's Sixth Avenue. It's now a business-sponsored mega-event, nothing like the small neighborhood affair it was once upon a time. From 1977 through 1984 several hundred, perhaps a thousand people at most wound their way through the neighborhood's narrow side streets towards Greenwich Village's heart: Washington Square Park.

In 1982 B.F. (Before Furry), I took advantage of the parade to indulge in a bit of pre-fandom animal dress-up. I assembled several Halloween masquerade beards into a mane, created a tail from a length of garden hose and transformed a pair of tawny-colored socks into paws. With the aid of a full-face cat mask I was now a fairly convincing, clothes-wearing anthropomorphic lion.

It was quite an experience. Along the way we passed a gigantic spider clambering up and down a nineteenth-century courthouse and sophisticated ghouls waving to us from their townhouse balconies. As we neared our destination we could see Satan himself atop Washington Square Arch, horned, dressed in red robes and waving his pitchfork as he urged us on.

In the park people mingled, danced and admired each other's costumes. I made the acquaintance of an attractive young harlequin who evidently had a bit of a thing for lions. (On my first visit to her apartment I pulled a random paperback from her bookshelf; it was a sci-fi novel featuring a lion-man on the cover very similar to the one I had been the week before.)

A few dates later we decided to re-don our Halloween outfits (except for my clothes) and indulge in a bit of private cosplay: she would be a naïve clown who wanted to prove her mettle by taming a ferocious circus lion.

The lion, who as it turned out was both ferocious and horny, quickly had her cornered. With one mighty paw he knocked the imaginary chair out of her hand, and with the other, the imaginary whip she had hoped to use on him. In the full-length mirror in my near-dark bedroom, under the influence of some primo cannabis, we saw a lion standing behind the clown, nuzzling and love-biting her neck, his claws ripping open her bodice to paw at her now-exposed breasts. An arousing sight to say the least, but in a few minutes we were no longer wearing any of our get-ups; at that point they would've just gotten in the way.

That said, there are quite a few furs that enjoy wearing and using a "murrsuit," a fursuit specifically modified for sexual interaction. Their videos can easily be found online in places like Xtube; after screening several I have to say it's probably more fun wearing one than watching someone else put his to use, with or without company. (Perhaps if the videos were shot in shadowy light to leave something to the imagination they might be more enjoyable.)

And just what makes the experience appealing? One murrsuiter [who asked to remain anonymous] gives this first-person perspective:

"It's an aesthetic appeal for me when I am in it. When I wear a [murrsuit] I know that I look sexy for the other person involved. When someone else is in it, however, it is about not only aesthetics, but feel. Fur feels excellent against one's bare skin!

"For me though, I like how I appear to others while [in the suit], but the feel of being in it doesn't do much for me. For others, being in a suit is often a headspace thing [imagining themselves as their anthropomorphic character]. In fact, I would say it is that way for a majority of murrsuiters. However, everyone experiences a murrsuit [and the sexual side of fur] differently. No one should claim to speak for an entire fandom or represent a fandom. In the anime fandom there are those that have sex in their cosplays. Hell, at comicons people will have sex in their costumes, too. Anyone who attempts to shame someone because sexuality is part of how they enjoy their fandom needs to reevaluate how they look at things. Most everyone has sex; I just happen to wear a fursuit while doing so sometimes."

For those who love the idea of unleashing their "animal side" in their sexual encounters, our good friend Second Life offers no end of pleasures that can be enjoyed for a few Linden dollars, and most definitely not just for furs. A 2014 business survey discovered half of Second Life's fifty most popular sims (places to visit) are rated A for Adult.[106]

Just as with any alternate online identity, anonymity is a big part of Second Life's appeal. In real life someone might see you drive into that hot-sheets motel or recognize you at a faraway bar with someone who's not your significant other; no chance of that happening when you're

---

106 *Half of Second Life's 50 Most Popular Sims Now Adult Rated.* New World Notes, (nwn.blog.com) Retrieved August 14, 2016.

online and anonymous. (Of course, someone might walk in on you while you're engaging in some torrid virtual sex; best to make sure the door's locked or at least have an alternate Internet tab ready in case of emergency.)

An equally large part of SL's appeal: you can actually get your rocks off in this place. Your might have a teeny-weeny peeny in RL, but not to worry: you can choose from over *seven thousand* penises in Second Life's Marketplace. (Most are human, but in a few minutes of browsing I've come across pony, dog and lizard ones—strictly in the interest of researching this book, of course.) They're controllable via a HUD—a "heads-up display" that lets you activate built-in motion commands.

"Me being a furry, I'm not that crazy sexual like most of these people are," my Second Life pal Big Z is telling me. "But one of my friends is like, 'Dude you need to get yourself a penis! Everyone has a penis.' 'But what if I don't want one?' 'It's so much fun to have one, trust me.'

"So he sends me a link, and it's a really cheap one but it has all these controls, like flaccid, slightly erect, super-erect, go down, less, less." Big Z brings up its display; each command is in its own separate box, just like his avatar's ear and tail controls. "A lot of people have really advanced ones; this is basic compared to them. You can also come, urinate, hide it or show it at your command."

"I'm always wearing clothes," Big Z says, referring to his wolf avatar. "Sometimes for shits and giggles, I'll be like—'unzip.'" He clicks on one of the controls; the avatar crosses its hands in front of its crotch and suddenly this purplish-pink thing appears. It doesn't look very penis-like, more like an unshucked ear of corn, if unshucked ears of corn were purplish-pink with some swelling at one end. Like Big Z said, it's a really cheap one; there are others in the marketplace that are much more realistic.

There are HUDs for all occasions. If you and a pal are into "D/s" (Dominance and submission) play, one will "make it easier for the sub to do his/her poses." Then there's the Male Masturbation HUD: "five animations included; offset feature stops shorter avatars from going through the floor." Good to know; the last thing you want when you're rubbing one out is your bottom half suddenly hanging from your downstairs neighbor's ceiling.

Then there are "poseballs"—round objects that trigger animations when they're clicked or sat on. There are almost 10,000 poseballs available in the SL marketplace; 291 are specifically for a non-consensual act that would get you locked up in the real world for a long time. (In consensual sex-fantasy roleplay however, variations on this are a guilt-free scenario enjoyed by many.)

Need a snooze? You won't have much chance to sleep in a sex bed. There are 14,000 of them to choose from. The Latex Fetish Sex Bed looks very attractive in red, all nice and shiny. It has over 1,100 animation options for varying genders and sexual orientations, and it's only L$5,995. Or you could go upscale and buy the VAW Eros Bed S4CS for L$9,550. It's preloaded with "146 realistic sex animations," fifty-four "hug, kiss, cuddle, sit, sleep solo animations" and "multiple-speed sex sets."

Furs are a minority in SL's massive, make-believe world; most people getting their freak on are regular folks. Still, in terms of viewable furry sexual interactions,

Second Life is definitely one of the best places for furs to explore their sexual sides.

Even though so much furry art exists that it might as well be mainstream, Furry may be the only fandom unfairly viewed by many—including other fandoms—as nothing more than a fetish scene. Other fandoms have their kinks but don't seem to have that problem. There's no shortage of tentacle rape and *bukkake*[107] *hentai* to be found in anime, for example, but they don't define the genre. *Yaoi* and *yuri*[108] manga abound without characterizing all Japanese comics as queer; Trekkers are not automatically thought of as "slash" (erotic Kirk/Spock fan fiction) enthusiasts.

There's no shortage of kinks in the mainstream world: BDSM, high heels, uniforms . . . There are chubby chasers, adult babies, people with a yen for non-western females, those who pine for pregnant women with bulging tummies . . .

Mainstream kinks with an element of animal make-believe (pony play or human pets for example) might overlap, Venn-diagram–style to a degree with Furry because of their subject matter. However, there's a D/s aspect to them for the most part absent in the friendlier forms of furry roleplay.

Still, there are a few kinks Furry has all to itself. While there are folks who have a serious thing for high-heeled shoes, the higher and pointier the better, there are furs every bit as fascinated by an animal's leathery pawpads, how they bulge out from its feet, how pleasant they are to

---

107 Look it up if you're really curious. (Don't say I didn't warn you.)

108 Yuri manga depicts same-sex female relationships.

the touch, solid yet slightly giving; they may collect art of anthros showing off their foot pads or own a fursuit with realistic looking (and feeling) silicone imitation pads.

Blow-up sex dolls are always good for a laugh (they say the newer models are much more realistic looking), and it's equally easy to chuckle at "plushies," furs who have a deeply personal and intimate relationship with a favorite stuffed animal. I'm in no position to pass judgment on anyone else. I understand from personal experience how something mundane or lacking an inherent erotic element can hold a hidden appeal. If nothing else, that stuffed animal has an identity for its significant other and a furry texture warm and pleasant to the touch.

Fur Affinity, the number-one furry-art website has a helpful "Browse" window that includes a "Fetish/Furry Specialty" locator. Most of those specialties are Rule 34F analogues of human kinks: bondage, water sports, overweight characters, muscled men, pregnant women and so on, but some are truly unique furry fancies: pawpads, inflation, macro or micro-sized furries, "vore"-acious characters[109] and human-to-animal transformation.

The specialties also include popular animation characters: Ponies, Pokémon, Sonic and the like, and General Furry Art, which covers just about everything else. The locator also lets you pre-select General, Mature and/or Adult art, which behooves me to point out it's equally possible for a fur to have a non-naughty interest in any of those specialties; they might just as likely be looking

---

109 As Maurice Sendak's Wild Things put it when Max decided to leave them, "Oh please don't go—we'll eat you up—we love you so!" *Where the Wild Things Are*, published 1963 by Harper & Row.

for G-rated fan art of Pokémon as a picture of Sonic doing the nasty dance with Rainbow Dash.[110]

Now that we've toured the sexy side of fur, please remember that the naughty bits are way in the minority compared to good-old wholesome furry fun, even if many people insist on seeing a few trees as the entire forest.[111]

There are plenty of furs willing to let it all hang out for me to acknowledge them with a chapter of their own. (A chapter I fear may lead many outside the furry community to say "you see?!" and ignore the rest of this book, and/or could cause many inside the community to accuse *me* of letting it all hang out.) Most of the hang-outers are shameless in a healthy way: free of the paralyzing, soul-crushing guilt that leads to self-loathing. Others, though, are shameless in the original sense of the word: lacking the common sense to know when enough is enough—when too much information is most definitely TMI.

And for all the naughty furry art I've seen in my time, I've yet to see a picture of the *real* sex organ, the part of the body that floats everyone's boat: the human mind.

---

110 Years ago I googled "furry art" to show a friend. The first image that came up was a drawing of Pepé Le Pew topping Bugs Bunny. I was shocked—because I had always assumed Bugs was a top and not a bottom. On second thought I realized Pepé has been chasing females his entire film career (and could rightly be tagged a sexual predator for his efforts) while Bugs has always had a thing for wearing women's clothes.

111 When I search Fur Affinity for art featuring popular 'toon stars, a quarter of the results vanish when I switch from FA's Not Safe for Work setting to Safe for Work.

CHAPTER TEN

The Spirit Is Willing,
but the Flesh Is Furry

"THERIANTHROPY" IS A WORD you don't hear much in general conversation. It refers to the belief that one is not fully a human being—that to whatever degree, you're an animal born by error in a human body—a "Therian." By contrast, "Otherkin" believe they're imaginary animals—dragons, gryphons and the like in similar circumstances.[112]

It's easy to mock people who imagine this kind of stuff, as if they're delusional, psychotic, or they suffer from Body Dysmorphic Disorder. Except it's none of the above—they're people with a spiritual belief. It's something they feel inside, a subjective truth they've known all their lives. They don't look in the mirror and see a tiger or a dragon; they see their human form, just as the world sees them. But as the old expression goes, it's what's inside that counts.

Do you believe you have a soul, a spiritual essence that

---

112 That young child I recently saw wearing an "I'd rather be a dragon" T-shirt may grow up to realize he is in fact an Otherkin himself.

exists apart from your body and will outlive it and you? What does your soul *look* like—a formless, ghostly apparition? An ethereal, transparent version of yourself? A ball of plasmic energy? Maybe you're not sure; maybe you've never stopped to think about it. Therians and Otherkin have, and they have no doubt what theirs look like.

Like so many furs, Therians and Otherkin have always had these feelings, but couldn't talk about them for fear of ridicule. And again like many furs, they discovered each other via the Internet and realized they were a community. They're a small but sizeable presence at furry conventions, mingling with furs who imagine and depict their animal alter egos in fursuit and art but don't experience it on a spiritual level.

That overlap has brought many into the furry community, enough to catch the eye of the International Anthropomorphic Research Project, who have focused particular attention and study on Therians and Otherkin; according to their latest data contained in *Fur Science!*, the two groups comprise roughly 14% of those surveyed.[113]

One of that group is "Abyssalrider," a twenty-three-year-old fur who identifies himself as "The Autistic Tiger-Wolf" in his online postings. "When most people get angry or annoyed at something, they usually hide it or scream and swear about it. My instinct is to growl at it—and more often than not, I do. It's something canines usually do—not humans. My theriotype[114] is some form of wolf; I

---

113 According to *Fur Science!* some furs with spiritual beliefs linking them to animals prefer not to be called Therians or Otherkins, just as other furs would rather not be thought of as furs. The study also found a sizeable number of furs who *did* have such beliefs but were unaware a name existed to describe them.

114 Theriotype: "The animal or animals that a therian believes they are inside

haven't found the exact species yet, but I think it might be the Arctic wolf. That said, I don't believe *I'm* a wolf, but I do believe I have some form of unusual connection to them, more than just an 'I really like them' type thing. Other than that, aside from being autistic, I'm perfectly normal.

"I've said it elsewhere and I'll say it here: I'm a therian, specifically the kind that believes he was a wolf in a past life. Do you know how much of a pain in the ass (no pun intended) it is to fall asleep on your back and feel like you slept on top of a limb you don't have? (In this case, a tail.) I've always found it much easier to relate to dogs than people, and not just because they're animals and easier to get along with. I've regularly managed to get dogs to do a new command or trick right from the start with minimal effort, [even] when an experienced dog trainer couldn't. Dogs usually seen as unfriendly run up to me and lick my face or try to play. All my dreams involving animals have me either as a wolf or with a wolf at my side; never has one been against me. I don't call that coincidence.

"My senses of hearing and smell are much sharper than my friends'. I can tell what color fireworks there were by the smell of the chemicals or metals that were used to make them, or what was used for bonfire fuel—burning newspaper smells differently than construction paper or magazines. Various types of wood have their own smell that can change depending on how dry it is. I can hear things most can't. (Electricity for one. Annoying as hell when I'm trying to sleep [when I've got] a migraine.)

"I hate house cats with a passion, but I like dogs. [Dogs are] good pets but I never felt that strong 'this repre-

---

or identifies as." Wikifur, (http://en.wikifur.com/wiki/Theriotype) Accessed November 29, 2016.

sents me' emotion about them that I do with wolves—specifically Arctic wolves. I've always had a fascination with Siberian tigers as well. When I learned there are white Bengal tigers with coloring similar to Siberian ones I immediately fell in love with them too.

"My fursona was a dragonhound, a wolf/dragon hybrid at first, but a couple of months later I changed it when I realized dragons just don't represent me that much. I like them and would love to be one, but other than the 'being misunderstood and judged before anyone gets to know you' type of thing, I don't identify with them.

"My new fursona is a Tigrol: a tiger/wolf hybrid. The tiger half is because not only have I felt a strong connection to them, but also because it's a direct contradiction to the wolf half—and I consider myself a walking contradiction."

A wolf might seem like an easy connection for a human to make, but what about a deer? A teenage fur wanted to share his cervine experience, but asked to remain anonymous . . .

"I've always had this subconscious connection to deer. Nothing empathetic or anything like that; it's just whenever I see or think of a deer, it always feels as though I'm looking at a physical manifestation of my internal mind, the mind that is always active, though I can never seem to express.

"Externally, I'm either a painfully awkward, distant guy with social anxiety, or a loud, goofy idiot with not a single crap to give. Internally, however, I feel like I'm one with nature. While an area with lots of trees will seem like nothing more than an area with lots of trees to most people, I can almost feel the life flowing through those trees. Have you ever felt or even heard a slight difference in the air when someone enters a room, even when they're being completely silent? That's what it feels like for me when surrounded by nature.

"Some of the more visible aspects of me can be compared to that of a deer. I'm thin, and very light on my toes. Despite heart disease running on both sides of my family, being diagnosed with asthma, suffering a pneumothorax and being exposed to a lot of secondhand smoke in my earlier youth, I have a very healthy cardiore-spiratory system. I exceed most of my peers when it comes to endurance running. I love to walk, run, anything that allows my legs to move.

"I always need to explore. Ever since I was old enough to go on walks around my city, it became my personal goal to see everything within a certain distance of my home. I discovered so many awesome locations, so many creepy locations (in a cool way), so many beautiful loca-tions, everything. And the greater my endurance got over time, the more that distance expanded, so [my] opportu-nities for discovery [grew]. I go on a six-mile walk almost every morning, and I know everything within a three-mile radius of my home. Anything that I'm capable of walking to, I need to discover.

"My favorite reason [for illustrating my connection with deer] happened a year or two prior to [my] becoming a furry. I was coming home from another one of my early-morning walks; the city was just beginning to wake up. I was walking right down the middle of a road when I saw a doe at the other end. We were quite a far distance away from each other when she locked eyes with me.

"Deer are uncommon where I live, and they'd usually

run off at the mere sight of a human. But this one just kept standing there, even knowing very well that I was headed toward her. At some point the doe actually continued her path in my direction. Neither of us stopped or attempted to take a different route, we just kept to our own paths at a delicate pace.

"Eventually the inevitable happened: we walked right past each other, about ten feet apart. If my memory serves, it was pretty cold that morning and I was close enough to actually see her breath! What I liked the most about that experience wasn't that I got that close to a deer, but that it didn't feel like I was passing a wild animal in the slightest. It felt like we were making some kind of strong connection. What that connection was is anybody's guess, but I felt like we understood each other in that one moment."

Therianthropy is perhaps the most intriguing aspect of furry spirituality, but it is not the only one. Some believe we all have a spirit or power animal guiding us through life, very often one that has chosen us without our being aware of it. Many Indigenous cultures see a particular animal as the tribe's totem and protector, and shamans would embody the animal through costume and ritual.

It took me a while, but once I found my fursona, it was like finding home. It wasn't of my own choosing but it seemed to fit; I was an *Alligator mississipiensis*. I started collecting gator things—figurines, lapel pins, little plushies and more that came to infest my apartment.

I found myself thinking about alligators more and more, considering how they looked and what their lives were like. I became entranced by the incredible variety of scales, textures and patterns adorning their leathery, near-invulnerable-looking hides: a knobby-nosed snout dotted with tiny black freckles; a set of gaping, grinning jaws; a flabby, scrotal neck goiter; the large scales that resemble a fishing net; the randomly sized and shaped scales along its body that somehow fit together like pieces of a jigsaw puzzle; their forelegs' delicately splayed fingers . . .

I was fascinated by the array of scutes on their armored backs, set in rows like parallel mountain ranges, each one a tiny alp as rough and bone-solid as the real thing. As their fearful symmetry advances down the animal's body, the interior rows vanish until the two remaining outermost rows merge into a single progression of dragon-sized plates at the end of its lengthy tail.

But apart from their aesthetic beauty, there's something about the alligator's timeless, ancient nature extending eons back to a time when mammals (never mind humans) didn't exist that makes me feel connected to that unimaginably distant past. The fact that they're at home on the land as well as in or under water makes them seem connected not just to the beginning of life on the planet but to all of life.

Some atavistic impulse was reaching out to me. It became easy to imagine myself as an alligator. There I was, basking on a river bank beneath the sun, its heat warming my armored back, my belly against the ground, embracing the Earth until it was time to lower my body temperature. The next moment I'd be instinctively sliding, gliding into the cool swamp water.

In the real world I'm swimming laps at the local pool, my eyes just above the water's surface, imagining my fellow bathers as yummy dinners or light snacks, while lazy undulations of my massive tail propel me through the weightless environment. Here, for the first time, I *am* an alligator.

There's an old French expression: *nostalgie pour la boue,* "nostalgia for the mud." In its original context it referred to well-off people who longed for a more primitive life. But I interpreted it on a more literal level; I longed to return to a *truly* primitive existence, the one my fursona had emerged from.

Swamps and alligators: they go together. In my mind there was something protean about the combination; there was something about entering a primal, fecund world that could connect me more to my inner alligator.

There's a kink out there known as "Wet and Messy"—WAM for short. Pie fights, getting covered with gunky, gooey stuff (anything from chocolate syrup to crude oil) and playing in mud; if any of the above appeal to you, you're into WAM. (Nickelodeon shows like *Slime Time* and *Double Dare* undoubtedly blessed a not-insignificant number of their viewers with a deep fondness for such activity.)

As with many other kinks, WAM has its fans within the furry world.

I knew a fur that actually had a small bog on his rural property, a low-lying area of soft ground that naturally collected moisture from its surroundings. For reasons likely similar to my own, he enjoyed the occasional sink while fursuited. Building up my courage to explain what I had in mind, I asked if it would be possible for me to visit and try it myself. Sure, he said, come on down.

I assembled a haphazard alligator costume out of a green shirt with a reasonably scaly-looking pattern, a green pair of shorts and a quilted card table cover that, once painted and folded into a narrow triangle, made an acceptable tail. A pair of swim gloves became my webbed hands and a store-bought over-the-head gator mask completed my outfit. The rest of me, the parts that remained human would be out of sight under the surface.

Two long-distance bus rides brought me to his front door. The day was bright and sunny but once we entered the overgrown woods beyond his house it might as well have been dusk. We walked downhill along a narrow dirt path until the ground leveled out. A few yards later there it was, just beyond some bushes—my friend's pocket bog.

I donned my haphazard costume and slowly sunk into the bog up to my hips. I leaned forward and let my weight drive my arms into the welcoming mud until I was lying on my stomach, eye level with the bog's surface. Only my masked head, gator-patterned back and attached tail were visible above the mud's surface.

I was now eye-level with the ground, viewing the world from the same perspective an alligator would view his. The trees that surrounded me a few minutes earlier now towered way above me. I luxuriated in the experience I had been looking forward to for months. The sensation of the bog holding me, *embracing* me, pulling on my arms when I tried to lift them, reluctant to let go of me . . . it was as if the Earth itself wanted me as its lover.

Finally, sadly it was time to leave; the day was turning dusky for real, the woods growing darker by the minute. I emerged from the bog's embrace, removed my costume and rinsed myself off in a nearby creek. I felt disoriented, spacey. (I didn't even notice my tail drifting downstream.) I'd felt a certain tingle after swimming in the past; as

I left the bog, a thousand-fold version of that sensation was coursing through my body. The feeling lingered for hours before at last fading into the background of my awareness.

My host had photographed the experience. One picture showed me bare-chested before donning my costume, my stomach a convex line curving away from my body. I'd tried for years to lose weight without much success, but the pot-bellied photo of me triggered something.

From that weekend on I stopped consuming the junk food and sweets that for years had been a source of comfort to me. I stopped cold. A half-finished bag of Oreos stayed that way for the rest of the year. (Visiting friends eventually consumed them.) It wasn't a matter of suddenly developing willpower, either; I'd simply lost the desire, the *need* for that form of self-comfort.

Over the next several months thirty-five pounds melted away; people who hadn't seen me for a while didn't recognize me or wondered if I'd been sick.

It wasn't until years later I realized what I had done: I had instinctively created a shamanistic transformation ritual that had connected me to primal energy. Was it a previously untapped internal strength, or a power already existing outside myself? There was no way of knowing, but the experience put me in touch with *something* that had never been part of my life before.

If someone else had told me this story, I'd think "New Age space cadet," or respond with a mocking "trust The Force, Luke" and walk away—but it was real, I experienced it, I lived it.

And it did physically transform me. Therianthropy describes the practice of shape-shifting—was that what happened to me? Am I a therian? Do I believe I possess an alligator spirit, that I'm truly a crocodilian sadly trapped inside a human body?

I can't say for sure, but the alligator who serves as my fursona was without a doubt my power animal, my totem.

And the alligator my niece saw, the one Groat drew?

As it turned out, that was indeed me all along.

Traditional western religions also incorporate animals into their beliefs and symbology. (The Gospel of John refers to Jesus as "the Lamb of God,"[115] and according to the Four Gospels, "when Jesus was baptized the Holy Spirit in the shape of a dove came down from the opening heaven and rested upon him."[116])

It would seem a tad unusual to pair faith with fur, but there are furry folks whose spirits rest comfortably in both the realm of animals and the spirituality of humankind.

Take, for example, Matthias Rat. He's a golden-furred rodent wearing a tropical-green shirt and cargo shorts, with pink ears, pink paws and a long pink tail he'll be holding in one hand while offering a friendly wave with the other. That's when you see him in person; online he's a steampunk triceratops, the captain of a dirigible airship constantly annoyed by the birds who enjoy nesting in his horns. His novel *Never Again a Man* won the 2004 Ursa Major Award for Best Furry Novel. Matthias is also a devout Catholic who ends all his online postings with *Dominus tecum*— "The Lord be with you." He's far from the only furry Catholic; he belongs to the online group Furs for Christ

---

115 "Lamb of God." Wikipedia. (https://en.wikipedia.org/wiki/Lamb_of_God) Retrieved December 3, 2016.

116 "Holy Spirit." The Jewish Encyclopedia, 2011. (http://www.jewishencyclopedia.com/articles/7833-holy-spirit) Retrieved December 1, 2016.

Illustration by Dr.West, courtesy of and © Matthias Rat

(fursforchrist.com) and moderates the Fur Affinity group Catholic Furries. In Matthias's eyes there's no conflict between faith and fur; in fact he feels the combination has brought him closer to Jesus.

"Like so many other furs I was furry for as long as I can remember. I grew up with Disney's *Robin Hood*; I stared in the mirror on the full moon to see if I could start changing; I watched the pig transformation scene from *Willow* in slo-mo; I wanted to be Gorbash.[117]

---

117 In the 1982 animated feature *The Flight of Dragons* a human's mind is magically transferred into the body of the dragon Gorbash to protect the human from an

"I was raised Christian, and like a lot of college kids I stopped going to Church and drifted for a couple of years. My girlfriend (now my wife) kept praying I would come back. In my senior year [of college] I became interested in Christian apologetics.[118] When I read what the Catholics had to say I found myself excited; it answered questions I'd struggled with and gave me reasons to believe again.

"I converted to Catholicism twenty years ago. The Internet had become a thing around the same time, and when I discovered the fledgling furry community I knew I'd found an online home.

"At first it was difficult being both Catholic and a furry. I think it goes without saying that the demographics of Furry are not heavily Christian, let alone Catholic.[119] Things changed as the Internet grew, and with it furry fandom.

"Back in the 2000s I discovered several active Christian Furry forums. I spent most of my time on Furs For Christ, a non-denominational forum. Catholic versus Protestant discussions took place regularly and were always pretty friendly. We loved to discuss ways in which Furry intersected with our faith and how to be both a Christian and a fur. My fellow Catholic furries and I do disagree on some things (I'd never wear my tail to Mass, though I've seen others do so).

---

evil wizard.

118 "[A] field of Christian theology that presents historical, reasoned and evidential bases for Christianity, defending it against objections." *Christian Apologetics,* Wikipedia. (https://en.wikipedia.org/wiki/Christian_apologetics) Retrieved November 9, 2016.

119 "About 25% of furries are Christian, though many indicated that they did not regularly practice their faith or attend church." From *Fur Science: A Summary of Five Years of Research from the International Anthropomorphic Research Project.* Retrieved October 14, 2016.

"Most of us who give it serious thought always end up asking ourselves [if it's okay to be a furry]. We've all seen fellow furs who ditch the faith because they found it morally restrictive (instead of freeing us from our worst impulses) or were offended by the hypocrisy of the hierarchy, or whatever. We don't want to be that person because we love our faith and know it to be true; it is the measuring stick against which we measure Furry.

"While there are aspects of the fandom we believe do not measure up, so much of the enthusiasm, imagination, joy and wonder that comes from man's relationship to the animals is there in Furry—and it is good. I need only think of the times kids and even grownups see me in my fursuit to know it.

"After becoming a father four years ago I'm no longer very active in Furs for Christ; I'm now one of the moderators of the Fur Affinity group Catholic Furries. We've tried to focus on specifically Catholic concerns such as Rosary meditations, Church teachings, prayer requests and occasionally controversial social issues. But we are Furry; I actually drew a picture of The Presentation of Christ[120] where the Holy Family and Simeon are all sheep anthros. I haven't shared it with non-furs, but one of my best friends is a fellow Catholic fur who is an actual artist; he told me that he is not comfortable depicting Jesus as anthro. Even so, he enjoyed the picture. One of the other moderators asked if I would draw similar scenes for the rest of the Mysteries of the

---

120 Forty days after his birth Mary and Joseph brought the infant Jesus to the temple in Jerusalem. The event has been depicted in many paintings throughout the centuries and is commemorated on Candlemass, forty days after Christmas. The event is one of the Mysteries of the Rosary, a series of meditations on Jesus's life.

Rosary; I'd love to but I'd need a long dedicated block of time which is unlikely to happen with a four-year-old daughter.

"One of the things that has always impressed me and drawn me to the Catholic faith was a love and a place for the animal world and the many incidents in the lives of the saints that revolve around animals.

"It's commonly known that St. Francis of Assisi preached to the birds gathered around him. They listened as he explained their role in God's plan; they waited until he was finished to disperse. It's also well-known he started the tradition of the Christmas crèche when he brought a donkey, cow, sheep and other animals into a Church and created the first Nativity scene to remind people of the humility, simplicity and poverty into which Christ was born.

"There are many, many others. St. Hubert of Liège was a hunter who converted when he was confronted by a mighty stag with a cross in his antlers (the inspiration for the Jägermeister logo). St. Christopher is supposed to have been a cynocephali[121] before his conversion. St. Jerome befriended a lion when he removed a thorn from its paw.

"There are patron saints for many, many animals and even an abbot who taught his monks humility by making them go about town wearing fox tails. Perhaps he's the patron saint of fursuiters! One Christian writer compared Jesus to a centaur because he is one person with two natures. Nor should we ever forget that the modern fantasy genre was started by a Catholic, J.R.R. Tolkien,[122]

---

121 A member of the legendary race of dog-headed human beings. After meeting the Christ Child, Christopher reformed, received baptism and became human in appearance.

122 Author of *The Hobbit* and *The Lord of the Rings* trilogy.

and an almost Catholic, C.S. Lewis, who peopled his world with animal folk.[123]

"It was a moral challenge at first to be Catholic and a furry. I found both at roughly the same time, and I struggled to understand and be both, which I think was the result of wanting things that were ultimately destructive for me.

"There is nothing in Furry that teaches me what is right and what is wrong, but it does help me see the world and how it all works together in ways I was unaware of. It's brought me into contact with a wide variety of people I would never have known otherwise. Furry is filled with good people and so much excitement that I could never leave it. And my faith helps me understand the proper place for Furry and helps me appreciate how much fun it is to be a Rat and to run around in my fursuit.

"I had essentially zero exposure to LGBT people until I found Furry. Many otherwise good, devout Catholics I know tend to lump them into one bucket and think of them as an interest group instead of a broad array of distinct human beings, each created by God. Furry helped teach me not to lump a group of people into a basket, [and not] to 'other' them [or] make them less than anyone else. I don't want it done to me (and it has [been]), and I will not do it to anyone else.

"Furry has [also] helped me see other species through their eyes and think about what life would be like with a tail or at their size. It's expanded my imagination and filled my eyes with wonder. And this can be seen in

---

123 C.S. Lewis authored *The Chronicles of Narnia*, a Christian allegory and series of children's books in which Jesus appears in the form of the lion Aslan.

all the stories I have written and shared over the years.

"I'm a Catholic furry and love it! *Dominus tecum.*"

FAITH AND FURRY, spirit and Furry, insight and Furry; there isn't a part of life that doesn't fold into our incredible community. Even the biggest, and arguably best, feeling of all can come from fur: love.

"How are you, you sexy gator?" read the unexpected instant message.

"I'll have you know I'm mostly straight," I answered, intrigued.

"'Mostly,' heh."

That's how our relationship began: an IM from "Furio," a fur I'd met at several conventions. Another aspect of having an alligator as both my spirit animal and online fursona is a fondness for cartoon gators, particularly the ones in *Fantasia*. (One of my favorite moments in the film is when a love-struck Ben Ali puts his hands over his heart at his first glimpse of Hyacinth Hippo—and they vanish under his flabby neck.) Being described as a "sexy gator" was far from the worst thing I'd ever been called.

I first introduced myself to Furio a few years prior, without knowing it was him. I saw him fursuited as his "Walrus Royce" character, a big-bellied, exuberant and nattily dressed *Odobenus rosmarus.* I told him I liked his over-the-head walrus mask because it left his human eyes exposed, not hidden behind an immobile toony pair. It's rarely done in fursuiting, but it allows for a much more emotionally expressive performance, eyes being the window to the soul and all that.

After that first meeting, and before his "sexy gator"

IM, I bumped into a tall, lanky fellow in a convention hotel hallway. I glanced at his con badge; "*You're* Furio?" I was far from the first person thrown off by the discrepancy between the human I'd just met for the first time and his chubby fursona; what I didn't know at the time was that I was talking to a man who found me very cute (an adjective I'd never think of applying to myself).

As for being "mostly straight," I considered myself heteroflexible or bicurious (and, I confess, not entirely unexperienced in that regard); I didn't have a problem with a man calling me sexy—especially one calling me a sexy gator.

"I worried that I had forced you or seduced you against your will rather than opened a door for you that you needed opened," Furio told me recently, not realizing that the door hadn't exactly been locked at the time.

Just what did he find so attractive about me? "You're always full of something interesting to enjoy and learn about, and eager to live and experience new things. I love how you seemed so animated and lively, like a living 'toon yourself."

"Like a living 'toon . . . " Furio definitely understood me! Perhaps that's why so many furs—regardless of their sexual orientation—couple up with fellow furs. If fur is just a hobby to you, like woodworking or belonging to a book club, you're more likely than not to have a non-furry spouse. But if fur is something closer to your heart, something central to your identity, if you're a "lifestyler," then you want to be with someone you can share *all* of yourself with.

Furio says "I feel 'safe' with you, like I won't be judged or looked down on. Your heart and mind are very open; I love you even more for that." It's almost word for word how I feel about him: I've no need to hedge my bets or keep parts of myself secret. I've spent too much of my life fearful of offending others, or of rejection by a mercurial family; I've never felt so totally accepted by anyone as I do by Furio.

For example, the pudding swamp. While Furio fursuits as Walrus Royce, his fursona is a bear. I'm very fond of bears (animal, not human ones) and we've drawn ourselves countless times as our fursonas. Furio knows about my shamanistic ritual, my "transformation" into an alligator in that bog. One night he surprised me with a special dessert he'd made to celebrate my visit[124]: a little PVC alligator in a dish of chocolate pudding, snout to snout with a plastic grizzly bear.

Furio thought I'd find it humorous, but I wept. I wept at not just his acceptance, but his embrace, his *celebration* of who I am, even (or especially) the "weird" parts I'd kept under wraps for years, always afraid no one would understand.

This was the truly amazing part. We weren't just having fun, fooling around, enjoying each other as friends with benefits. We fell truly, deeply—and unexpectedly—in love. We became partners—and as our human selves, not as our fursonas. Alligator, walrus, bear, Komodo dragon . . . those masks are fun to wear, but it's not Komos and Furio who are in love, it's Joe and Marc.

---

124 Furio lives outside of Washington D.C., while I live on the island off the coast of the U.S. known as Manhattan.

CHAPTER ELEVEN

I Read the News Today, Oy Vey

FURRY'S VERY FIRST mainstream coverage was actually quite positive. It occurred completely by accident—and I happened to be there.

I was one of the Sci-Fi Channel's first employees, helping it get up and running in time for its September 1992 launch. The furry coverage happened a few months later in January 1993. My furry pal Peter convinced me to fly cross-country with him to attend ConFurence 4 in Costa Mesa, California, my first furry convention. I was still quite deep in the furry closet, keeping my anthropomorphic interests separate and apart from the channel—and frankly, from just about everyone who knew me.

At ConFurence 4, I was on the other side of the continent from Rockefeller Center and my co-workers. There was no way I was going to let them know I'm part of a fandom that considers cartoon animals sexy, because they wouldn't get it and I'd just as soon—

"Hey Joe, there's a crew here from the Sci-Fi Channel."

My pulse rate must've doubled that moment—*busted!*

The crew was from the channel's only original series, *Sci-Fi Buzz*, a magazine-format show covering the genre. I chatted with the segment producer—without telling her I worked for the company that had sent her to the convention. As it turned out, *Buzz* was doing a feature on fantasy author Mercedes Lackey; when they discovered she was appearing as a Guest of Honor at something called ConFurence, they followed her to the convention—two segments for the price of one!

I made sure, damn sure, to keep out of camera range for the rest of the weekend, except for one brief moment when I decided I wanted to be represented after all. Dig up the segment on YouTube ("Sci-Fi Buzz Confurence") and look closely at the lower-left corner of the screen, around 1:21 in. You'll catch a glimpse of the only part of myself I let wind up in the segment—the bottom of my shoe.

It was a positive piece; the fandom equals fursuiting and Furry equals kinky memes had yet to develop. Furry art filled over a minute and a half of the four-minute segment; a mere twenty-five seconds were devoted to fursuiters. The rest of the segment was filled by an assortment of folks thoughtfully explaining Furry to the uninitiated. It was an art-to-'suiter ratio never to be seen again.

In March 1994 Furry got the front-page treatment from *WIRED* Magazine. Performance artist Laurie Anderson was the cover story, but the last of three other stories hyped read "MUDs: Sex with the FurryMuckers."

The 6,200-word article was titled "Johnny Manhattan

Meets the Furry Muckers: Why playing MUDs is becoming the addiction of the '90s." Even though Josh Quittner's article is an overview of "the hundreds of MUDs, Mucks, Mushes and M-whatevers that are propagating on the Net like jackrabbit warrens," the furry one winds up on the cover—linked to the "S" word, of course. Just in case you're not sure what Quittner's take on FurryMUCK is going to be, an early paragraph informs readers "you can live in a world of vampires on Elysium, or be a cartoon character on ToonMUD or be a sleek, post-pubescent otter on FurryMuck, where you can have Netsex with a fish." ("Netsex" as Internet slang never quite caught on.)

About halfway through the article Quittner finally gets around to actually describing FurryMUCK, taking care not to disappoint readers who bought the issue on the basis of that cover blurb: "'[T]he first anthropomorphic MUD . . . It makes LambdaMOO look like the Young Republicans. People describe themselves as furry cuddly animals; more times than not, they have furry cuddly animal sex. FurryMuckers like to write long, loving, animal-sexy descriptions of themselves . . . " Quittner quotes an "animal-sexy" description in full, of which a few excerpts here will suffice: "Jynx . . . is a Salusian male . . . he has big clear blue eyes and is covered with a shining light-brown fur... [Alendia] is a very attractive squirreloid in her later teens. Her soft red fur clings damply to her body . . . The fur of her inner thighs is orange and damp, becoming thinner and steamy near the uppermost edge. Her waist is very narrow and her body curves up towards her firm breasts, making a nearly perfect hour-glass shape . . . "

You get the idea. Not surprisingly, "FurryMUCK gets a [temporary] deluge of sex-seekers."[125] I can't blame Quittner for zeroing in on some steamy roleplay, but wish he hadn't ended with, "It also goes a long way to explaining the Usenet group, alt.sex.bestiality."

Being written up in a well-known venue like *WIRED* wasn't shabby at all, but Furry's next mainstream appearance was about as high-profile as it gets: an appearance in the *New York Times*.

On October 27, 1996, the paper's Sunday magazine section ran a brief item with the headline "WILD ABOUT FUR." Alongside a photograph of a husky young man wearing a skunk suit with his face painted to match, the story described Wisconsin doctoral student James Firmiss and his "skunky" alter-ego A.J. Skunk.

According to the item, James/A.J. belonged to a "growing national subculture of furry-suit hobbyists" who roleplay online as animals and attend "conFURences." The payoff, according to Firmiss was the freedom to reveal a private alter-ego, in his case a skunk who is "more expressive about his emotions" than his human counterpart. The item mentioned that A.J. would be appearing, apparently for no particular reason, Thursday in downtown Madison.

A respectable little item, accurate for the most part, although the author did mistakenly use "conFURences" as a generic term to describe all furcons. Later on I would meet A.J./James Firmiss at a sci-fi convention (I didn't recognize him at first because he now had a skunk head to accompany the suit), but more recently I tracked him

---

125 Wikifur, *History of FurryMUCK*. (en.wikifur.com/wiki/Hisory_of_ FurryMUCK) Retrieved January 3, 2016.

down to learn how he became known to the "newspaper of record."

Firmiss explained the writer came across his website detailing his costume's construction and followed up with a "fairly straightforward" phone interview. Next came a pair of photographers, who he later found out specialized in photographing "eccentrics."

The part-time skunk was less than overjoyed with the final article. "[The writer] didn't put that negative a spin on the fandom, but he had re-worded some of the things I said yet kept them in quotes. The thing that upset me the most was that it said 'on Thursday he will strut his skunky stuff in downtown Madison.' It was published October 26, and a lot of people didn't realize Thursday was Halloween. I got a flood of phone calls afterwards asking for interviews; I'd say more than half the callers thought I wore the costume every week. I think at some point Rush Limbaugh even mentioned me,[126] probably an example of the 'human debris' he's talked about occasionally. People from *The Daily Show* called; they were rather rude, calling it 'your little costume thing.' Screw you, *Daily Show*."[127]

The calls dwindled in number as the month

---

126 In 2005 Limbaugh spoke about Further Confusion, which was about to take place in San Jose, California. Although he didn't mention Firmiss, Limbaugh kept referring to "inter-species fantasies" and finished his report with "[w]e've got a war going on and the tragedy of the tsunami. Isn't this furry convention a little bit too festive and too costly? There's a real furball for you liberals, eh? Ha ha. 'Shut 'em down! Shut 'em down, it's perverted!'" "The Rush Limbaugh Show." Wikifur, (http://en.wikifur.com/wiki/The_Rush_Limbaugh_Show) Retrieved September 19, 2016.

127 Prior to 1999 *The Daily Show* was hosted by Craig Kilborn. During the pre-Jon Stewart era "[t]he show was slammed by some reviewers as being too mean-spirited, particularly towards the interview subjects of field pieces." Wikipedia, *The Daily Show*. (https://en.wikipedia.org/wiki/The_Daily_Show) Retrieved September 19, 2016.

progressed; by the end of November his fifteen minutes of mephitic fame had come to an end. "I was rather glad it was over—but in a way I kind of missed the attention."

Media-wise, it was all downhill from there. A May 2000 article on ConFurence 11 in the Los Angeles *New Times* wallows in a "look at the weirdos!" mode, turned up to eleven. Attendees include "skinny teens in dog collar tags . . . gentle giant computer geeks . . . hoary biker wolves . . . like *The Island of Doctor Moreau*, only air conditioned." One fur "stares flatly through wire-rimmed glasses," while "disgust ripples through [the] corpulent form" of another. The author wonders "what sort of claustrophobic phantasm of bobbing cartoon faces might squeeze those sweat-fogged pinhole eyes."

While acknowledging—very briefly—furry fandom isn't 110% kinky, the article spends an enormous amount of column space describing, in great detail, furry porn, animal dildos, strategically placed holes and other aspects of furry fandom that no, you wouldn't want your mom to know about. If I hadn't already been part of the fandom for over a decade, I wouldn't want to hang out with a group like that myself.[128]

"'HEY THAT STUFFED CHIPMUNK IS TURNING ME ON!' Inside the bizarre sex-fetish world of 'plushies' and 'furries,'" drooled the March 2001 cover of *Vanity Fair*. Furry fandom hit the big-time media—and vice versa. Heralded by a shocked write-up ("one of the most

---

128 Mark Merlino's take on negative furry coverage: "[P]ublicity helps us find more of our furry kin . . . I believe it is worth the controversy caused by any negative publicity if it means that more furry people can find their way 'home.'" (From the ConFurence 10 program book, 2009.)

astounding, irritating and disturbing things I've ever read about weirdo adults . . . yucky pornography . . . and creepy sex") by Liz Smith in her daily gossip column, the high-society magazine spends nine pages looking at a handful of furs to reach their conclusion: people dressing up as animals? Disgusting—except for the soulful-looking gorilla who happens to be a Hollywood actor in expensive prosthetic makeup on the contents page and further in, the photo spread of Tim Roth and Helena Bonham Carter pretending to be primates for Tim Burton's misfired *Planet of the Apes* remake.

George Gurley, author of "Pleasures of the Fur," built his article around a visit to the first iteration of Midwest FurFest in 2000.[129] In spite of Gurley's seemingly neutral voice, the article nonetheless reeks of condescension. ("Some have googly, glazed, innocent eyes. A few are crazy-eyed . . . something happened to them after a youthful encounter with Bugs Bunny or Scooby Doo or the mascot at the pep rally." Sorry, George. It goes a lot deeper than that.)

Gurley lets many furs speak for themselves—which in spite of some thoughtful, even poetic comments[130] ("there's something just inherently cheerful about ducks"), in the context of this article, it was equivalent of giving them enough rope to hang themselves. Gurley's grasp of

---

129 MFF was originally the popular "furry track" at the mainstream DucKon science-fiction convention but outgrew that con and became an independent convention. Three-hundred eighty-eight furs attended the 2000 MFF; by 2016 attendance had grown to 7,075. (DucKon wasn't held in 2015 or 2016 and for all practical purposes no longer exists.)

130 "If the main character [in a furry story] was a mouse or a rabbit, then the fox would be the evil villain . . . if the main character were a lion, the fox is a bumbling sidekick. It depends on basically the line of the food chain with who's the star."

furry history is fairly solid, except when he says furry conventions started in the early nineties, when the first ConFurence took place in 1989. (There's a passing reference to the "nexus of furrydom [located] near Disneyland," almost certainly a context-free allusion to the Prancing Skiltaire.)

Gurley spends a lot of time, an *awful* lot of time, with Fox Wolfie Galen, a plushophile (and one-time zoophile) with a mountain of stuffed animals in his room and perhaps not the world's greatest set of social skills. (The inference is he's only a degree or two further divorced from reality than the average fur.) Some friendly comments from a good-natured army lieutenant observing the convention come to an end "when he learns he has been chatting with a guy who might *really* want to be a raccoon." (Gee, I wonder who told him—and besides, maybe that guy simply enjoys pretending to be one at conventions.) From there the article travels into some *definitely* weird and non-furry tangents involving fans of "smush" and "crush" videos.[131]

Furrydom: *terra incognita* (or even worse, a scary nightmare land) for the high-society celebrity-worshiping magazine. In *Vanity Fair*'s defense, 2001 was still fairly early in the fandom's existence, but even so, it's easy to transcribe an audio interview or offer a patronizing description of a fur or fursuiter; Gurley's failure is his refusal to get under the fur, to understand, empathize, or God forbid, respect the people he's interviewing; it's

---

131 "A crush fetish is a fetish and paraphilia in which one is sexually aroused when someone crushes objects, food and sometimes small animals (frequently insects) with their body, usually under their foot, or when crushed oneself." "Crush fetish," Wikipedia. (https://en.wikipedia.org/wiki/Crush_fetish) Retrieved March 20, 2017. The description applies equally to "smush" videos.

easier and much more fun to write a "lookit the weirdoes" piece.[132]

The final nail in the coffin of Furry's early reputation came early in 2002 with the MTV airing of *Plushies and Furries* in their "Sex2K/True Life" documentary series. When early on a guy in a tiger leotard claims "anyone who says Furry is not a sexual-based fandom is really kind of fooling themselves," you've got nowhere to go but down. Title cards like "Fursuiters: people who get turned on by dressing as big stuffed animals"—apart from being entirely inaccurate—just compounded the damage. (Just as in the *Times* item, the documentary kept referring to all furry conventions as "confurences.")

Clips of fursuiters marching through hotel hallways or pairs in close, *very* close, physical proximity abounded; a fur who gives advice on where to add strategically placed holes to facilitate fursuit sex suggests "somewhere in the crotch and somewhere probably near the ass for most furs." The documentary's main focus was on Mike Sano, aka "Yote" (as in coyote), and his deepening involvement in furry fandom. In the film Yote confesses his furriness to his mother and models his newly purchased fursuit for her benefit. It's too much for her to handle; she's unable to grasp the significance fur plays in his life. ("It's hard for me to accept my son as anything else than my son.") Her fears that people who have been "talking to him online and seducing him online are going to be there [at his very

---

132 I contacted George Gurley in September 2016 to learn more about how "Pleasures of the Fur" came to be. "I'll do my best to answer your questions," he responded. "I'll reread the story in the meantime, been a while." I never heard back, perhaps because my questions were on the order of "were changes made to your manuscript, either in length or tone?" and "from the perspective of fifteen years later, do you have any regrets over 'Pleasures of the Fur'?"

first] convention trying to get into his pants" come true. ("It was great," Yote shares about one such encounter. "And I was in a fursuit while he wasn't, and we had sex . . . it just kind of happened.")

Not long after the documentary was broadcast questions began surfacing as to its truthfulness. The documentary was the work of one Rick Castro, who presented himself as "a fur working on a personal project" but was actually "a professional filmmaker, producer of documentaries involving the porn industry and a professional fetish photographer as evidenced by his adults-only website at RickCastro.com."[133]

The conversations between Yote and his mother? An anonymous online poster claimed "the scenes between Yote and his mom were arranged and faked on camera at the request of the director, Castro. The convention depicted was not only his first convention, but his mother knew about his interests long before the cameras rolled."[134]

No matter. The die is cast, opinions are frozen. For the next several years the rest of the media take their cues from *Vanity Fair* and MTV, and for a long, long time thereafter scores of furs decide it's best not to discuss their furry lives in public.

In 2007 an author named Christopher Noxon published *Rejuvenile: Kickball, Cartoons, Cupcakes and the Reinvention of the American Grown-up*. Noxon spends 288

---

133 "Plushies and Furries," WikiFur. (http://en.wikifur.com/wiki/Plushies_and_ Furries) Retrieved September 20, 2016. Castro's website is now vacant; the URL is currently occupied by a page of random links and a "buy this domain" banner.

134 (http://pressedfur.coolfreepages.com/comments/anonymous-sex2k.html) Retrieved September 20, 2016.

pages celebrating adults who have retained their youthful playfulness—except of course, for "the foxes and bunnies and pandas known as furries, men and women whose fondness for a particular animal or animated character has evolved into a love of dressing up in (and occasionally having sex wearing) cartoon-animal costumes." In case that's not enough, he spends another paragraph explaining plushies and adult babies to the uninitiated.

I can understand Noxon's distaste for fursuit sex or adults who wear diapers for reasons other than incontinence, but grown-ups wearing fursuits and pretending to be animals for fun doesn't count as "rejuvenile"? (Much like most writers who don't "get" Furry, Noxon is unaware of furry art.)

The same year an article appeared in a Connecticut alternative weekly[135] detailing the author's undercover visit to the nearby "FurFright" convention in search of that raunchy decadence she'd heard so much about. (At the time FurFright had a "no media" policy, thanks to the lingering impact of the *Vanity Fair* article.) She instead found nothing beyond the equivalent of what might be seen at a mainstream sci-fi convention: "No superhero capes, but plenty of animal tails poking out from shirt bottoms," the adult material "rare and hidden from view," and the adult behavior? "If I peeked behind every hotel room door I probably would've found something, but that's true of any gathering of hundreds of people far from home." Her bottom line: "The furry convention wasn't a sex thing but the exact opposite: an innocent world of children's-book

---

135 Jennifer Abel, "Hell Hath No Furries," The Hartford Advocate, November 1, 2007; (jenniferabel.blogspot.com/2008/04/hell-hath-no-furries.html) Retrieved September 23, 2016

animals, where a three-year-old can roam with impunity and a [self-described] maladjusted kid [with a skunk fursona] can enter the room with nobody leaving."

A touch idealistic perhaps, but where some people can only see decadence and social misfits, others understand and respect the fantasy.

As awareness of the fandom grows, so does coverage. A WikiFur page charting the fandom's media mentions[136] lists a single item, or perhaps two or three, per year in the early 1990s, then a handful per month from the late nineties into the early 2000s. Come the late double-0s the list explodes: suddenly there are dozens of articles and TV segments per year, sometimes as many in a single month—more than this book could ever hope to cover. At first they're only from U.S., Canadian or British outlets, but soon they're from France, Germany, Australia, South Africa, Russia, Norway, Brazil, Sweden, New Zealand, Hungary . . .

It's inching towards a more balanced perspective, but still has a way to go. There's always a Howard Stern, who calls furs fetishistic sickos then spends the rest of a nineteen-minute segment discussing—in great detail—a Swedish-accented fur's interest in bestiality. Or a syndicated, tabloid-style news-magazine show like *Inside Edition* that crashed Further Confusion in 2015.

Inside Edition released a one minute, forty-five second segment that leaned so heavily on the incredulity button they likely broke it. ("*Can you believe* more than 1,300 people showed up? Many posed for photos, like any family portrait—*only a lot weirder* . . . A hotel guest *could hardly*

---

136 "Timeline of media coverage." WikiFur. (http://en.wikifur.com/wiki/Timeline_of_media_coverage) Retrieved September 23, 2016.

believe what was going on . . . Furries are triggering *fierce criticism* from some: 'fursuits *creep me out*' . . . others call furries '*weird*' and '*losers* . . . '")[137]

Even my beloved Jon Stewart, the man who kept me sane through W's presidency, got in on the act.

In an April 2015 *Daily Show*, Stewart reports Angie's List is putting their Indiana expansion plans on hold in response to the state's anti-gay "religious freedom" law. Stewart pretends to be offended: "Without Angie's List, how are you going to find a trustworthy contractor to remodel your house?" With a graphic behind his shoulder of a giant teddy bear head resting atop a small house, he continues: "craigslist is no good—they'll just dress your house up as a furry and rub themselves on it. You don't want that!"

The 100% non-sequitur punchline (craigslist equals furries? Domicile frottage?) triggers a strange mixture of laughter, groans and applause from an audience evidently familiar with furry fandom—or at least its reputation. A disbelieving Stewart responds, "That just resonated *way* too high," generating another round of laughter; for an otherwise hip program, this was an unfortunate throwback to the Craig Kilborn-era *Daily Show*.

Thankfully there are also outlets like the UK's *Guardian*, the British newspaper that published a 1,600 word myth-busting article in their "Fancy dress and

---

137 When I said "crashed" above, I meant it. Denied media access to the convention based on their past coverage of the fandom, *Inside Edition*'s correspondent and cameraperson went inside posing as plain-old furs to produce their sensationalist piece. "We find it inexcusable," convention organizers said later, "that *Inside Edition* chose not to make those filmed aware that they would be on TV. We apologize for this intrusion into Further ConFusion, and will do our absolute best to prevent similar events from happening in future years." (*Inside Edition*: Official Statement. (http://www.furtherconfusion.org/inside-edition/) Retrieved March 17, 2015.

costume" section: "It's not about sex, it's about identity: why furries are unique among fan cultures."[138] The title is defensive, but considering the stereotypes still believed by many, it was a necessary introduction to an article that sets out to disprove those stereotypes one by one. Its first sentence reads: "Furries tend to get a bad rap as perverse fetishists when in reality, the subculture is about playful escapism and a fascination with what links humans to animals." It goes on to interview a busy suitmaker, describing a few of her three hundred creations to establish their individuality. (. . . "Zeke the Hyena, cartoonish with hand-stitched stripes and airbrushed abs, and Blaze, a vixen with flirty eyelashes and [a] curvaceously padded chest.") The *Vanity Fair* article is namechecked as is the notorious-among-furs *CSI* episode, "Fur and Loathing"; furry researcher Kathleen Gerbasi and Anthrocon CEO Sam Conway offer their thoughts throughout the article. (A major blooper on the writer's part, however: Conway does *not* own or wear a samurai cockroach costume.) Conway hits the nail on the head when he explains "Furry fandom is unique among fan cultures in that we are not consumers, but rather creators." He continues, "*Star Trek* fans are chasing someone else's dream. Furries create our own fandom."

Familiarity breeds content(ment): It was a bit rocky at the start, but Pittsburgh has come to love the furs, who since 2006 visit their city every Fourth of July weekend to take part in Anthrocon, the world's largest furry

---

138 It's not about sex, it's about identity: why furries are unique among fan culture. theguardian.com, February 4, 2016. (https://www.theguardian.com/fashion/2016/feb/04/furry-fandom-subcultureanimal-costumes) Retrieved September 22, 2016.

convention. Coverage has evolved from head-scratching "WTF?" to "Hey, the furries are back!" Newspapers run friendly stories; TV reporters try on ears and tails at the convention. NPR's *All Things Considered* takes note of the phenomenon with a three-and-a-half-minute piece, "The Furries Have Landed—and Pittsburgh is giving them a great big bear hug." Listeners hear thumbs-up sound bites including a ten-year-old's deliriously happy "I love it more than anything in the freakin' world! There are unicorns!"

NBC News runs a six-minute, eighteen-second Anthrocon report of their own[139] so furry-friendly it triggers tears of joy—and thousands of comments from furs grateful for the positive coverage. ("Finally, a video that isn't insulting!" . . . "Thank you for understanding" . . . "LET'S CELEBRATE GUYS" and so on.) The unnamed reporter explains what a furry is and points out the vast majority of suits are peoples' personal fursonas, not movie or TV characters. Dance-off and rave footage is shown, the kinky/adult side of fur is acknowledged with brief glimpses of collars, harnesses and a chat with the publisher of naughty furry fiction ("it's just a different way of looking at the same sort of romantic themes [as in human-starring works].")

At segment's end the reporter bravely tries on a tail, wags it a bit and with an embarrassed laugh says, "This is pretty weird, so it's not for me—but it seems to 'suit' [the furries] just fine."

Unfortunately, TV coverage is rarely this friendly, and there are reporters who just can't handle the fur.

---

139 "Meet the Furries." Published on YouTube, August 14, 2014. (https://www.youtube.com/watch?v=xHZ9SwTk2UE.) Retrieved September 24, 2016.

In 2014 the Midwest FurFest was disrupted with a middle-of-the-night chlorine-gas attack in a hotel stairwell that sent everyone into the cold December air for hours. To this day the incident remains unsolved, still "under investigation" by the local police.

The incident was reported on MSNBC's *Morning Joe* news program.[140] With a local newspaper article filling the screen co-anchor Mika Brzezinski began reading her copy and almost immediately hit a snag. "Nineteen people were hospitalized at a [confused pause] . . . 'furry' convention in, in, Illinois, in what's called an . . . intentional . . . leak . . . of chlorine...ga—" Mika is slowly losing it.

A man's voice asks, "What's a 'furry' . . . convention?"

Mika responds, "Did I get that wrong?"

The man's voice is heard again: "Oh gosh . . . "

Video of the exiled hotel guests, many fursuiters among, them replaces the news article. Mika and company are silent as the footage—which is also silent—rolls. For a few seconds all that can be heard is scattered laughter from the technical crew.

The footage ends; Mika, co-anchor Joe Scarborough and news reader Willie Geist are onscreen. Willie manages to keep a straight face and, tongue slightly in cheek, continues describing the event ("many still dressed in their furry, furry costumes") but Mika, head down, is covering her face with both hands while Joe looks away from the camera, hand over his mouth. Joe tries to face the camera, his mouth clamped tight to keep from bursting out in hysterics, but unable to make eye contact with the

---

140 Mika Brzezinski Learns About 'Furries. Published on YouTube, August 7, 2016. (https://www.youtube.com/watch?v=CAFsUKmNL_M) Retrieved January 3, 2017.

camera, he bows his head and stares at the desk. Meanwhile Mika, quietly squealing with suppressed laughter has practically collapsed onto the desk, her hands still hiding her face.

We next see video of Sam Conway in front of the hotel explaining the situation. ("We have a lot of costumers out here with big fluffy costumes keeping people warm, so at this point we're not worried.") Then we're back in the studio, Willie still reporting the story. "We just told Mika what the convention is about," explains Joe before noticing Mika running away in the background. "Where are you going? Hey, come back!" Mika, now way in the distance, is still fleeing. The report returns to video of the exiled conventioneers, and even though Willie is still reporting, we hear Joe say "Come back?" in a losing-hope voice, and finally "Could you check on Mika and see if she's okay? She's over there somewhere."

Perhaps if Mika had kept up with her own network's news coverage she wouldn't have found the idea of people wearing animal suits so hysterical; she obviously missed NBC's thoughtful report that aired just a few months prior to her on-air crack up.

If Furry's reputation as a nonstop kink fest lives on, it's in no small part due to furs who happily participate in perpetuating that image.

In August 2009 "midori8" posted the following to LiveJournal's "FursuitLounge" page:

. . . my boyfriend got this message on Facebook today. I think it's a little fishy . . .

Subject: The Tyra Show

Hello,

My name is Brooke and I am an Associate Producer for "The Tyra Show." We are in the research stages of an upcoming show and I'm looking to speak with furries in relationships. If this applies to you or anyone you know please give me a call at [redacted]. Thank you so much and I look forward to hearing from you.

Sincerely,
Brooke Townsend

The now-cancelled *Tyra Banks Show* (or simply *Tyra*, as the show identified itself on air) was a daytime talk/interview show offering its viewers celebrity interviews, discussions of social issues, fashion and beauty advice—and plenty of less-than-high-minded episodes. People with bizarre eating habits, teen sex workers, plastic-surgery addicts, self-proclaimed womanizers, gay teen exorcisms: they've all had their televised moment of fame thanks to *Tyra*.

Some of the comments following midori8's posting were wisely skeptical: "I can just see [Tyra] talking about it then going SO DO YOU LIKE TO SCREW IN THOSE SUITS? They will probably just fish for the info they want to hear" . . . "We can tell them how we never stop yiffing and we met at a Starbucks while wearing our suits" . . . "It's all tacky, sensationalist crap and I wouldn't touch it with a three-meter pole."

The skeptical furs were right. But *Tyra*'s staff eventually found their furry couple.

The next month the lights went up on *Tyra*'s stage, revealing three couples lounging in silk pajamas on queen-size beds. A smarmy introduction gets things off to a rousing start: "They all say their sex lives are completely normal, but what they do behind closed doors is going to surprise you!"

Tyra Banks herself invites the audience to guess which couple enjoys group sex parties, which wife sleeps with two different husbands and which couple are furries, "meaning they have sex in animal costumes."

The audience guesses right; on bed number one lounge Chelsey and Steve. While Chelsey explains "furries are people who have an inner animal they like to celebrate . . . by drawing ourselves and wearing animal costumes, and other such things," a superimposed title cuts to the heart of the matter as far as *Tyra* is concerned: "Chelsey and Steve: furries; they have sex while wearing animal costumes."

"When you go to Disneyland do you guys get turned on?" asks the ever-curious Tyra as the audience laughs. "Looking at Mickey Mouse going 'Hi,' do you go [shaking her hips] 'Ooh, *yeah!*'?" Assured by Chelsey that wasn't the case, Tyra continues.

"Do you have sex when you have the costume on?"

"Yes."

Tyra gasps as if she's never, *ever* heard of such a thing before; the camera cuts to a woman in the audience shaking her head and doing a facepalm in disbelief and disgust. "There are strategically placed holes" Chelsey helpfully explains, prompting an audience-wide groan.

Tyra drops the B(estiality) bomb, but Chelsey quickly defuses that hypothesis: "Not in any way. It's just an alter-ego–type thing, that's all it is." Steve, who's been the silent partner up to this point, fetches his fursuit head, part of his costume that he "would wear normally, to, like, a social event . . . " (Too late, Steve. This audience doesn't care about furry social events.) He tries to explain his ("Tom Kat") and Chelsey's ("Chew Fox") fursonas . . .

"Are you for real?" a skeptical Tyra interjects. Steve answers in the affirmative, to audience laughter. "Are you furry monogamous, are you furry polygamous?" "It's just the two of us," Chelsey assures her, clasping hands with Steve. This time the audience responds with a romantic sigh, as Chew Fox and Tom Kat's five minutes and forty-two seconds of fame come to an end.

Their fandom infamy, however, was about to begin.

"Major fail, and she and her boyfriend will never live this down," began a post-broadcast thread on Live-Journal. "If you are going to 'represent the fandom' at least do it somewhere where the focus isn't sex." "It sad [sic]," posted another fur. "We in the fandom, we have our Galens [of *Vanity Fair* ignominy] and Chewfox[e]s, exhibitionist[s]s who [are] willing to sellout the fandom for fifteen seconds of fame."

The anger spilled over onto Fur Affinity. Chew Fox's journals answering her critics generated an unprece-dented number of comments, crashing the popular furry website.[141] While most questioned her and Tom Kat's wisdom in appearing on a show reinforcing the fandom's unsavory reputation, many—too many—attacked Chew

---

141 Chew Fox's journals and the thousands of responses were soon expunged from the website.

Fox in over-the-top personal attacks. A more level-headed fur criticized her critics:

> [T]he vitriolic response on this girl's journal is remarkable and simply unacceptable, an attack on her person that just goes well beyond "what you did was foolish." If anything, reading through those posts brings me as much if not more shame than the fact that this girl went on Tyra in the first place.

Chew Fox and Tom Kat told the inside story of their *Tyra* experience in Dominic Rodriguez's documentary *Fursonas*,[142] although each of them had a slightly different perspective on what had taken place.

"It's not what we said, it's that we said it at all," Chew Fox smirks in response to her online critics. "Everyone likes to pretend [fursuit sex] doesn't exist."

Things get more interesting when Tom Kat reveals "they kind of lied to us to get in there, but that's what a lot of them do. They said to hype up the story and make it," he air-quotes, "'real.' They told us we were going to be paired up with two other couples and we were going to be the people who have sex in their fursuits. We're like, 'We don't do that.' 'No, but we want you to *say* you do that.'"

There's a brief digression as the couple disagree on

---

142 In this fur's humble opinion, *Fursonas* itself did little to enhance the furry community's reputation. Apart from presenting a sympathetic portrait of Boomer the Dog, a good portion of the film was a hit job on Anthrocon's Sam Conway for supposedly appointing himself supreme ruler of all furdom, followed by an interview with the creator of a line of animal dildos demonstrating their ability to ejaculate artificial semen.

whether or not they actually *do* do that which ends with them sheepishly admitting, well, perhaps, "a little bit."

"At the time," Tom resumes, "we said, you know what, forget it, let's just go on there and try to portray it the best way we can—and it totally backfired. Looking back, we shouldn't have done it, but hindsight is 20/20, what's done is done."

Chew Fox begs to differ. "I don't regret it. I don't think we personally did anything that wrong. The first question [was] 'what is the furry fandom?' I answered that, but any question after that was solely about what goes on between us."

If Chew Fox and Tom Kat agreed to pose as the "fursuit sex" couple, they weren't so much "selling out" the fandom, as some of their accusers insisted, as letting themselves be used by an exploitative TV show perpetuating the fandom's negative stereotype. Chew Fox's accurate description of the fandom doesn't do much good if the on-screen title is telling the audience "they have sex while wearing animal costumes" at the same time.

People who insist there's no sexual aspect to Furry are kidding themselves every bit as much; Chew Fox and Tom Kat simply believe it shouldn't *represent* the community—even if that was exactly the result of their appearance on *Tyra*.

As Furry gets better known, it starts appearing more often in news and entertainment shows, which in turn helps the fandom get better known and so on, *ad infinitum*. There are more news reports about the fandom on YouTube than any one person (or one chapter of this book, or an entire book for that matter) could keep up with. Somebody really should watch at least a sampling of these reports and rate them for accuracy and attitude . . . oh wait, somebody already is.

In April 2016 a fursuited fox named "Aberguine" began posting *Furries in the Media* videos on YouTube, beginning with an examination of a clumsily staged segment featuring two supposed fursuiters on *Storage Wars: Texas*. Aberguine, relaxing in a chair in what looks like her living room, addresses the camera as she analyzes the segment at hand in bite-sized pieces. ("No furry would greet a stranger at the front door with their suit on, especially one this hideous...and they're already starting in with the howling," she adds, facepalming—or should that be facepawing?)

Forcing herself to watch the good, the bad and the ugly of the media fur sightings, Aberguine rates each news report or TV episode based on how accurate its depiction of the fandom is, as well as the spirit of the clip. (The *Storage Wars* segment earns 55% for accuracy but only 20% for its attitude towards the fandom, averaging out to a meager 38%.) Each video ends with her thoughts on the program just reviewed. ("This feels like a lazy attempt by the show to keep viewers interested or at least keep ratings up.")

Aberguine published forty *FitM* videos to YouTube in 2016, including examinations of the notorious *CSI* episode, Boomer the Dog's appearance on *Dr. Phil* and the aforementioned *Tyra* show episode. Her candidates for best and worst news segments, respectively: NBC's lengthy report ("positive overall coverage, even addressed the NSFW side in an understated, respectful manner") and an L.A. TV station's coverage. ("[They] couldn't even get rental animal suits or a real therapist, [they] exploited a local troupe of performers who happened to wear furry costumes [and they] referenced *CSI* as though it were a credible source.")

As Furry grew from a handful of people into a fandom, the feeling we were a family grew along with it; as we kept growing that sense of family expanded until we saw ourselves as a community. Because we all shared something similar, something we once thought was our own private fascination the world at large was incapable of understanding, our discovery of each other bought us together in a bond deeper than "Hey, I like *Star Trek* too." Beyond tiffs, politics and grudges (endemic to families as much as to any field of commonality, social or professional) we thought we were immune to extremes of emotions—and in particular anger. Especially anger so white-hot with rage it would inevitably, irresistibly lead to violence.

On September 25, 2016, we unfortunately discovered we weren't immune after all. At that moment, a part of the idealized image of our community withered —the part that believed in the innate goodness of each and every fur.

The previous day, the media reported on the 25th, three California furs were murdered by a fellow member of the furry community. If he and his victims hadn't all been furs it would've been just another crime of passion, an unstable man murdering the parents of the daughter they kept him from dating.

The fact that these killings were between people who knew each other over a personal conflict that could have taken place in any group of people with a common interest, and that it wasn't the work of a lunatic who imagined the fandom as a satanic cult, is of small comfort. The "people who dress up as animals" angle made this tragedy unique and attention-getting. (Somewhere down the road we may even have our own made-for-TV movie "based on actual events.")

According to police reports, a twenty-five-year-old fur had been dating the seventeen-year-old daughter of a furry couple. When the parents told the young man he could no longer see their daughter, he arrived at their house with another fur who did the actual killing, shooting the parents and a friend who had the misfortune to be visiting. The tragedy shocked and terrified local furs who worried their own safety might be at risk—and wondered if the media would use the story to once again depict Furry in the worst possible light.

For the most part the coverage had a "just the facts, ma'am" approach, but the media consistently felt the need to explain Furry to audiences who'd never heard of the fandom. The usual fursuit-focused explanations predominated ("the alleged killers and their victims were members of a local 'furry' community . . . which involves dressing up as anthropomorphic animals as a hobby"), although some took the trouble to give a fuller picture of the fandom. The most accurate and succinct description of furry gatherings I'd ever read appeared in a local CBS news report:

The suspects and victims attended "furry" events where some participants dress up in colorful animal costumes.

Not *all* participants as is usually assumed, not most participants, but the far more factual *some*. Simply put, most furs *don't* suit up.

And "*colorful* animal costumes." That one word

makes all the difference. It implies creativity and individuality and equates fursuiting with other, better-known dress-up occasions: cosplay, Halloween, Mardi Gras and the like. Stories that describe furs as wearing generic "animal costumes" for no particular reason just makes the whole thing sound weird.

A reporter finally got it right in a single, short sentence. It sucks that sentence had to appear in a murder story—and as it turned out, that crime of passion wasn't the only cruel deed committed by people who considered themselves furs. Furry is a free-form, open-to-all "big tent" community. There's no entry exam, no ruling body to bestow membership on applicants. If you feel furry, you're a furry; if you say you're a fur, you're a fur. That openness is one of Furry's most attractive qualities. Sadly, for a miniscule number of individuals the form their furriness takes is monstrous. For years we've had to tell people that no, except for among the kinkier members of our community, Furry isn't a sexual fetish; now we'll have to tell people, no, except for these monsters, we don't wear fursuits to entice and sexually abuse children.

At first I thought it was a one-off, a needlessly sensationalized story intended to show Furry in the worst light possible. A 2016 report on a Michigan news website about a man accused of child rape was headlined "'Furry' enthusiast accused of repeatedly raping boy, lying to investigators." The Furry equals child-rape connection was reinforced by the report's first sentence: the arrested man "apparently is part of the 'furry fandom' movement that involves dressing up like cartoon animals." Four paragraphs down the article mentioned the child was a *relative* of the accused, making it unlikely he needed a fursuit to entice the boy. In fact, a comment posted under the report claimed the accused didn't own a suit until the following year. The reporter defended her story later in the comment thread, claiming "he could have lured [the child] with a big fuzzy cute costume—just the sort of thing kids like."[143]

But it wasn't a one-off. In late January 2017 a similar story appeared on a Philadelphia TV station's website: "Men Dressed Up as Animals Sexually Abused Boy During 'Furry Parties.'"[144] Beginning in 2009 a group of men who considered themselves furs repeatedly sexually abused a nine-year-old boy in Pennsylvania, a practice that continued until they were exposed in mid-2016.

According to a Washington Post article,[145] "Beginning in 2009, Parker [one of the men in the group] would transport the boy to a house, where, as the victim described, men donned full-body animal costumes. The boy, now fourteen, noted that Fenske's fox costume consisted of 'full long sleeves and pants, a zipper in the back, paw gloves and a fox head with pointy ears,' the Associated Press reported. Fenske told others to call him by the name 'Lupine' while he was in the fox suit." Perhaps the weirdest detail in the story was "[t]he child, meanwhile, was made to dress in a Tony the Tiger outfit."

---

143 'Furry' enthusiast accused of repeatedly raping boy, lying to investigators. (http://www.mlive.com/news/muskegon/index.ssf/2016/10/furry_enthusiast_accused_of_re.html) Published October 24, 2016. Retrieved November 21, 2016.

144 Men Dressed Up as Animals Sexually Abused Boy During 'Furry Parties' in Bucks County: Officials," nbcphiladelphia.com. Published January 29, 2017. Retrieved February 17, 2017.

145 Prosecutors: Boy sexually abused at 'furry parties' by 'network' of men, washingtonpost.com. (https://www.washingtonpost.com/news/morning-mix/wp/2017/01/31/prosecutors-boy-sexually-abused-at-furry-parties-by-man-who-wore-foxcostume/?utm_term=.83c62220585f)) Published January 31, 2017. Retrieved February 17, 2017.

In their press release, the Pennsylvania Attorney General's office attempted to even-handedly describe the fandom[146] with a bit too general "[f]urries are people who dress up as animals and identify as the chosen animal. For some, although not all, being a Furry is a sexual fetish." While making the same "furries all dress up" assumption, a local newspaper[147] acknowledged "authorities said can be a form of a sexual fetish." I'd emphasize the *can*.

Some outlets attempted to explain Furry in a little more depth. The Philadelphia TV station's website's description started with the standard "they all dress up" assumption but went on to add "[i]t mostly consists of visual art, conventions, games, toys and online communities" before wrapping up with "in rare cases it also involves a sexual fetish," *rare* being a much better qualifier than the attorney general's "some" or the local paper's "can."

However, Ben Guarino, author of the *Washington Post* story, went into surprising depth when describing Furry:

"Furries" are members of a subculture who take on identities based on anthropomorphic animals, called fursonas. It may involve wearing mascot-like costumes... (Many furries argue that the media has, during the past two decades, overplayed the sexual aspect of the subculture. Only about 15 percent of furries own full fur costumes, and even fewer say they are sexually attracted to stuffed or cartoonish animals. One of the few social

---

146 Bucks County man ordered held for trial on child rape charges during 'Furry party.' (https://www.attorneygeneral.gov/Media_and_Resources/Press_Releases/Press_Release/?pid=3375) Published January 29, 2017. Retrieved February 17, 2017.

147 5 charged in 'Furries' child predator sex ring,(http://www.lehighvalleylive.com/news/index.ssf/2017/01/bucks_man_is_latest_charged_in.html) Published January 30, 2017. Retrieved February 16, 2017.

psychologists to study furries, Niagara County Community College's Kathleen Gerbasi, told the BBC in 2009 that, "for most, the furry fandom is a hobby," likening it to "'Star Trek' fans or such.")

How did Guarino know so much about Furry? Because he took the extra step of actually researching the subject before writing his article. "I hunted around a bit in Google Scholar and LexisNexis, and found Professor Gerbasi's interview with the BBC," he explained in an email. "[A]s a reporter who cut my teeth at digital news startups, I'm used to casting a wide net over the Internet, and often [head] down Google or Reddit rabbit hole[s] . . . I also vaguely recalled that there was some sort of outrage over a bad *CSI* or *Law and Order* episode that included furries."

Perhaps more importantly, *why* did Guarino go to the trouble of spending a few minutes online? "I anticipated that the horrible nature of the crime, frankly, would draw quite a bit of attention to a smallish and occasionally misunderstood fandom. It was important to convey to readers this was not representative of the fandom writ large. I'm aware of how easy it is for the Internet to magnify certain aspects—particularly those involving sex—of small subcultures or quirky hobbies."

CHAPTER TWELVE

Anthrocon:
The Convention that
Conquered Pittsburgh

A PRIDE OF LIONS, a school of fish, a congregation of alligators . . . As people who have adopted animal identities, furs deserve a group name as well.

I nominate "a convention of furs." That is, after all, where we gather. Those sixty-five furs who attended ConFurence Zero in 1989? The tiniest of blips compared to the 45,000 furs who attended conventions worldwide in 2015.[148]

The lion's share of those fans—about 35,000—gathered at the forty-plus furcons held in North America, from Reno, Nevada ("The Biggest Little Furcon") to Edmonton, Canada ("Fur-Eh!"); eleven of those conventions attracted over a thousand furs; several, multiple thousands. Furry conventions have been held across

---

148 An approximate number since not all conventions post their total attendance on WikiFur. Feel free to deduct a few hundred from that total to allow for furs who attended multiple conventions. (I go to two or three a year myself.)

Europe,[149] in Australia, New Zealand, Japan, Taiwan, the Philippines—the list goes on.

The world's three largest furcons take place in the U.S., the country where Furry was born: San Jose's "Further ConFusion," "Midwest FurFest" just outside of Chicago and the biggest of them all: Pittsburgh's "Anthrocon."[150]

It's eighty-two degrees in downtown Pittsburgh on this particular July afternoon. It feels a lot hotter in the sun, yet hundreds of people are gathered on a street in front of the David L. Lawrence Convention Center. The street continues through a tunnel-like space just under the massive structure, where several hundred smarter, cooler folks line its sidewalks or sit atop the concrete stanchions protecting the building's supporting columns.

They're waiting for a parade—the Anthrocon fursuit parade—to begin. In the past only furs attending the convention were able to view the event, which until today had never left the convention center. Many in the crowd hold yellow signs reading "I ♥"—with a pawprint inside the heart—"Anthrocon," distributed by convention volunteers.

The crowd cheers as the first 'suiters come into view: a fox tapping a marching rhythm on a cymbal, the famous ballpark mascot the San Diego Chicken (one of this year's Guests of Honor), followed by two tigers, several dragons, a polar bear and a green-and-white husky. (Huskies

---

149 Just to mention a few: "Confuzzled" (England), "Eurofurence" (Germany), "Furtastic" (Denmark), "Futerkon" (Poland), "Rusfurrence" (Russia), "WUFF" (The Ukraine), "Zampacon" (Italy).

150 Midwest FurFest is closing in on Anthrocon's record as the world's largest furry convention: in 2016 MFF attracted 7,075 furs vs. Anthrocon's 7,310.

and their upward-curling, plushly furred tails are quite popular among canine fursuiters.)

Close behind them is a round-faced gentleman with close-cropped black hair and a curly-wired earpiece affixed to the side of his head. He's carrying a large bull-horn and wearing a white lab coat. On the back of the coat is a picture of a frantic-looking man hunched over a workbench, operating an enormous, antique electrical machine, sparks flying. The words "MAD SCIENTIST'S UNION / LOCAL # 3.14" frame the picture.

Some 1,400 fursuiters will follow in his wake, but in the meantime he raises the bullhorn to his lips and speaks.

"Thank you, Pittsburgh! This is all for you! This is our way of giving back to you to show our appreciation of how very kind you've been to us."

Ladies gentlemen, people of all species: meet Uncle Kage.[151]

Uncle Kage, or as he's known in that mundane realm we call "real life," Sam Conway, is a fascinating gentleman. A few years ago, I asked to interview him about his furry career. We met in a bar in Philadelphia's Thirtieth Street train station. Conway held one of the several glasses of wine he would imbibe during our conversation while explaining his unusual fursona—and how he came to be the public face of furry fandom.

"I always liked cartoons," he said between sips. "I would run home after school to watch them. The characters intrigued me. Bugs Bunny was cool—there's not a person in the world who thinks otherwise.

"To a certain extent they were real to me; they were cool friends to have. Most of the kids around me were

---

151 Pronounced "KAH-gay."

Sam Conway (Photograph courtesy of and © Vovchychko)

fairly brain dead. I didn't grow up among intellectually stimulating peers—I got more out of cartoons than anything else.

"I was at the 1989 Worldcon when I saw a booth with a sign reading 'Furry Fandom.' 'Furry Fandom, what the hell is that?' Just out of curiosity I went to check it out.

"They had comics, including one called *Albedo*. I leafed through it—and for the first time I saw 'funny animals' that aren't being funny. I'd grown up indoctrinated: 'When you see a [funny-animal] cartoon character, a piano is going to fall on him [on the next page].'

"I turn the page; no piano. He's getting shot in the chest by a laser; his fiancée is grabbing him and sobbing. I was captivated.

"This was pretty close to the beginning—furry fandom was just getting rolling. I was intrigued, so I bought [the comic] and a few other issues, then I went to a comic book store and bought some more serious funny-animal comics. I saw *Omaha, the Cat Dancer.* It was intriguing, but not my kind of storytelling; I preferred Stan Sakai's *Usagi Yojimbo,* which was coming out around that time. *Usagi* was sort of the nail in the mental coffin for me, of leaving the real world behind.

"I always loved [the work of Japanese filmmaker Akira] Kurosawa, even before I knew who he was. There was something about the storytelling and artistry of his films. I had seen *Kagemusha* in college—it just blew me away, one of the greatest films of all time. *Usagi Yojimbo* had characters that could've stepped out of a Kurosawa movie, but happened to be animals in heroic tales of feudal Japan. I remember in particular being really intrigued by Lord Hebi, the villain's second-in-command who happened to be a snake. I started to realize names of his characters reflected their species—*usagi* is Japanese for 'rabbit.' Some of Stan's *Usagi* stories will leave you in tears.

"In 1991 I got my Ph.D. and was shipped off from Vermont to the south side of Chicago for a post-doctorate assignment. I'd grown up in the farmlands of Pennsylvania, I did my graduate work in the mountains of New Hampshire, I was living in Vermont—and now I was by myself in the Big City. It wasn't anything like *Sesame Street*—it was much more like 'Avenue Q.'[152] I very quickly learned I'm not an urban person.

"I was living in a dreadful apartment in a dreadful city.

---

152 An adult Broadway musical with a puppet cast.

I hated my job—I was completely miserable. I didn't really have any friends, and I was *not* about to step out that front door. The job was all science; my co-workers were all chemists. Most of them were afraid to say anything because the boss was a tyrant who liked to set people against each other. It was a toxic work environment and I was very, very unhappy.

"About a month into my sentence, I still had a slip of paper someone had given me with a code on it to type into my crappy little computer—'telenet one-dot-three, yadda yadda.'

"This was back in the early days of the Internet when you used an IP address to connect to a site. I had just tele-netted into one called FurryMUCK and I was immediately immersed in a text-based world. I'm an old *Dungeons & Dragons* player, so text-based [stuff] is fine for me—I don't need pictures like the kids do these days.

"FurryMUCK was populated by animals, anthro-pomorphic animals. The idea of playing an animal and having to live as that animal was familiar to me from *Dungeons & Dragons*. People could interact with each other as animal characters here.

"It was sort of like a cartoon, a serious cartoon world. We had an otter whose [webbed] fingers always got cold in the wintertime because he couldn't wear gloves. He could wear mittens but then he couldn't manipulate anything he owned. I still remember that character complaining about his cold hands. He had a home by the river, in a burrow like Bugs Bunny with a rug on the floor, a TV set and a stereo. I was captivated by the roleplay aspect of it. I was lost in this world, happily lost—and I finally had people I could relate to, could roleplay with online. I very quickly met a unicorn named Luagha. It turned out his name Ron and he ran the help desk at the University of Chicago where I was studying."

The FurryMUCK forum started Uncle Kage on a life-long furry path, but even before he discovered the fandom, he'd had some unique interactions with animals that influenced his furry nature later on.

"I actually slept [next to] a wolf once [not in a sexual way, but actual dozing]. I took an internship at a raptor center after I graduated and before I went to Chicago. The interns lived in a cabin, a small bungalow.

"They had a visit from some people from Wolf Haven in Colorado who brought along some of the wolves they used for education. One of them was a puppy—a 110-pound puppy with jaws that could shear through my upper arm as though it was made of glass. We let them sleep in our bunk beds because they were our guests, and we spent the night on the floor in sleeping bags.

"The puppy was happily gnawing on her favorite toy—which was a deer leg. I'm lying on the floor watching and all of a sudden she just . . . who knows what goes through an animal's mind? She stopped and she looked down at me. She dropped the deer leg, jumped off the bed and started sniffing around my face. She decided she'd much rather sleep down there on me than on the bed. She turned around three times and—*plop!*—right on top of me, one hundred and ten pounds of wolf.

"I lay there for a little bit. When I kind of tried to shift her off she went *arrrhhh*. Alright, okay, fine, no problem. Her handler was watching. 'Isn't that cute? She likes you.'

"At 4:30 the wolves woke up and the handlers took them outside to do their business. It was foggy outside. I looked out the window. I could just see the wolves in the fog and they started to howl.

"It was a magical moment. I didn't have an animal identity of my own on FurryMUCK yet; I started thinking, 'maybe a wolf fursona, wolves are cool.' I dabbled with a wolf character for a while. But it really wasn't what I wanted, and for one thing there were already like fifty wolves there.

"When I joined FurryMUCK, I wanted something unique, something nobody else had. I bought a used copy of the *Peterson Field Guide to Mammals of North America* and sat at my computer, looking through it. I started at A, ant bears or whatever, going through badgers, bears, flipping each page: me, me, no, not me. [I considered coyotes], but there were eight coyotes already. Dogs, eagles, foxes—how many foxes are already online? Four thousand! Okay, not foxes. G . . .

"That's when I saw something moving out of corner of my eye. I looked up at my computer and crawling across the top was the biggest, most monstrous, blackest, greasiest Asian cockroach you've ever seen in all your days. This thing was like a *kaiju* out of a Japanese horror film.

"It got to the middle of the monitor. I guess it saw me looking at it and it stopped. I'm a country boy, and I *freaked out*. I was screeching and screaming. On TV you turn the light on and they run away—this was full daylight! I took the book and was waving it at him— '*shoo, shoo, go away, go away!*'

"This little bastard just turned and faced me and reared its legs up. I stared at it and thought My God, that's a ballsy little roach!' My fear sort of drained away and became fascination. I got a glass and a piece of paper and nudged him towards the glass. He grudgingly went in and stared out at me.

"The wheels started to turn. Remember that Kurosawa movie *Kagemusha*? Kagemusha in Japanese means 'the shadow warrior.' It just so happens the word *mushi* in Japanese means 'bug.' I suddenly had this revelation: this little character, this samurai cockroach—*Kagemushi*, The Shadow Bug!

"I created Kagemushi, gave him samurai armor, two tiny swords and everything. He became my FurryMUCK personality. He was an immediate hit; no one had ever seen a cockroach character before.

"When he was online he'd entreat some kind individual to pick him up and put him on his shoulder so he [wouldn't be] looking up at everybody, and [he'd] sit there stoically like a tiny Toshiro Mifune. People were charmed by that. Even though he was my character, they would refer to me as Kagemushi or 'Kage' because Kagemushi is far too many syllables to say.

"I became friends with an otter online who kept telling me about ConFurence, [and offering to let me crash in their hotel room.] The problem was that ConFurence was out in California, and I couldn't afford the $300 airfare— that was like a month's pay for me.

"I'm certain I'm going to hell for this even though I've since confessed my sin. Never in all my days have I lied to my mother. But I called my dear, sainted mother: 'Mom, I'd like to go to a conference in California but Professor Eaton won't pay my travel expenses.'

Technically, it was an absolutely true statement. Mom didn't ask what *kind* of conference it was; she sent me the money and I bought a plane ticket.

"The otter had said some people wear fursuits at Confurence, but I didn't own one. What *should* I wear? The only thing that set me apart was my lab coat, so I wore it to the convention over a shirt and tie because it looked more professional than over a scruffy T-shirt. That was my costume at ConFurence 3.

"It was 1992 and this was my first furry convention—and it was a different kind of world. Oh my God, [there were] *lots* of furs, people who didn't have to feel guilty about taping daytime cartoons so they could watch them when they got home from work, people who idolized the scientific genius of Wile E. Coyote. I met people I'd been talking to on FurryMUCK: 'You're Kelly? Oh, wow, you're Timber! I pictured you taller with big ears.'"

While we were waiting for Conway's next glass of wine, I asked him for the secret of his success: what transformed him from just another furry fan to the man who is essentially, at the moment, the public face of the fandom?

"I think it started at ConFurence 6 in 1995, at a hotel across the street from the John Wayne Airport in Santa Ana. I was in the lobby, I'd had a little bit of this . . . " Conway leaned towards my recorder and explained "on the tape I'm holding up my wine glass," then continued with his story. "I'm a terrible drunk—I get loud, I get talky. I was sitting with Colin Frisanti, a furry artist who's now a professional chef, and a few other folks I'd met online, telling a story. I'm pretty sure I was complaining about my job in Arkansas working for a woman I hated.

"I couldn't help notice a crowd was gathering and was getting bigger. I'd acted in high school and college—I'm a natural ham so I started playing to the crowd, adding gestures and roaring into peoples' faces.

"When I finished the story everyone applauded; Colin grabbed my sleeve: 'Tell us another story Uncle Kage.' That's where it began.

"The rest of the night is kind of a blur. I was back home after the convention when I received an email from someone on the ConFurence programming staff: 'Would you like to come back next year and do that as an event?'

"'Do what, complain about my job?'

"'Yes.'

I've been going to cons for years—I was always the guy sitting in the audience looking up at the panelists. 'Okay, if you guys are that hard up for programming I'll do it.' The next year they gave me a chair in the lobby. A bunch of people showed up, and I just blithered and blathered and talked.

"The next year, 1997, I was approached at ConFurence 8 by a fur who's known online as 'Rigel.' He told me he was putting together a convention back east in New York later that year, Albany AnthroCon, and asked if I would attend."

And thus the yarn-spinning Uncle Kage became a fixture at what would eventually blossom into the world's most successful furry convention (and he into one of the best-known personalities in the furry world)— but Anthrocon still had a ways to go before that could happen.

Trish Ny had some furry goodies for sale. A table in the Philcon dealers' room would be perfect, but in 1994 they were all already spoken for. Did the old-school, main- stream sci-fi convention have it in for the sizeable number of furs who congregated at its November convention? Did they treat the furs like second-class animals and refuse to allot them their fair share of tables?

Actually, no. Philcon reserved its tables for returning dealers from previous years, leaving little or no room for new ones to get in on the action. It made no difference; if Ny couldn't have a dealer's table at Philcon, she'd start her *own* convention, with plenty of dealers' tables.

Come November, Philcon had company. Just down the hill from the Adams Mark hotel, Ny's "Furtasticon" was taking place in the Holiday Inn. According to furry historian Fred Patten, the East Coast's first furry convention attracted some 230 folks, furs who (thanks to the free admission Ny offered to Philcon badge holders) split their time between the mini furcon and the big convention up the hill.

Truth be told, there wasn't that much to Furtasticon: a small dealer's room housing Ny and perhaps a dozen other furry entrepreneurs, and an events room offering a limited amount of programming. But Ny had pulled it together at short notice and the results were impressive enough to try again next year. This time, however, Ny's convention would stand on its own, not as an adjunct to a nearby mainstream convention.

On October 13, 1995, at the Holiday Inn by New Jersey's Newark airport, Furtasticon was reborn as "ConFurence East," a title courtesy of furry partners Mark Merlino and Rod O'Riley who lent Ny the name of their well-known west coast gathering. It too was a success, attracting a decent-sized crowd of 449 furs. Almost $11,000 worth of furry art changed hands, making both artist and buyer quite happy, while $1,000 was raised for Ny's favorite charity: an Indiana wolf preserve, making both her and presumably the wolves quite happy.

But the first rumblings of discontent were heard. To some, Ny seemed intent on making ConFurence East a one-woman operation, unwilling to delegate authority or accept advice from people with more experience running a convention—and refused it in a less than politic way.

"When Trish was organizing ConFurence East I did some research." Nearly twenty years later, Mitch Marmel, a first-generation East Coast fur, remembers his experience. "Hotel rates, room sizes, that sort of thing. I typed it up and emailed it to her." Without a decades-old email on hand, Marmel paraphrases her reply: "'That stuff's no good, we're gonna do it the way I do it.' Not a 'thank you, but,' just a very rude 'piss off and die,' basically. She wound up alienating a lot of people who could've been very helpful otherwise."

Then there are others who see her as a heavy-handed rule-maker getting in the way of their light-hearted fun. One fur who was on the scene offers his assessment:

"With the exception of a couple of cases of food poisoning from the hotel restaurant, all had a good time. Well, almost all. It seems that a few people wanted to play around and prank a lot at the hotel, and Trish can be (or at least tries to be) stern sometimes—this was her first hotel experience and she wanted it all to go well so she could try again next year. She came down hard on a few pranksters (maybe more than she should have, I don't know), and some people got upset that she was harshing their buzz.

"Trish made enemies."

In 1996 ConFurence East moved 453 miles west to

Cleveland, Trish's hometown. Jim Groat, the furry wise guy we met earlier in the book, was planning one of his "Silly String assassinations," in which he and friends bury a "lucky" victim under several cans' worth of the sticky stuff.

The free-spirited Groat chafed under Ny's strong-willed style. According to Groat (whose storytelling style tends towards the dramatic) when word of the planned attack reached Ny, "she stood on a chair and said, looking right at me, 'anyone caught using Silly String in the hotel will not only be fined and prosecuted for vandalism but will pay all cleanup expenses.'"

I recently asked Groat if he thought Ny had a point. "She knew I ran Silly String assassinations and didn't like the fact I organized them and they were a big hit."

A fur who doesn't share the animosity many felt towards Ny offers a different perspective on the event: "Trish made the inexcusable mistake of finding out (from the hotel manager, who heard it from several of his staff, who heard several people talking about it) that there would be a Silly String attack in the hallway outside the art show. The hotel had just laid a new marble floor and had not yet sealed it; there are neon fluorescent dyes in Silly String and the hotel manager didn't want red, pink and green squiggles on his expensive new marble. He and Trish came into the dealers' room and said there would be *no* Silly String attack. The 'Get Trish' squad took this as Trish snooping on them and making the con no fun."

A "Get Trish" squad? Evidently so. In spite of an unexpected November blizzard, over 500 furs made it to the con; all fifty dealers' room tables were filled and over

$12,000 worth of furry art and goods were sold—none of which stopped rumors and outright disinformation from flying around, some of it emanating from the convention's own Internet room. ("Trish pocketed all the charity money . . . she gave them the money, but under her own name to get a tax write off . . . this con is like a ghost town . . . there are more dealers than fans here . . . ")

Nonetheless, ConFurence East's sophomore year was a success. At the con's conclusion Ny announced the convention would return to Cleveland next year and for several years thereafter, but under a new name all its own: "MoreFurCon."

But the rumors didn't let up. If anything, they grew in vitriol and volume as 1996 gave way to 1997: "Trish never paid the hotel . . . never paid the artists . . . the dealers had terrible sales . . . " The "Get Trish" squad was in full gear, some of them planning a convention "ten times better than this sorry excuse of a con."

In February of 1997 Trish Ny gave up: there would be no MoreFurCon. She announced her decision in a posting on the alt.fan.furry message board that read, in part:

> . . . there are those out there who tear at my spirit. Rumors surface and resurface... the feeling of competitiveness is escalating and taking a malicious edge. It has ceased to be fun. It's not been an easy decision. But the stress, the anger is building within me. It's affecting my family life, my health. And given the choice between my family and this convention, I'm certain I've made the same choice all of you would make . . .

Ny's announcement generated several trolling online responses; a fur surveying them counted "several 'GREAT!'s, one 'There IS a God,' and someone singing 'Ding, Dong, the Witch is Dead.'"

There was indeed a "Get Trish" squad—and it got Trish. The squad included several people involved with the July-scheduled Albany AnthroCon, some of whom privately admitted it to friends. A fur on staff known as "DACC" who enjoyed—*literally* enjoyed—a reputation for heavy trolling couldn't resist bragging online:

> *I'm back . . . one of the people who is tip-top _proud_ to say that they chucked a few pieces of their toolkit into Trish Ny's machinery. Those of you who don't like that, well...bite me. She needed taking out, and anyone with half a brain who's not upset about losing their _inside meal ticket_ . . . can figure this out. For those of you who can't...hey.*

On Sunday, July 6, the first Albany AnthroCon ended with a post-mortem session where staff and attendees discussed what worked and what needed improvement. A fur who was there recalls one moment in particular:

"The thing I remember most was during the dissection on Sunday. I don't know who said it but to this day I want to shake their hand: 'We don't mind Joe Ny [Trish Ny's husband] showing up, we just wish he'd leave his dog home.' The whole room laughed. Tells you something right there."

Yes, it does. .

SAM CONWAY ACCEPTED Rigel's invitation to the premiere Albany AnthroCon. "Albany's only four hours away [from my home in suburban Philadelphia], so what the hell—I went."

Conway was one of 500 or so attendees at this new convention, conducting his "story hour" on the hotel's pool deck.[153] He soon discovered the people behind the convention were running a less-than-tight ship. "The art auction was supposed to begin at one p.m.; at a quarter after we were still waiting for the auctioneer to arrive. Finally, a staffer tried to start the auction himself. The poor boy was terrified—I know stage fright when I see it. He was stammering, mumbling, he had no idea what he was doing. The audience was rolling their eyes, 'what are we here for?'

"I've enjoyed the performances given by some of the finest amateur auctioneers in science-fiction fandom; I loved watching them. Meanwhile this poor guy was going to pieces and I couldn't take it anymore. I went up to him, 'Can I try one?' and channeled one of the auctioneers I'd seen. It worked, I got bids. The guy said, 'Do the rest!' I'd never conducted an auction before, and it was exhilarating—my God, people were actually reacting to this!"

Conway's inherent hamminess, his ease entertaining an audience and his take-charge-when-necessary resourcefulness would soon come in handy for more than just conducting an auction.

Albany AnthroCon grew out of occasional parties organized by local fur Roger Wilber, aka "Aloyen C.

---

153 Other programming included now-standard furry convention fixtures like a charity auction that raised $2,200 for therapy dogs, a fursuit dance and what furry historian Fred Patten speculates was the very first fursuit parade. (*Furry Fandom Conventions, 1989-2015*, McFarland and Co., 2016.)

Youngblood." As with many other furry gatherings, his parties grew in popularity until more people started showing up than could fit in his apartment, at which point Youngblood relocated the gathering to a meeting room in a local hotel. It was a one-time occurrence that set the stage for the full-fledged, hotel-based furcon to come.

Was Youngblood part of the "Get Trish" squad? One observer believes it more likely others involved in Albany Anthrocon's launch were responsible rather than Youngblood himself. In any event Youngblood may have had better people skills than Ny, but in terms of running a convention, he was not even close.

A power struggle developed among Albany Anthrocon's staff over "DACC's" participation because of his admitted role in sabotaging Ny's convention plans. The uproar ultimately led to DACC's ouster from the official convention staff, but not from the convention itself.

When money due to exhibiting artists failed to reach them weeks after its conclusion, it was discovered that Albany AnthroCon '97 had seriously overextended itself. The cash went to the hotel to pay down the convention's way-larger-than-expected bill. (Ironically, stiffing the artists and the hotel—the same accusations made against Ny—were this time true.)

In 1998, a few weeks before the start of Albany Anthro-Con's second go-round, Youngblood suddenly resigned, leaving the convention rudderless—just as Conway, now on the convention's mailing list, was taking a growing interest in its operation. A self-described "buttinsky," he found himself "unable to stay quiet when I saw an idea coming across. I'd been going to conventions for about fifteen years by this time—not only furry cons, but sci-fi cons: Balticon, Philcon, Worldcon, con after con after con. At this point I had a pretty good idea how a convention works.

"The AnthroCon staff would come up with an idea I knew wouldn't fly. I would hesitantly send an email back, 'I know it's not my place, [but] can I talk to you about this? If you do that, I can envision the following happening,' or 'It's a great idea on paper, but . . . ,' 'You know how fans are. You might want to try this instead,' et cetera.

"When the chairman resigned they contacted me, 'will you take over?'"[154]

In spite of a complete lack of experience in running an enterprise of any sort, Conway said yes. "[I'd said do it], 'but not just this year.' I told them up front that I learn from watching everybody else. I learned from Philcon and talked to its organizers—I've been friends with them since I was sixteen. I told the people running Albany AnthroCon: 'After 1998 I will run the organization for you, but we must do it on my terms.'

"'First, you've got to move to Philadelphia—four hours away is too long a commute for me.'" Actually, Conway's decision was based on more than the time he'd save driving. "One thing I noticed about Albany on the Fourth of July weekend, the city literally closes—the Subway [sandwich shop] was closed, for God's sake! The only place to eat that was still open was a little Chinese restaurant—and they ran out of food Saturday afternoon! The hotel restaurant cost $17 a meal, which in 1998 was a giant chunk of change.

---

154 Rigel, the fur who first approached Conway at ConFurence, has a slightly different memory: "After Aloyen dropped out we were discussing how to move forward; no one wanted to take charge, so Sam stepped up."

"I remember standing in the middle of Albany's main drag, the equivalent of [Philadelphia's] Market Street, looking in one direction, then the other. It was like something out of *The Omega Man*: newspapers blowing by, no cars, no pedestrians, no human beings, the city was fucking deserted! This was not a good place for a con. I thought about Philadelphia. It's alive all the time, it's cheaper to get to because it's a major airline hub. How the hell do you get to Albany? You've got to connect somewhere—there are [few major] direct flights to Albany.

"I told them 'AnthroCon has to move to Philadelphia, and I don't believe this can be run as a bunch of people having a party. If we're going to run a convention, it'll be run as a business. If you agree, I will take the job.'"

Conway had taken a jump into the deep end—but it was a well-thought-out jump. "At the time I was on the board of directors of a nature center near where I lived. One of the others was lawyer who dealt with such things so I sat down with her. She educated me in incorporating as a non-profit entity," which was done under the name Anthrocon, Inc. "We went 501.c7: a 'fraternal organization,' the same as the Elks Club or the local Lionel Train Society. The rest was on the job training—I had to teach myself.

"I was living next door to the Valley Forge Hilton. I was familiar with the place; my favorite Japanese restaurant was there. I told the hotel we had a convention with 500 people. Once you say that, they're your best friends in world: 'We'll give you this, we'll give you that, we'll give you this . . . ' One thing [I learned from my friends who ran Philcon is that] if it's not in writing, it never happened, so I made sure it was all in the contract.

"This was 1999, and I'd told the hotel we had 500 people coming. I thought it would take us five years to fill the hotel; we filled it that year." The actual attendance turned out to be 845 furs, a whopping 69% increase over the previous year. "Every room was ours—the hotel was overjoyed. Next year we had more people than the Hilton could handle and we had to take a second hotel for the overflow.

"The hotel wanted us to stay but we were pushing out the walls. I called Anthrocon 2000 'the goldfish con.' [Attendance had increased by almost a third over the previous year, from 845 to 1,128.] I started looking for another venue."

Anthrocon spent the next four years, from 2001 through 2004, at Philadelphia's Adam's Mark Hotel, a modest venue at the very edge of the city. It was already a familiar spot to many who'd attended the furry-friendly Philcon there before Anthrocon existed.

But Anthrocon refused to stop growing; 1,457 attended the 2001 gathering; three years later 2,404 furs showed up. Everyone assumed 2005 would see an even larger crowd—but at the end of 2004 the Adam's Mark was sold, closed and replaced by a Target department store. Anthrocon found temporary refuge in a downtown Philadelphia hotel the following year—temporary because a search for a new, permanent venue with plenty of growing room was already underway.

"Anthrocon had outgrown the Adam's Mark. They could only handle 2,000 people and we were pushing 2,400—we had to find bigger digs. We looked at Harrisburg, Pennsylvania; Washington D.C.; New York City . . . Trying to find, one, a place we could afford and, two, a place able to fit 3,000 people under one roof where hotel rooms don't cost $300 a night.

"While we were searching I got a call from Visit-Pittsburgh, the people who try to bring new business to town: 'Why not consider us?'" Conway gives out with a delighted laugh. "I'm a native Pennsylvanian: 'Pittsburgh is a cess pit, it's a steel town—gritty, filthy and gray.' I didn't know the steel mills had closed down. The last time I was out there was 1979. Bethlehem Steel was spitting 400 trillion cubic yards of carbon a year into the air—the city *was* gray and gritty. Besides, I'm not going there, it's 300 miles away.

"A week later, people from the bureau happened to be in town and invited me to lunch.

"'Are you paying?'

"'Of course.'

"I picked the most lavish, expensive restaurant I knew, the Bahama Breeze, a gorgeous place. I figured I was playing these people in exchange for a free lunch.

"They were at a big round table; people from the mayor's office, the city's convention and visitors' bureau, the Westin convention center hotel, the Omni William Penn Hotel. They all stood up, grinning and happy to see me.

"I ordered the most expensive dish, the most expensive wine the place had—I'm going to show you people. Then they started: 'We'll give you this, we'll give you that, we understand you're paying $110 a night [for a hotel room]—we'll give you that rate, we'll give you thousands of feet of convention space for a ridiculously low price—we'll give you, we'll give you, we'll give you, we'll give you . . . '

"I held up my hand. 'Will everybody stop? I want

to make sure we're all clear—you understand this is a *furry* convention, right?' One of the gentlemen reached under the table and pulled up—I didn't know they made three-ring binders this big—five six-inch thick, *enormous* binders. He had printouts: my web page, Anthrocon's web page, several webpages of the kind we try not to let people see . . . they basically had all of furry fandom printed out. 'Oh my God, you've really done your homework; you really want us to come out there?' 'Absolutely,' they said.

Jason Fulvi, Executive Vice President of VisitPittsburgh, the city's tourism agency, said that indeed, they'd absolutely done their homework. "That's what we do for every group," he continued. "We want to make sure that any customers we bring to the table for our hotel partners are going to be a viable, profitable piece of business for them."

"I started thinking, 'Well they're earnest,'" Conway recalls. "I felt a little bad—all I had been doing was trying to get free lunch out of them. They said, 'Just pick a Saturday and come out and look, that's all we ask.'

"I took them up on it. I hadn't seen Pittsburgh in twenty years. The grit, the gray-brown clouds were gone. I saw green, I saw flowers—it was beautiful. They took me to the Westin and gave me a big room, wined and dined me in the Fish Market [an upscale restaurant inside the hotel].

"The next day we toured the convention center—it was magnificent. They built the place but they weren't getting business they anticipated." Which might be an understatement.

The $373 million David L. Lawrence Convention Center wasn't delivering the bang for the buck its builders had promised Pittsburgh. Conventions, trade, public shows and attendance in general—all were dwindling compared to the Center's first year of business in 2004, which itself was unimpressive. One local politician wondered if the all-white building had become "a white elephant" on the banks of the Allegheny River. (Beginning in 2006 there would be no shortage of fauna whatsoever *inside* the Lawrence.)

"Pittsburgh was hurting for business," Conway continues. "They were desperate for us, and they'd offered me the moon and the stars.

"I took their offer back to the board, and I put it on the Anthrocon web page: 'What do you people think?' Seventy-five percent said yes. The New England furs were crying and screaming and whining and kvetching, 'It's too far for us.'[155]

"We decided to go for it, but we had to—the Adam's Mark was sold out from under us. We had to rush to make it happen in 2006. We were so scared—we didn't advertise Anthrocon 2007 because we weren't sure if there'd be one—2006 was a make or break year for us.

"We made it to Pittsburgh in one piece, and we broke the attendance record: 2,489 people came. Anthrocon was still the largest furry convention in world.

"What's more, Pittsburgh loved us. The city went Furry that weekend." There must've been some degree of culture shock, I ask Conway. "For the first five minutes, yes. When you've got 200 people in bunny suits, you've just gotta have fun!"

---

155 Beginning in 2003 New England furs averse to long-distance travel could forego Anthrocon in favor of FurFright (recently renamed Furpocalypse), a Connecticut-based, Halloween-themed convention successful enough to attract some 1,455 attendees in 2016.

Sometimes people need to have "fun" explained to them. A few blocks away from the Lawrence Convention Center stands the Omni William Penn, a massive hotel occupying an entire city block. Unlike the more modern Westin adjacent to the Center, the William Penn is definitely old school, with an ornate marble lobby festooned with enormous chandeliers and maze-like floors that angle in all directions. While Anthrocon completely occupies the twenty-six-story Westin (leading to an endless traffic jam to board one of its four snail-slow elevators), only a limited number of rooms at the Penn are reserved for furs; fursuiters are nowhere as prevalent here. In order to cushion their more sedate guests from furry culture shock, the hotel thoughtfully provided an explanatory leaflet at the registration desk:

Dear Guest,

Please be aware that Pittsburgh is hosting the annual city-wide conference known as Anthrocon.

Anthrocon is the world's largest convention for those fascinated with anthropomorphics, which are humanlike animal characters. Attendees are a collection of artists, animators, writers, costumers, puppeteers and just everyday fans who enjoy cartoon animals. Guests will dress in costume, and you most likely will see such costumes in the hotel and throughout the city this weekend.

"This is what I like to see," Conway continues, "furs

showing up and the public just having fun because that's what it's all about—furry fandom is about having fun, and people did. By the end of the first year we won them over, by the next year they were eager to see us back—the local businesses were painting pawprints on the sidewalk and posting 'welcome Anthrocon' signs in their windows. We'd never seen this before. We'd always [see] 'oh my God, the weirdoes are coming, maybe we should go on vacation.'

"At that point we realized we'd made Pittsburgh a furry city, and decided to stay there."

The feeling was mutual: VisitPittsburgh estimates Anthrocon and its furry attendees have infused some $41 million into the local economy since their 2006 arrival while raising over $189,000 for a variety of local animal-related charities, from the local Humane Society to Pittsburgh Parrot Rescue. But the relationship between Anthrocon and Pittsburgh is deeper than money, as a story about money reveals.

Fernando's Café is a small fast-food eatery on Liberty Avenue, just around the corner from the Lawrence Convention Center and steps away from the overflowing-with-furs Westin hotel. Fast, convenient, affordable and quite good, it's been popular with furs since Anthrocon first landed in Pittsburgh.

It took a few years for Pittsburgh to embrace the furries, but owner Fernando DeCarvalho got it right away; the first year Anthrocon was in town, DeCarvalho drew chalk pawprints on the sidewalk leading into his café,[156] a

---

156 The Pittsburgh Post-Gazette reported that year DeCarvalho's restaurant did three months' worth of business over the convention's four days. (http://www. post-gazette.com/local/city/2012/06/16/Pittsburgh-cafe-gets-a-hand-or-paw-from-a-loyal-group-offurry-friends/stories/201206160160) Published June 16, 2012. Retrieved January 24, 2016.

gesture his fellow merchants were much slower to adopt.

A few years later DeCarvalho took a brick to the head and suffered a fractured skull while protecting his furry patrons from a local moron. No small amount of affection grew between the furs and the owner of their favorite establishment, who renamed his store "Furnando's" during Anthrocon's annual visits.

Early in 2012, however, under the burden of a weak economy and a heavy debt load, DeCarvalho was about to declare bankruptcy and shutter Fernando's. In a video on the *Post-Gazette*'s website he described what happened next. "[Sam Conway,] the CEO for Anthrocon found out that we were not going to be here this year. He said to me on the phone, 'How much money do you need to stay in business?' I was taken aback, but he was persistent. I said why don't you pay for May? I can stay here thru June and be part of the convention."

On the video Conway picks up the story. "I put word out [on] various social media. I simply said, 'This guy has been there for us, he is an honorary furry, furries help each other.' I expected maybe three, four thousand dollars, that would've been really cool.

"We had $4,000 by the end of the night. Within three days we had about $20,000. By the end of the week the total was $23,800. These weren't giant corporate sponsors, these were ordinary people putting in $10, $15, $25—hundreds of donors. We handed him the bulk of the money on April 20. He was at first a little reluctant, but I put [the money] in his hand and said, 'Here we are, this is for you.' Whatever came up next, we were going to be his first customers."

"I believe God worked through the furries," said

DeCarvalho, "because I really was in need."

"I believe God worked through the furries"—definitely the highest compliment the furry community has been—or, in all likelihood, will ever be—given.

Anthrocon is so much a part of Pittsburgh that it's become a tourist attraction in and of itself. In 2012 *USA Today*'s "Pop Candy" column invited Pittsburgh readers to "name their city's top pop-culture hot spots/events." Anthrocon came in third, right after the Andy Warhol Museum and just before movies filmed in the city:

> *The annual Anthrocon—Lions, tigers and bears—oh, my! I'm not referring to the Pittsburgh Zoo but rather the people who feel comfortable enough to dress as their favorite animal characters roaming the streets for Anthrocon.*
>
> *The annual gathering attracts thousands to Pittsburgh each year. If you plan on visiting Pittsburgh during the convention, chances of finding a hotel are slim, but odds are good that you'll see someone dressed as your favorite cartoon animal walking about.*[157]

Way back when, before Anthrocon was Albany AnthroCon, before Albany AnthroCon existed, it was just a bunch of furs congregating in a friend's apartment, furs who had no idea where their fandom was heading.

---

157 Pop Traveler: 10 reasons to visit Pittsburgh. USA Today. February 20, 2012. (http://tinyurl.com/hst22bs) Retrieved January 30, 2016.

Three cities and thousands of furs later, Anthrocon takes over Pittsburgh every July. It's the time of year the city sees fursuiters on the downtown streets—and Uncle Kage in the local media. Sam Conway is the face and voice of Anthrocon, and as far as the good people of Pittsburgh are concerned, of Furry itself. And with great media attention comes great responsibility . . .

"I used to be a volunteer with Red Cross where I had a few uncomfortable run-ins with the media because I hated them in disasters. I consider [the media] vultures, and I probably said some things that were—improper.

"A house collapsed—in Philly it happens all the time, these old houses fall down. I'm there, trying to help its residents. An elderly woman walks up, carrying her groceries. She stares at the building and her eyes go wide. I realize she lives here and I try to comfort her. Just then a reporter with a microphone got ten feet away from her, 'We have just learned two of the occupants in this building have died!'

This poor old lady threw up her hands and screamed in agony, fell down, crying, sobbing. These reporters ran up, shoving their microphones in front of her lips, 'How do you feel about this, tell us how you're feeling?'

The captain of our team ran up to protect her and told me 'get them out of here!' I said, 'Guys, please, talk to me.' Then, of course, I said the wrong thing: 'You're a bunch of fuckheads!'

"After incidents like that my superiors at the Red Cross realized I was a bit of a loose cannon, so they sent me to media-relations classes [to learn] how to deal with the media in times of disaster. Now, Anthrocon isn't a disaster, but it is a stressful thing and one must keep his nerve. I was trained to speak to the media, and I consider myself qualified to be spokesperson for the fandom because I know what I want the folks at home to take away. I know what I don't want them to take away—and I know in particular what happens if they see you sweat: they come in for the kill.

"The Pittsburgh press has been very positive to us—they adore us. I won't credit myself, but I will [share] one of the things I carefully orchestrated. One of the questions I naturally got early on was 'why did you come to Pittsburgh?' There's a long-standing rivalry between Pittsburgh and Philadelphia. I told them, 'We started in Philly, but the very second we laid eyes on Pittsburgh, there was no going back—when you compare the cities, it's like night and day.' That immediately put us on good terms."

VisitPittsburgh's Fulvi offers an example of Conway's ability to finesse the skeptical: "Early on most people had a negative perception about Anthrocon and the furries. That was the approach a local radio station took—they were saying all kinds of disparaging things on the air, how strange this thing was, how weird the attendees were. We helped Sam get in touch with these people and have a good conversation. He talked to them on air, and before you knew it the station became their fan, and now they promote the heck out of it."

So does Fulvi's boss, VisitPittsburgh CEO Craig Davis. "It's always funny because whenever people ask what we do, I tell them that we bring all the conventions into town. [They'll ask what.] 'We bring the furries.' Sometimes they say, 'I heard that there are problems.' I tell them that Anthrocon's been here for years now and we would not invite them back if the community didn't want them; if the hotels didn't want them, we wouldn't have them back. [I tell the skeptics that the furries] are the most harmless, nicest bunch of people that you'd ever want to meet. People just kind of smile and say, 'You know, you're right.'"

However, "there were some rough instances the first year," Fulvi recalls. "Some attendees staying at the Westin put the convention in a negative light; they weren't allowing the housekeepers into their rooms. When they checked out the housekeepers found their rooms extraordinarily messy [with] soda cans stacked to ceiling. It took a whole day to clean a single room.[158]

"We got in touch with Sam and told him the issues. 'We've got to figure this out because if this is what the hotel is going to deal with every year, I don't know if it's a profitable piece of business for us.'

"Sam's group came in, and in a very professional manner took copious notes on all the details. They focused on the specific rooms where there were issues, and they were able to pinpoint [whose rooms those] were. Sam went to certain individuals and told them they weren't allowed back next year because of the position [they'd put the conference and tourism board] in. We didn't have to take care of anything. Sam and his team took care of it all—they policed themselves, and the next year they had their own security. And quite honestly, we haven't had problems since."

"It's something we're very proud of talking about,"

---

158 Many of Anthrocon's 7,000-plus attendees are young, first-time convention goers unfamiliar with hotel etiquette, sharing a room with numerous friends to make the trip affordable. The Westin's special Anthrocon "Please come back later" door hanger now advises furs: "Every room has been provided extra garbage bags. If you generate more trash than the bins in the room can handle, please place excess into the garbage bags and place the bags by your door. Additional bags are available at the front desk if needed."

declares Davis. "I think it says a lot for Pittsburgh and for Anthrocon that we kind of embraced each other." Fulvi adds, "We like the different vibe Anthrocon brings to our city. And it reminds people that you don't have to be so serious every day."

CHAPTER THIRTEEN

That's Entertainment?

SOMETIMES I'M SURPRISED Furry isn't better known considering the amount of attention showered on us, not just in the news media but on primetime TV. Then again, considering how we're usually portrayed, maybe that's a good thing.

Hollywood is definitely aware of us, judging from how often episodes are built around or reference Furry. Sometimes it's just a throwaway gag that avoids the "F" word, but it's obvious just the same to those of us with working furdar.

My favorite of that ilk was "Love 'em or Leash 'em," a 2005 episode of the animated Nickelodeon series *My Life as a Teenage Robot*. In order to distract a part-canine robot, one of the human characters says, "I swore I wouldn't wear this outside the feline fan convention, but now I have no choice." ("Feline fan convention"? Close enough.) He ducks into the men's room and emerges looking like a cat— not a kid in a cat suit, but a 1940s *Looney Tunes*-style cat.

With three lead characters that happen to be sentient fast-food items, *Aqua Teen Hunger Force* is pretty strange to start with, but their 2008 episode "Hoppy Bunny" featured an equally strange assortment of fursuiters, all dancing on their front lawn. In the *ATHF*-verse 'suiters wear oversized heads that cover their entire bodies, their arms and legs sticking out of strategically placed holes. A few are wearing more conventional suits, like a shapely fox gal or the pink unicorn humping "Frylock" with his pixilated penis. Hoppy Bunny's head is so huge its occupant can stick his own head out of an armhole to make a phone call. (He happens to be a surgeon specializing in brain transplants, thus proving a lot of furs are very accomplished professionals and not basement dwellers.[159])

The same year *Back to You*, a sitcom set in a Pittsburgh TV station newsroom, used Anthrocon as the episode's B-story. A reporter realizes he's about to be assigned to cover the convention: "Oh no, no—not Anthrocon!"

Off to a rousing start. Mistake number one: "It's an annual convention for people who like to wear animal costumes." That's right, every last one of us likes to wear animal costumes.

Mistake number two: "These are the people Trekkies beat up."

A joke organizational chart called "The Geek Hierarchy" can be found online. At the top are literary sci-fi fans, followed by comic book superhero fans, writers of erotic fanfic, Pokémon fans over the age of six, etc. Finally, at the very bottom, the group they all feel superior to:

---

159 He's also very serious about fursuiting: "Furry bunny hands make me a bad surgeon? It may be weird to you, but it is my religion!"

"Furries." (Trekkies are three levels higher.) The episode's writer apparently consulted this chart before coming up with that gag.

Mistake number three, and in my book the biggest of them all: every last "fursuiter" in the episode is wearing a generic animal suit straight from the costume rental agency—saggy, baggy and completely personality-free.

The most off thing about the episode, apart from the suits: the 'suiters take offense at the reporter's "insulting" jokes, even though they're the kind 'suiters might tell each other in real life—and they're funnier than the script's actual jokes. ("There's no excuse for those teeth," the reporter tells a bucktoothed bunny who's a dentist in real life; he then asks a canine couple if they ever do it "people-style," and so on.)

The 'suiters get their revenge though. At episode's end, the reporter, surrounded by the now-menacing 'suiters, nervously tells his viewers, "Anthrocon's nothing to joke about—just good, clean, well-adjusted fun." Other than the convention's name, they got everything wrong. Gee, thanks a lot, *Back to You*.

In a 2002 episode of his sitcom Drew Carey dates an attractive blonde, not realizing she's a fursuiter until she brings him to her apartment, excuses herself, then returns wearing a generic squirrel costume straight from the rental agency. "Silly me," says Carey, "I was expecting a negligee." "I know this is a little unusual, but this makes it more . . . exciting for me," she explains while fondling the chubby comedian's thigh. "Is that a problem?" "It's a problem," he answers, "but not mine." Evidently, though, he's willing to give it a shot: later in the episode he's wearing a squirrel nose, ears, tail and a set of paws—

while dressed in his pajamas. "You look so hot," she sighs, as they vanish into her bedroom. "This is going to be a *most* fluffy evening."

Of course, the worst furry offender of all time is *CSI.* Or, as I like to subtitle it:

CSI: The gift that keeps on giving . . . furries grief.

On October 30, 2003—the day before Halloween— CBS aired an episode of *CSI* titled "Fur and Loathing." The episode was promoted in a half-page *TV Guide* ad, unusual for the show: "WHEN PARTY ANIMALS ATTACK! The wildest case ever . . . really." The ad depicted two of its stars surrounded by generic-looking fursuit heads.

A fursuiter found shot dead after being hit by car in the middle of nowhere leads the CSI investigators to a furry convention—or at least a TV version of a furry convention. Whopper after whopper follow, from the latex-lined fursuit (as if wearing a fursuit alone isn't stifling enough), to the civet oil used as a supposed aphrodisiac, to the generally creepy vibe of their imaginary furry convention (scored to eerie music) with almost everyone suited, to the writhing furpile ("all the animals start rubbing and wiggling, some of the animals start to . . . do things" says a participant), to a suspect staying fully suited while being questioned in a police station, to the dead 'suiter supposedly poisoned by somehow licking ipecac off another 'suiter from inside his own fursuited head . . .

Aberguine scored the episode's accuracy at 11% and its spirit 6% in one of her YouTube *Furries in the Media* segments; to this day she considers "Fur and Loathing" the all-time worst depiction of Furry in an entertainment program. "The writers were lazy; the show gave an inaccurate picture of furries. It was clear they didn't give a fuck and [didn't] bother to do some research."

Actually the producers did consult an L.A.-area fur who managed to tone down some (but not all) of the original script's excesses,[160] which were evidently inspired by Rick Castro's discredited MTV "Sex2K" video.[161] Other than a few actual fursuiters who participated in the filming, the other suits all came from the good-old costume-rental agency.

While other CSI team members indulge in snarky remarks ("Well, I like hairy chests, but I'm not about to bop a six-foot weasel"), Grissom, the most thoughtful member of the bunch, is given to a few reflective thoughts ("Think of stuffed animals as a Jungian archetype"). I would've loved the show to acknowledge the existence of furry art with one of Grissom's associates discovering him buying a portfolio of spicy furry pinups. "Oh, hi, uh . . . it's strictly for research purposes, you understand, right?"

By the way, the unfortunate dead "raccoon" in the episode? Seems he was poisoned by a jealous fur, got out of his girlfriend's car to throw up, was hit by a passing car and was then shot dead by a farmer who mistook him

160 The fur put the word out to the local furry community: "I have spoken with the Director and Production Assistant about the script and this is going to show Furry in a good light . . . Here we go guys, another positive chance to put furry in the limelight!!!!" (*Attn SoCalFurs!* Posted to SoCalFurs (Yahoo group), August 28, 2003. Retrieved June 8, 2014.) A week later he was not as optimistic: "I am going to continue to work with the CSI team to fix a lot of stuff . . . I am not going to watch one of the best TV shows on TV mudilate [sic] Furry for misinformation. I am being proactive so I can at least say 'Hey, I tried' if it bombs out, and not be like a lot of people and say 'Jesus, did you see what they made us out to be?'" (*As promised, a CSI Update.* SoCalFurs (Yahoo group), September 4, 2003. Retrieved June 8, 2014.)

161 "I'm Not Really an Actor; I just play One on TV." kayshapero.livejournal.com, September 16, 2003. Retrieved April 21, 2014.

for a coyote . . . happens at least five or six times at every furcon I've been to.

American Dad's take on furry is every bit as kinky—but somehow a lot more fun.

In the 2008 episode "One Little Word," Stan and his CIA boss, Bullock, are having an ongoing conversation even though they're in a new location (and dressed to match) every few seconds: a night club, a goth bar, a western barn dance, playing spin-the-bottle with teenagers and, finally, at a furry convention. Stan is wearing a pink bunny suit and Bullock, a brown bear suit. A squirrel walks into frame (again with the squirrels!) and shows off his butt to an uninterested Bullock. The squirrel walks away disappointed—and bumps into a guy wearing a car suit. The squirrel happily lies down on the floor, and with a "vroom-vroom!" the car starts humping the squirrel! ("Oh yeah, I'm a squirrel and I feel *great!*") Yes, there's nothing like roadkill sex. The beauty of it: they start with the fursuit sex cliché, then transcend it with a completely ridiculous twist that makes fursuiting itself seem normal by comparison.[162]

The show revisited the furry-as-a-kink trope in the 2013 episode "The Missing Kink." Stan is horrified when his wife reveals her spanking fetish. Roger, the flaming Paul Lynde-soundalike alien, assures him, "Everyone has something a little different that they like, something a little naughty, a little *keen-ky.*" He escorts Stan to a sex dungeon he was evidently unaware existed in his own basement and launches into an elaborate production

---

162 It tickled an actual squirrel fursuiter so much he and a friend re-enacted the scene at a furry convention—right down to the naked-legged "carsuiter's" black shoes and socks.

number, "He's Got a Kink," with the dozens of kinksters already there singing along.

It's a full-tilt fetish festival: traditional whips & chains, bondage, human furniture, women's feet, adult babies, super fatties, even a singing donkey. The song comes to an end with the camera landing on a traditional furpile: "So if you like us old or fat or furry . . . " the purple bear removes his head, revealing it's Stan's boss Bullock—"you won't be judged, we're not a jury, 'cause way down deep inside we've all got kinks!"

It must be hard for Bullock to decide between his brown and purple bear suits on any given night. Perhaps it depends on which sex dungeon he's heading towards; you don't want to clash with the décor.

College Humor (collegehumor.com) also took note of Furry with a trio of cartoons starring the "Furry Force." If you can imagine every negative stereotype of Furry as a non-stop, over-sexualized kink fest turned up to eleven—no, make that thirteen—that's "Furry Force."

Animated in a pitch-perfect knock-off of 1980s low-budget TV animation—complete with an exuberant "Now back to *Furry Force*!" announcer—the Force arrive in their paw-shaped airship to confront the villainous Victor Vivisector.

"Ha, how are four kids going to stop me?" sneers Vivisector, who will shortly regret asking. With a cry of "fursona trans*fur*mation!" the quartet turns into their furry forms: an exceptionally well-hung effeminate lion-man, a wolf-taur,[163] a super-boobed squirrel gal and a six-breasted cow-girl. One of Vivisector's minions exclaims

---

163 The lupine equivalent of a centaur.

"whoa, why are they so sexy?"—and it's not a compliment.

The four go to work: squirrel gal traps one minion between her superboobs, wolftaur staggers the other with his "power musk" ("Ugh, smells like wet fur and sex!"), lion-man traps Vivisector's rocket punch in his mane ("Ew, could you please release my hand, your fur's all sweaty and matted!") while cow-girl frightens off Vivisector's robots with her six swaying breasts.

The four leap into a floating, writhing furpile and merge into their combined form: a giant, gigantically endowed furry hermaphrodite. The sight scares off Vivisector and drives his two henchmen to suicide.

And that's just "Furry Superheroes Are Super Gross," the first of the three cartoons. Two follow-ups ensue, each grosser than its predecessor. The final one ends with the entire world, human and animal alike, transformed into anthropomorphic beings who drown in a tidal wave of . . . never mind.

The cartoons' ultra-exaggerated furry stereotypes were accurate enough to make actual furs cringe . . . with laughter. While not all furs were pleased (and the furry haters did their usual hating) many responded with comments like "I found this hilarious . . . the writer knows his shit! . . . fucking awesome!... can't get enough of the stereotypes, they slay me . . . " and so on.

In fact, furs so enjoyed being skewered by *Furry Force* that they gave it the 2014 Ursa Major award (our Oscars, or maybe our People's Choice awards) for "Best Short Work or Series," beating out *Bojack Horseman* and even the beloved *My Little Pony: Friendship Is Magic*.

What could possibly counterpoint these exploitative or

affectionate parodies of Furry? The answer: an episode of a popular primetime network series that hints, without the tiniest touch of condescension two of its young attractive supporting characters might very well be furs. To be exact, a 2015 episode of CBS's *NCIS: Los Angeles*, "Blame it on Rio."

In a brief, mid-show vignette, tech geek Eric and his close friend Nell, the team's intelligence analysts, are discussing renaissance fairs. Nell wonders if they're similar to furry conventions. When a surprised Eric asks if she's been to any, Nell confesses she's been to Califur a few times. The subject of fursonas comes up, a concept it turns out they are both familiar with.

Flirtatious banter ensues as Nell wonders if Eric owns a fursuit. Playing coy, he asks if it would be "weird or cool" if he did. When she replies it depends on the suit he mentions several species; a platypus, aardvark, or musk ox suit would be weird, she declares, but a narwhal suit would be cool. Then, in a slow, deliberate voice, Eric mentions another species: "Komodo dragon."

"*Very* cool" answers Nell.

"Califur," "fursona," "fursuits," all spot-on. Thank you, CBS, for making amends for *CSI* at long last; and thank you, *NCIS: Los Angeles* for declaring *my* Komodo dragon suit "*very* cool."

CHAPTER FOURTEEN

Furrywood:
or, "You'll never work
in Toontown again!"

IF YOU INVESTED in a live-action movie starring a talking animal, overseen by one of the most successful filmmakers of all time, you would've made a bundle off Steven Spielberg's *Who Framed Roger Rabbit*—or lost your shirt on George Lucas's *Howard the Duck*.

Anthropomorphic animals are no strangers to movies: turtles, chipmunks and raccoons star in big-budget live-action movies rubbing shoulders with human beings, while entire menageries of anthropomorphic animals inhabit equally expensive animated features. But if talking animals rule Hollywood, why does the animation industry keep its distance from the furry community?

The 2005 animated feature *Hoodwinked* was a Little Red Riding Hood send-up in the form of a crime investigation, and also the most obvious hat tip to furries I'd ever seen in pop culture at the time. The police, led by a gruff grizzly bear and assisted by dapper frog detective Nicky Flippers, attempt to unravel the conflicting stories of Red, her Granny, the Wolf and the Woodsman to discover the identity of the Goody Bandit, a mysterious figure who has been stealing the forest inhabitants' dessert recipes. No one is who they seem to be at first, and each character's story is an overlapping piece of a mosaic that eventually uncovers the real culprit.

As we learn in the DVD chapter titled "Wolf's 'FURsion' of the Story," the wolf is Wolf W. Wolf, an investigative journalist and columnist for the *Once Upon A Times* forest newspaper. We see Wolf go undercover as a health inspector, chatting with the proprietor of an outdoor sandwich shop—who happens to be a surly-faced human in need of a shave, wearing an open-faced white-tiger suit. "I will tell you, my furry friend, food is dangerous."

A human in the midst of a forest full of talking animals, wearing an animal costume, addressed as "my furry friend"? So totally a call-out to us that I had to write Corey Edwards, the film's lead director, and ask him about it. "The guy in the tiger suit running the sandwich shop—'my furry friend'—seems to be a pretty obvious nod in our direction," I queried. "I'm wondering if you can fill me in on how/why that reference wound up in the movie, how you heard about the fandom and what was your perspective on it at the time?"

"This is by far the strangest question I've ever been asked about the movie. I have to say, I barely know what you're talking about."

Oops.

Edwards's reply continued. "If I read the context of your email correctly, this is referring to fur fetishists? There's not really any connection between *Hoodwinked* and that world. The sandwich shop guy, whom we called "Wade," is a joke about the world these characters live in. The character was simply born from one sight gag, where Red passes a raccoon wearing a business suit, then passes a business man wearing a raccoon suit. To be honest, I don't think anyone ever really was as amused by this character as we were.

"We put the raccoon-suited guy in the sandwich shop because we imagined that in that world, some people running businesses just dress up like animals to get more customers. More than anything, he's really a throwback to the Lost Boys in Disney's *Peter Pan*, who all wore animal skinsuits. The character is in no way a nod to any kind of "Fur Fandom" or "The Furry Scene" of which you speak. Sorry to disappoint! But we do enjoy seeing what others get out of this film . . . I'm sure the other guys will get a big kick out of knowing that there is another niche world out there that feels represented."

Furry still has a way to go before the animation industry learns to if not love, then appreciate us. (Although I would settle for tolerate.) There are several folks I remember from the furry scene now working in Hollywood who have cut their ties with the fandom—the better to avoid a metaphorical scarlet letter "F" pinned to their careers.

A now-retired animation writer/producer who was actively involved in furry fandom's dawning days in the mid-1980s offers his perspective:

> *Furry's relationship with the animation community? Well, there are plenty of folks in the biz who might be considered furry...but it really boils down to your definition of "furry."*

I never hid any of my interests at work. But I also never let any of my personal life into my work life. Back in the seventies, eighties and nineties one's politics, sexuality or "kinks" were left at one's home. It was called being professional. Human, monster, unicorn, it shouldn't matter on the job. Today? Well, I'd say by the output of many studios that lots of folks have an interest in the furry community. Whether they are "furry" is another matter.

"Furries are pretty widely known about amongst professional animators, but primarily, I think, stereotyped as sexual fetishists. I think they were first defined to me as 'fuzzies' and 'plushies.'" The speaker is Jeff Goode, creator of the 2005 Disney Channel series *American Dragon: Jake Long (ADJL)*.

Jake was a Chinese-American teenager able to shapeshift into a dragon to protect the world against supernatural menaces.[164] The series wasn't Goode's first foray into anthropomorphism; in 1993 his stageplay *The Eight: Reindeer Monologues* featured Santa's reindeer (portrayed by actors wearing fuzzy antler headpieces) spilling the beans on the fat guy's sexual harassment of his transportation team. In 1999 *Poona the Fuckdog and Other Plays for Children*[165] featured the title canine, a

---

164 In the *A Bug's Life/Antz* Department of Amazingly Similar Premises That Premiered at the Same Time, Cartoon Network simultaneously aired *The Life and Times of Juniper Lee*, about an eleven-year-old Chinese-American girl who also fought supernatural menaces. (She did not have the ability to turn into a dragon.)

165 Poona the Fuckdog" stagedirect.com. (http://www.stagedirect.com/poona) Retrieved December 6, 2016.

frog, a fire-breathing dragon and sundry other creatures. (The play received some marvelous reviews from high-class outlets like the *New York Times* and the *New Yorker* who weren't put off by the F-bomb in its title.)

"My first real contact with furries was shortly after *ADJL* first aired," Goode told me. "RodsO [Rod O'Riley] called me and asked me if I would be a guest at Califur, which he described as an animation and comic book convention.[166] Naturally, I said yes, and only later learned that there was probably a bit more to it than that. But by then I was too curious and had to go see what was what.

"I don't know that I was particularly anthropomor-phically minded, but in hindsight, I did notice that I had written a handful of things that could be considered anthro. *Reindeer Monologues* is my best-known stage-play, and I'd written dragon characters into several plays and TV shows. I was certainly not anthropomorphically averse."

Goode was so taken with his experience at Califur, he wrote *Fursona Non Grata* in 2012, a play furry-friendly enough to be performed at the convention in 2013.[167] Goode's website offers the following description: "A woman-raised furry brings her fiancé home for Thanks-giving to meet the family for the first time. Fur-larity ensues." A less imaginative playwright would have had the woman bring her fursuited fiancé home to visit her

---

166 I used to use the identical euphemism to describe furry conventions to friends and family until I said "the hell with it" and came out of the furry closet.

167 Wild Nights Fursona Non Grata Highlights. YouTube. Published July 1, 2013 (https://www.youtube.com/ watch?v=u7Yvw4mHdt4) Retrieved December 6, 2016.

staid family, but Lisa, the bride-to-be's family, includes (as per the play's *"Dramatis Fursonae"*),[168]

ZEBRINA - Lisa's mother, orange zebra
BUCK/CARL - Lisa's father, a talking bobcat
NICK - Lisa's brother, a Siberian husky
YAVA - Lisa's high-school sweetheart, a weasel

—and just for the sake of variety, "ALEX - Lisa's sister, a goth lesbian vampire," and "TERI/PAUL - Alex's wife, a mid-op transsexual." I look forward to seeing the play someday, if only to hear exchanges like this:

LISA: Mom, I specifically asked you to be normal.
MOM: Why do you think I made cookies?

STOP ME if you've heard this one: "A furry artist took his portfolio to a major animation studio and showed it to the director."

It's not the first line of a furry joke. A fellow greymuzzle is repeating an oft-heard anecdote that's been circling the fandom for years. He mentions the artist's name but asks me not to print it since he's passing on gossip, not sharing something he witnessed firsthand. I've already heard the story several times from several people, but I respect my friend's request and leave it out of his telling. "'Here's what I do—because I know you guys like this stuff. I'll fit right in because I like it too.' Evidently he had superbly rendered and colored cel-type art of characters, singles and in groups, posed provocatively, things like that; he thought that was an in with people."

---

168 Goode, Jeff. *Fursona Non Grata*. Script. Retrieved December 6, 2016. (http://www.jeffgoode.com/scripts/fursona/fursona.pdf)

"Basically, he was shown the door—politely but firmly, and really quickly. The person who told me the story said the artist had completely violated the unwritten law: the animators do naughty pictures *for each other*. It's an accepted part of the culture, but it stays inside the studio. It's not just funny animals either: 'How sexy can you make Olive Oyl?' It can gross people out, but more likely it's a challenge, a who-pays-for-tomorrow's-lunch [kind of thing]. 'Here's my Olive Oyl—and here's Bluto's reaction.' They get pinned to the wall of the animator's cubicle, and if the director asks for some of the better ones as a gift, they get pinned up on *his* wall."

I remember Floyd Norman's comment several Anthrocons ago: "Walt didn't [have a stash of naughty pictures], but a lot of the animators did."

"I HEARD YOU were trying out for a job at an animation studio and you showed them a portfolio that included some art that was, let's say 'a touch risqué," I ask Steve Martin.

This isn't the "wild and crazy" Steve Martin. This Steve Martin is a long-time furry artist who does indeed create slick and shiny furry art of nubile female anthros, some of which is definitely more than a touch risqué.

"It was Warner Bros.," Steve tells me as we're enjoying brunch at an IHOP not far from his Orange County home. "They said bring your best artwork. I brought one of my paintings, 'Tiger Waterfall' or maybe it was 'Tiger Falls.' It was a picture of a tiger-man holding a tiger-woman, very tastefully done." Steve pauses to take a bite. "The guy had a penis, but nothing risqué showing.

It was no worse than a Victorian painting. From what I heard, that somehow became legend. I couldn't believe it."[169]

"How'd other people hear about it?" I follow up.

"The story got around from the studio."

"And the rest of the art was standard funny-animal–type stuff?"

"The rest of the art was just animation-type stuff they would expect to see, storyboard tests, that kind of stuff."

"That must've bummed you out a bit," I offer.

"Well, you have to remember the American media, [and] Americans in general, [if] you mention 'children,' peoples' brains automatically shut off and run on pure emotion—nothing's grinding back in here. That's why we have this school system. We put on this big show on one side, how much we love our kids, and on the other side we treat them like shit."

Which may be true to one degree or another, but wasn't quite germane to what was until then our topic of conversation: the Hollywood animation industry's relationship—or lack thereof—with furry artists.

Steve tells me about the genesis of Lola Bunny, a character created to costar with Bugs in the 1996 live action/animated feature *Space Jam*. A furry protégé of Steve's is hired to design the new character and comes up with a pleasantly attractive female rabbit boasting shapely legs,

---

169 WikiFur, the furry version of Wikipedia, backs up Steve's story while adding a few additional details: "Steve's work interview at Warner Bros. TV Animation in 1991 turned into a now-classic fiasco when he showed *TazMania* director, Douglas McCarthy, adult furry artwork during the course of an animation portfolio review, assuming that the director wouldn't have a problem with it. A lot of furry fandom detractors have used this incident to bolster the theory of furry blacklisting within the animation industry." (http://en.wikifur.com/wiki/Steve_Martin) Retrieved December 6, 2016.

a narrow waist and a healthy but not overdone bosom.

"Then," according to Steve, "came the battle of the bunny boobs. You had some folks in the Warner Bros. hierarchy telling the artist to tone it down, make her boobs smaller, make her hips smaller. On the other side were the marketing people saying, 'Sex her up.' You can see [from the artist's original drawings] how much he had to erase the boobs and the rest.

"They took the [toned-down] designs to McDonald's marketing department for the cups and all that other shit for *Space Jam*. Ronald McDonald takes a look at the concept art and says—" Steve shifts into a goofy, clowny voice—"'We love Bugs and the *Looney Tunes* [characters],' who can't love them? 'But me and the Hamburglar, we got a problem with Bugs Bunny kissing and making out with this young boy.' They rejected the design [that had the smaller boobs and hips].

"The irony is [that the tone-her-down camp] at Warner Bros. cleaned up and cleaned up and cleaned up Lola Bunny to the point she was obscene." I'm confused; how can a desexualized cartoon rabbit be obscene? "You have to work on the assumption [the audience] won't know who these characters are" if they've never seen them before, Steve explains. "To make them appealing they have to stand on their own.

"They cleaned her up to the point where she looked like a young boy. They took a man hugging a woman and cleaned it up to the point it looked like pedophilia," thus putting the McDonald's deal in jeopardy.

Steve's passionate retelling of the episode concludes with the president of the studio's marketing department angrily returning Lola to her original curvaceous appearance[170] to the chagrin of the studio's middle management.

As our IHOP brunch draws to an end, I ask Steve's opinion on something Mark Merlino had told me earlier in the week: "Furries are the new gays in Hollywood, but they try not to be openly." "Isn't that a little exaggerated?" I ask Steve.

"Not too much. A lot of them show up incognito at furry conventions. You see somebody not dressed like a real furry: his shoes look awfully nice for a fanboy, and isn't that an Armani shirt he's wearing? Plus his badge is inside out so you can't read his name . . . they're looking for ideas to steal. You have to remember—this is fucking Hollywood."

ON JUNE 11, 2015, Disney's teaser trailer for *Zootopia*, their spring 2016 animated release, appeared on YouTube.

"In the world of *Zootopia*, humans never happened," the announcer (supposedly Jason Bateman) casually begins. Onscreen against a white background, the word "humans" is obliterated with a scribble, as if by an invisible crayon.

A sly-looking cartoon fox (who will be voiced by Bateman in the film) walks into the frame; he's not wearing any clothes. "Animals in *Zootopia* are anthropomorphic," the announcer continues, as "anthropomorphic" pops up onscreen, a syllable at a time. "That's a big fancy word that means they walk around on two feet, they do not go

---

170 It wasn't long before numerous uninhibited furry artists started creating fan art of Lola that would definitely upset those who preferred the "desexualized" Lola. "Fans vs. Time Warner: Who Owns Looney Tunes" by Bill Mikulak, an insightful essay about the studio's discovery of and reaction to X-rated Internet drawings of their characters, can be found in *Reading the Rabbit: Explorations in Warner Bros. Animation*. (Rutgers University Press, 1998.)

around nude—" the fox quickly coves up his non-existent genitals; this is a Disney cartoon after all.[171]

The teaser goes onto describe *Zootopia*'s world and introduces the fox's bunny adversary. Finally, the movie's title appears onscreen. A sentence appears beneath it, the words popping in one at a time, as the announcer says them: "Like nothing you've seen . . . " He pauses for a beat, then adds in a sly voice as the last word pops into view—"be-fur," giving the final syllable an extra bit of verbal eye-wink.

The furry community went nuts: "They know we're here—*they're talking to us!*"

Were they, or weren't they? Why did they need to define "anthropomorphic?" Why the "be-fur" pun? Hasn't Disney been creating anthro animals since (never mind *Steamboat Willie*) Walt's Kansas City *Alice in Cartoonland* shorts in the 1920s?

The discussion and speculation continued non-stop[172] until the film's U.S. premiere on March 4, 2016. However the smoking gun had already appeared two days earlier in a BuzzFeed news item: "Proof Disney Is Actually Marketing *Zootopia* To Furries."[173] BuzzFeed reported

---

171 This cartoon sight gag has been used so often it's earned a TV trope all its own: " . . . if a half-dressed character loses their shirt they will suddenly realize their crotch is exposed." Half-Dressed Cartoon Animal, TV Tropes. (http://tvtropes.org/pmwiki/pmwiki.php/Main/HalfDressedCartoonAnimal) Retrieved March 8, 2017.

172 A Reddit thread dedicated to the subject had eighty comments posted to it within days of the teaser's release. ("Is it just me or is Zootopia suspiciously furry?") The speculation spilled over onto non-furry pop-culture websites like Inverse with the December 2015 item Disney Prepares to Cash In on the Furry Demographic with 'Zootopia,'") and *Vanity Fair* (Disney Seems to be Embracing Its 'Furry' Fan Base.) All retrieved December 7, 2016.

173 https://www.buzzfeed.com/katienotopoulos/proof-disney-is-actually-marketing-zootopia-to-furries. Also retrieved December 7. Also retrieved December 7.

FurLife, a Seattle-based meetup.com group, received an email from Allied Integrated:

Hello Furlife,

My name is [name redacted] and I am representing Walt Disney Studios. Our next film being released is ZOOTOPIA and it is about a world inhabited by animals all living in peace together. The pictures of the members of your group all looking like animals are incredible and align perfectly with the film. All of you could live peacefully in Zootopia. It would be great for you all to share these photos on social media platforms such as Instagram and Twitter. You can take new photos of each other and share these new photos online using the hashtags #Zootopia and #ZooU. You can be representing ZOOTOPIA and the participants can receive film-based items such as the poster and rabbit or fox crowns. This can be a lot of fun and your group seems perfect to participate. If you are interested start posting the photos today and email me at xxxxxx@ alliedim.com. Thanks!

The BuzzFeed item ended with a "no comment" from Allied and the sound of crickets emanating from Disney when asked about the report. (Admittedly, it's possible the email was the work of an over-eager staffer at Allied who came across a suited-up photo of the FurLife group and contacted them on his own; had he done his homework he would've discovered hundreds of online furry groups and websites.)

For me, however, the real smoking gun came from the mouth of Byron Howard, the film's chief director and first listed of its nine writers. In an online interview[174] conducted shortly after the film opened, Howard confessed:

> *I grew up on* Robin Hood. *It's not the most popular Disney film, but it made a huge impression on me as a kid, so there's a lot of Robin Hood's DNA in this movie. There's that great Disney appeal.*

Howard credited the film, which came in 1973 just before he turned five years old, in each and every interview. And in the movie's publicity notes he called it his "favorite childhood film." *Robin Hood* starred a dashing fox in the title (who bears no small resemblance to Nick Wilde, Bateman's character in the film)—and countless furs credit him as the character who set them on their individual furry paths that ultimately led them to the fandom.

Five is an awfully impressionable age. Might Byron Howard be one of those closeted Toontown furs Steve Martin spoke of?

I was invited to a *Zootopia* press junket the week before the film premiered and was granted one-on-one time with Byron and his directing partner, Rich Moore.

---

174 Interview: Rich Moore and Bryan Howard for Zootropolis. The Hollywood News, March 24, 2016. (http://www.thehollywoodnews.com/2016/03/24/zootropolis-interviews-rich-moore-byronhoward/) Retrieved December 7, 2016.

I immediately—and perhaps not too wisely—asked if the teaser was a "dog whistle" to the furry community. Howard deftly dodged my questions, and not long after the interview I received an email from my upset editor, who'd been contacted by an upset Disney PR person.

Oops again.

So who knows. Perhaps there was more than a wink and a nod to furs in *Zootopia,* perhaps Howard himself is one of us—and perhaps not. Realistically, though, there's no way Disney is unaware of their furry demographic. (Like that poster said, "Disney: Turning kids into furries for over ninety years"). It's pretty obvious they're reluctant to take to their bosom a community they see as a font of pornographic art of their characters and/or a fetish scene.

Either way, furs and non-furs alike flocked to *Zootopia*, generating over a billion dollars at box offices around the world and earning it 2016's Academy Award for Best Animated Film—and I'm sure it sent no small number of millennial and post-millennial kids on their own furry paths.

As it happened, I already owned a tropical-green patterned shirt, basically identical to the one Nick Wilde wore in *Zootopia.* (I made sure to wear it to my interview with the directors.) It was impossible to resist: I had to track down a blue-and-red striped tie identical to Nick's (although the stripes on mine ran in the opposite diagonal from his). Furio lent me a fox tail he just happened to have in his own furry wardrobe, and we strolled the streets of Old Town Alexandria, Virginia, a few weeks after *Zootopia* premiered, my first time cosplaying anywhere.

A kid who couldn't have been more than eight spotted me. "Nick Wilde!" he shouted.

I'll probably see him at Anthrocon a few years from now.

CHAPTER FIFTEEN

The Future of Fur

Be a good animal, true to your animal instincts.
—D.H. LAWRENCE

EARLY IN 2016 the *New Yorker* printed "Beastie Boys and Girls: The New Anthropomorphism."[175] In addition to the furry "movement," the article reported on a pair of phenomena that had escaped my notice: "On the Web, a virtual wilderness of humans tweet vicariously as bears, rhinos, owls, cobra, ferrets . . . to say nothing of cats and dogs."

The tweeters weren't basement-dwellers either; the people using Twitter as animals "included ministers, [museum staffers] and a health-care researcher." The animals' tweets tended towards zen-like koans (due in

---

175 Published February 10, 2016; from the author's reference collection.

large part to Twitter's 140 character limit per tweet) on the order of "I think I would like to have more eyes" (@A_single_bear), "You've really got to admire Carmen San Diego" (@bronxZoosCobra) or "TOOK A NAP ON THE WAY TO TAKING A NAP AND DREAMED I WAS TAKING A NAP WHILE ON THE WAY TO A NAP napception WE MUST GO SLEEPER" (@sockington, a Massachusetts cat; the human behind Sockington says a lot of the cat's tweets were the result of "building a fantasy life living inside the cat.")

The bear has almost 73,000 followers, the cobra 162,000 and the cat *one-point-four million*, dozens of whom respond to his every tweet. There's no small number of canines tweeting their doggy thoughts as well; to paraphrase that legendary *New Yorker* cartoon, "On the Internet no one knows you're *not* a dog."

Anthropomorphism is the practice of giving animals and inanimate objects human qualities, but when furs suit up or wear tails, they're turning zoomorphic—giving themselves animal qualities.

The *New Yorker* article also reported the experience of Charles Foster, a British naturalist who took the pursuit of zoomorphism way beyond what the most passionate fur might ever attempt: living like a feral, in-the-woods actual animal.

Early in *Being a Beast*,[176] his retelling of the experience, Foster refers to the boundaries between species, presumably including humans, as "if not illusory, certainly vague and sometimes porous." Together with his eight-year-old son, Foster emulated badgers as best he could. Unable

---

176   Metropolitan Books (Henry Holt and Company), 2016.

to burrow into the ground, Foster and son dug a trench, covered it with vegetation to create an imitation badger sett and slept in a nest of ferns; they lapped water from a pond, went about on their hands and knees and attempted to find their way around primarily via scent. He attempted likewise as an otter, a dumpster-raiding urban fox, a red deer and (with the aid of a parachute) an aptly named fast-flying bird known as a swift.

Foster eventually admits his quest to live an animal's life—not just physically but mentally, to project his mind into an animal's, to imagine himself as one—was doomed to failure. Like me, Foster admits, "I preferred my ideas of badgers and the wild to real badgers and real wilderness."

Thomas Thwaites had better luck when he decided to become a goat. In *GoatMan: How I Took a Holiday from Being Human*[177] Thwaites wonders, as so many furs have, "Wouldn't it be nice to be an animal just for a little bit?"

Thwaites describes his attempts to "become" a goat, a species he chose based on the advice of a Danish shaman—a country not generally known for producing spirit healers. A prosthetics specialist constructed a pair of arm extensions, enabling him to assume (exactly like a furry quadsuiter) a four-legged posture. He traveled to a goat farm in rural Switzerland, ate grass and successfully blended in with a herd of Alpine goats. (His only faux pas: trying to graze further up the mountain slope than the more dominant members of the herd.) "And so perhaps for a while the goats thought of me as a goat and I thought of myself as

---

177 Princeton Architectural Press, 2016.

goat, and so maybe for a moment . . . " Thwaites doesn't finish the thought, but my guess would be "I *was* a goat."

Tweeting as animals or living like animals: two more ways people who have probably never heard of Furry join us in imagining themselves as animals. The Zeitgeist rolls on.

Furs wearing tails are a common convention sight, as its the easiest way to signify your fursona and transform, if only slightly, into your animal form. It's not a new idea either.

The celebrated nineteenth-century French actress Sarah Bernhardt was a character and a half. She claimed to have had over a thousand lovers, slept in a coffin and kept a champagne-drinking alligator and a lion as pets.[178]

It's likely an apocryphal story or one she invented herself. As the legend goes, "She once told a group of dinner guests that she had, that very day, consulted an eminent surgeon to find out if it would be possible for him to graft a living tiger's tail onto the end of her spine as it would be so satisfactory to lash it about when she was angry."[179] Sadly, the doctor informed her it was a medical impossibility.

That was the past; had Bernhardt lived in the imaginary tomorrow of *The Simpsons* "Future-Drama" episode, she could have visited Springfield's Plastic Surgery Center, an establishment specializing in "Celebrity Buttocks, Nipple Relocations," and now popular in the future, "Fluffy

---

178 The instant expert: Sarah Bernhardt. The National Arts and Life. October 19, 2011, (https://www.thenational.ae/lifestyle/the-instant-expert-sarah-bernhardt-1.436567) retrieved November 5, 2016.

179 "Sarah Bernhardt On Stage In Findlay." The Courier, October 1, 1999. (http://thecourier.com/historical-highlights/1999/10/01/Sarah-bernhardt-on-stage-in-findlay/) Retrieved October 20, 2016.

Tails." (Marge's sister Patty emerges sporting a particularly fluffy one.)[180]

Technology might soon make that sight gag a reality. In 2012 the Japanese company Neurowear introduced "Shippo," an electronic tail designed to respond to the wearer's brainwaves and heartbeat via body sensors worn along with the tail. A video on the company's website shows a young girl wearing the fluffy tail (quite similar to the one Marge's sister now sports) that wags happily when she smiles thanks to a "neural app" included with the device.

The app does more than set your caudal appendage in motion: it displays both your mood (via emoji) and location on a smartphone map viewable by your friends, a tip-off to your frame of mind before they find you (or based on that emoji, decide to stay away).

Rather anthropomorphize your top than your bottom? The company also sells "necomimi": cat ears affixed to a headband. According to the company's website the device reads your brainwaves and sets the ears in motion, "express[ing] your emotional state before you start talking." As an online article[181] explained, "Depending on the signals decoded by the sensors the ears can twitch, wriggle or even flop down, letting everyone around you know your true mood."

---

180 A few people have tried to physically transform themselves into an animal in real life, as far as their human bodies will allow. Dennis Avner, a U.S. Navy veteran also known as "Stalking Cat," was the most ambitious of them. He subjected his face to saline injections, surgeries and tattoos, and wore an animatronic tail in an attempt to resemble a tiger, his totem animal. His unique appearance earned him a slew of TV appearances, but facing personal and financial troubles after his temporary fame faded, Stalking Cat took his own life in 2012.

181 Cat Ears Pick Up on Brainwaves and Act as Furry Mood Rings For Those Around You. gizmodo.com, May 5, 2011. (http://gizmodo.com/5798892/cat-ears-pick-up-on-brainwaves-and-act-asfurry-mood-rings-for-those-around-you) Retrieved November 13, 2016.

If a fluffy tail and a set of cat ears aren't enough, how about replacing your unexceptional human face with a cool animal one? It's not a real-life possibility at the moment, but "FaceRIG," a $15 computer program, will turn you into a variety of anthropomorphic beasts for your online chat or blog.[182] The sophisticated software maps your expressions onto a computer-generated, customizable character that animates in real time. Its avatar gallery includes a dashing red panda, a *muy* sexy wolf (in the online demo video he purrs, "Oh yeah, I *totally* know the way to grandma's house"), a powerful-looking dragon, a cool tiger and other animals. (Human/humanoid and video game characters are also among the avatars.) As the demo video so temptingly puts it, "With FaceRIG, you'll never have to settle for plain reality ever again."

Are the Minotaur and the sphinx furries? How about the satyrs? All combine the human and the animal, although not in the manner of your standard furry character. These are more of the cut-and-paste variety: the minotaur sports a bovine head on a human body; the horned satyr walks on goat legs and flicks a goat tail; the centaur, as the old joke goes, is "a man with a horse where his pants ought to be."[183]

Millennia have passed but these fabulous beings continue to fascinate us. One of their ilk is not as well known today: the chimera, a fire-breathing beast with a lion's head, a goat's body and a snake as its tail.

A modern chimera is something quite different: a being

182 facerig.com, retrieved November 25, 2016

183 A 2003 Princeton University Museum show of antiquities depicting these beings was titled "The Centaur's Smile: The Human Animal in Early Greek Art."

created by combining DNA from two separate species. The concept is scary to some, tempting to others—specifically furs eager to embrace (literally as well as metaphorically) the possibility of actual anthropomorphic beings living among us. Beings blending the human and animal are a science-fiction staple, notably with H.G. Wells' 1896 anti-vivisection novel, *The Island of Dr. Moreau*. In contemporary pop culture they've taken the form of human/kangaroo hybrid "Rippers" in the *Tank Girl* movie and comic, while the set-in-the-future animated TV series *Batman Beyond* featured "Splicers," people who alter their DNA to become semi-bestial for kicks.

The concept did not appeal to the second President Bush. In his 2006 State of the Union address, he asked Congress "to prohibit the most egregious abuses of medical research: human cloning in all its forms; creating or implanting embryos for experiments; creating human-animal hybrids; and buying, selling or patenting human embryos."[184]

Congress never got around to it. In fact, according to *Wired* magazine, "animal-human chimeras have been around for several decades"[185] utilizing existing gene-editing techniques. But in 2015, the National Institute of Health banned the funding of experiments inserting human stem cells into animal embryos. (Stem cells have the potential to turn into any cell composing the human

184 President Bush's State of the Union Address," *Washington Post*, January 31, 2006. (http://www.washingtonpost.com/wp-dyn/content/article/2006/01/31/AR2006013101468.html) Retrieved December 10, 2016.

185 You Can Soon Grow Human-Animal Hybrids, But You Can't Breed 'Em, wired.com, August 5, 2016. (https://www.wired.com/2016/08/new-nih-ruleslet-grow-pigoons-cant-breed-em/) Retrieved December 7, 2016.

body.) The move disappointed scientists who saw the possibility of creating various types of tissue or even organs within chimeras for transplantation into human beings. The following year the NIH eased its ban and instituted a review process that proposed experiments involving changing an animal's brain functions would have to pass before continuing. (Projects that would allow chimeras to reproduce or inject human stem cells into primates were still prohibited.)

Someday, somebody is going to go all the way. It's already been the subject of *Splice*, a 2009 sci-fi/horror movie about husband and wife scientists who secretly create a human/animal chimera, with, to put it mildly, less-than-ideal results.

That was fiction. If the gloves were off, if there were no legal or moral restrictions,[186] if every biological obstacle could be overcome, what would it take to create a truly anthropomorphic being, a fully intelligent, speaking individual halfway between human and animal in appearance? In other words, an actual living furry?

I asked Robert K. Streiffer, a bioethics professor at the University of Wisconsin-Madison, for his thoughts on the subject:

> *We already have lots of animals with human cells in them, typically to study the way those cells behave in a living system and to explore their potential for future transplants into humans. And we already have lots of humans*

---

186 The subject of what rights such beings might enjoy—human rights, animal rights or, like themselves, some mixture of the two—is a subject of much debate, mirroring the one currently raging regarding non-human animals.

with animal cells in them (e.g., animal-derived medicines, humans with heart-valve replacements from pigs). If you what you are talking about is an individual who was a really thorough mix of human and animal cells from the beginning (imagine an early-stage embryo with half human cells and half animal cells), then how that individual would develop would depend on which parts of the individual were derived from the animal cells and which from the human cells.

We know from animal/animal chimeras that they can display a mix of morphological characteristics. For example, a sheep/goat chimera can end up with wool on parts of its body and hair on other parts of its body; a quail/leghorn chick chimera can have black quail feathers on parts of its body and yellow chick feathers on other parts. In order to make changes that would result in an animal possessing human intelligence and speech, you obviously would have to dramatically affect the development of the brain and also the development of the skull (too small a skull limits how complex the brain can be) and the mouth, tongue, and other parts underlying our ability to speak. You would also probably need to use a species that has a relatively long gestational period and continuing development after birth, as this is part of what provides humans with the opportunity for the development of more complex brain architecture. We sometimes have the ability to direct *cells into one specific cell or tissue lineage, so one could imagine generating an individual who was mostly animal but for whom some part was all human cells. Attempts to introduce human cells into an animal embryo typically result in the human cells not being very competitive and losing out to animal cells over time. This would need to be solved, somehow. And one would need to introduce the human cells in a way that they weren't incompatible with successful pregnancy in the surrogate mother in whom the embryo was implanted. Very much science fiction compared to the current state of research.*

Of course if we're talking science fiction, there would be no obstacle to gestating the embryo to its birth in a laboratory environment, a "test-tube" furry as it were. But the ultimate step—the ability to transform *ourselves* into furries, to truly become a Splicer—would it be possible? Streiffer continues:

To take an already developed human being and reassign him or her, so to speak, would probably not involve chimeras but rather genetic therapy. The introduction of cells into an already developed individual will have very limited impact on the overall development of the individual; to get such an impact, you usually have to introduce the cells at the embryonic stages of development of the organism. But with genetic therapy, one can use a virus which targets and

> *infects certain kinds of cells and which can insert into those cells DNA that we have introduced into the virus. That DNA can affect how the infected cells behave and can be passed on to the daughter cells of the originally infected cell.*

Genetic therapy? Sounds a heck of a lot easier than creating an embryonic chimera. I suspect no small number of furs would gladly volunteer for that kind of therapy and actually, physically *become* their fursonas. I might even be willing to give it a shot myself; there are days when the idea of drifting lazily through swampy waters sounds awfully appealing.

CHAPTER SIXTEEN

The Peaceable Kingdom

THIRTY YEARS AGO we were a handful of people in a hotel room trading sketchbook art and watching cartoons. Today you can find us across the globe in every country on the planet, well over a million of us—and our numbers grow larger every day.

Furry wasn't born in a vacuum, and it isn't new to the twenty-first century. The anthropomorphic instinct has been part of the human race ever since there's *been* a human race. We're denied the power and freedom of the beasts, their amazing bursts of speed, their ability to coast on the highest winds and plunge into the ocean's depths. We can mimic them using our brains and our tools, but where they're one with the environment, we've never stopped changing (or destroying) it to suit our needs or whims of the moment.

Might Furry at its heart be an atavistic longing to rejoin the animal kingdom and escape the loneliness of being the only "intelligent" species on the planet? Perhaps that's why animal stories, from Reynard the Fox in the thirteenth century to *Zootopia* in the twenty-first, show different species living side by side as friends, lovers or rivals, not as predator and prey.

Furry seeks to bridge the divide between us and other animals, to meet them in the middle, as it were: make them more human via art and storytelling, while we attempt to make ourselves more animal via fursuiting and roleplay. We can enjoy the Edenic natural world they represent in our imaginations without leaving the safety and comfort of our human lives.

Predator or prey, animals' lives can be (to quote a pair of old expressions) nasty, brutish and short, red in tooth and claw. From our civilized vantage point we can observe them on TV or in their zoological captivity while we pet, play and care for our companion animals.

In recent years, society at large seems more receptive to the anthropomorphism we've made—take your choice— our hobbies, lifestyles, and/or spiritual pursuits. One of the most popular and critically praised TV shows of the moment is *Bojack Horseman*, which centers on a neurotic, self-destructive Hollywood star—a vulnerable, complex cartoon horse—and is set in a universe shared by humans and anthropomorphic animals. A few years ago the only place you would have found mature stories about anthro animals and humans sharing the same world would have been in furry comics or novels.

Furio explained Furry to his mom by reminding her of her crush on lion-man Vincent in the 1980s *Beauty and the Beast* TV series. I find it easier every month to tell people about my alligator totem, to show them pictures of me as Komos—and more often than not, they're impressed.

Furry may have started as a fandom, but before long we became a community; 'fandom' is way too tiny a word to encompass the many flavors of Furry. One can be a fan of Bugs Bunny or the Ninja Turtles, but a "fan" of therianthropy? Calling it a subculture is a bit of an improvement, but a subculture of what? Furry evolved out of sci-fi, funny-animal and animation fandoms. I've used the word occasionally myself (in this book's subtitle, for example) but it's really not all that accurate. "Community" nails it.

A fur I know points out the difference between a fandom and a community: being a fan is a passive act, whereas being a member of a community is active. "You're not a 'fan' of yourself doing something; you're a fan *of someone else doing something.* When you're part of a community, you're a doer, not a fan." (Although there's no reason one can't be a fan of something *within* the furry community.)

And for many furs, Furry is more than a community—it's a family, a welcoming place for people whose furriness (or their autism, or their gender fluidity) made them outcasts among their peers. Those outcasts weren't the only people who discovered Furry via the Internet, the central nervous system of the twenty-first century, but until they discovered us, they might have felt the loneliest.

Furry fandom was created by Baby Boomers and the earliest Gen-Xers. The original furs have crossed the line into middle age and beyond.[187] It's no longer "our" fandom; we've been joined by the next generation—high-

---

187 Not that younger furs are exempt: anyone over thirty (!) is welcome to join the Facebook "Greymuzzles" page.

school kids, college students and twenty-somethings. Many experienced their own "I'm not the only one!" moment when they discovered Furry on the Internet and realized they weren't alone; others took a look, liked what they saw and joined in.

I suppose Furry never really was "ours" to begin with. As Rod O'Riley pointed out, no one invented it, we simply recognized something that was there all along—we recognized ourselves. Furry long ago ceased being simply sketchbooks, funny-animal comics and cartoons. It's fursuiting; it's people who feel a spiritual connection to their animal identity; it's entrepreneurs and artists who've discovered they can earn a living sharing their creativity with the community.

Furry's been around long enough to be a Thing. Like smart phones and the Internet, as far as younger furs are concerned, it's always been here. When they discover Furry online or via friends, they see how *big* it is. They're not struggling with the same degree of isolation the original furs felt, and they join without hesitation. (In a decade or two, Furry will belong entirely to them.) The Internet trolls still post "yiff in hell furfag," but as our numbers grow theirs shrink. Meanwhile, that *CSI* episode, while still many people's only exposure to Furry, is over thirteen years old and drifting further into the past every day.

According to the sociologists and marketing experts who are paid to notice these things, the millennials and their follow-up, Generation Z, want to belong, to feel like they're part of a group. They want to be recognized for their skills and creativity. They're entrepreneurial and open Café Press, Etsy and Red Bubble stores to sell their personal creations. They share their ideas, feelings and creativity online.[188] They're also more open-minded than any generation before them. Ethnic or cultural differences often count for little; they're more accepting of LGBTQ people, more ready to acknowledge their own sexuality without fearing rejection.[189]

The millennial and Gen-Z furs feel the same way. "Coming out," the figure of speech furs often use to acknowledge their furriness to others, isn't necessarily sexual, despite its origins in the LGBTQ liberation movement.

You come out as a fur when you discover you're not an isolated atom, a weirdo who thinks about this stuff way more than you should, way more than anyone else does. You come out because now you have friends who understand you, who share that very central and no-longer-so-unique part of yourself. You're now part of something larger than yourself—and there is strength in numbers. Check out some of the increasing number of thumbs-up articles and news videos about Furry on the Internet; people are beginning to get it.

Comics (not just graphic novels, but plain-old comic books) and superheroes are now mainstream entertainment; they're no long just for geeks and nerds. In fact nerd- and geekdom—knowing every detail of an obscure TV show, a video game or an entertainment franchise—is practically hip. (Stephen Colbert proudly demonstrates his all-encompassing *Lord of the Rings* knowledge at every TV opportunity.)

---

188 "How to engage millennials? Appeal to 3 core values, 3 core traits." GreenBiz, October 24, 2014. Retrieved November 15, 2016. (https://www.greenbiz.com/blog/2014/10/24/engage-millennials-and-gen-z-appealing-values-and-traits)

189 "Millennials Are the Gayest Generation." The Daily Beast, March 31, 2105. Retrieved November 15, 2016. (http://www.thedailybeast.com/millennials-are-the-gayest-generation)

Cosplay has gone mainstream too—it's become cool, a fun hobby. A double-page photo spread in *Entertainment Weekly* shows a massive group of cosplayers on the steps outside San Diego Comic-Con—dozens of superheroes on one page facing down an equal number of supervillains on the other, and it's obvious everyone is having the time of their life.

Then there's that trivia contest in an episode of *The Flash* TV series. One of the main characters apologizes for picking the wrong answer. "Maybe [the other team] will get it wrong too," his friend consoles him. "Oh yeah," says a third character. "I'm sure that the team named 'Pride and Padawans' doesn't know the name of Han Solo's ship."

The camera pans to the other team; they're dressed as *Star Wars* characters, including someone wearing a home-made R2D2 costume. (The robot's domed top is worn like a hat.) A TV show ten years ago would've mocked them as pathetic losers, but here in the second decade of the twenty-first century, because cosplayers or their friends are very likely *creating* those shows, they're just folks having goofy fun.

Fursuiters are beginning to be treated likewise. The 2015 *NCIS: Los Angeles* episode was a near-historic breakthrough: two attractive young people, *regular cast members* flirt with each other—by knowledgably discussing furry conventions and fursuits without the tiniest bit of condescension.

In an age of a million fandoms and mainstream kinks, weirdness is no longer so weird. Perhaps weird is even the new normal: cool, different and challenging.

My favorite observation on the subject was in an

exchange between two furs in an online comment thread:

"I also like robots with Sexual AI. ALSO video game journalism. I'm not making these up, I'm just a weird bag of weirdness."

"Your weirdness is what makes you wonderful."

IT'S LATE SATURDAY NIGHT at Anthrocon. A furry rave is going full blast in the enormous Spirit of Pittsburgh ballroom in the David L. Lawrence Convention center. Lasers are flashing, colored lights are twirling overhead. The DJ onstage is creating the beat, the soundtrack for an event that is at once primal, pagan and ecstatic. He's bookended by dancing fursuiters on either side of his console.

A conga line of revelers snakes past me, both human and animal, under the spell of the DJ's propulsive audio environment. Man and beast dance together as equals, alternately silhouetted and illuminated by the ever-shifting lights. I see someone in an alligator suit so awesome I follow him like a puppy, high on the "reality" of being a few feet away from my spirit animal.

I need to cool out and escape the over-stimulating environment for a while. I leave the ballroom and head towards the Allegheny River just behind the convention center. There's a walkway alongside the quiet river, at the moment the most tranquil spot in all of Pittsburgh.

A young crowd is there, Furry's next generation. Some are in full fursuit, some have taken off their heads, many are dressed regularly or sporting a tail. A few folks are enjoying beers; every now and then a whiff of cannabis drifts by.

The animals, the half-animals and the humans, no

matter what their genders, no matter what their species, no matter who or how they love—they're all sharing the moment.

It may not be Eden, but for me *this* is the peaceable kingdom.

Acknowledgments

Furry Nation is the result of many years of writing and research (and a few of procrastination). This book would literally not exist without the generous help and support of no small number of my fellow furs who gave so freely of their time.

At the top of the list are Mark Merlino and Rod O'Riley, they of the Prancing Skiltaire and organizers of the very first furry convention. Right alongside them is Fred Patten, whose selfless contribution to Furry is the stuff of legend; right alongside Fred are Ken Fletcher and Reed Waller, whose publication *Vootie* was the first to showcase the work of funny-animal fan artists and set the stage for just about every furry art book and comic to follow. And alongside them all: Sam "Uncle Kage" Conway, who's done more than anyone else on the planet to introduce Furry to the world at large.

I must also thank Ray Rooney for that surprise furry party invitation, the ultimate result of which is the book you now hold in your hands. Kudos to Mitch Marmel, whose recollections of the fandom's earliest days and knowledge of online fur were invaluable. Huge gratitude is also due to Kathy Gerbasi and Courtney N. "Nuka" Plante of the International Anthropomorphic Research Project.

And then there are the many, many furs to whom I spoke along the way: the Greymuzzle twins Eddie and Marty Lee, Boomer the Dog, Matthias Rat, James "AJ Skunk" Firmiss, *Furries in the Media* host Aberguine, Fur Affinity director

Dragoneer, furry historian Dronon and BigZtehwuff, my guide to the wonderful world of Second Life; artists Steve Gallacci, Tim "Tim Kangaroo"/"Tympany" Fay, Heather Bruton, Kjartan "Karno" Arnórsson, Lucius Appaloosius, Vander, Pickelle, Steve Martin, LeeLee and Thad; suit-builders Lance Ikegawa, Robert King, Denali, Charleston Rat, Temperance and Artslave, who brought Komos to three-dimensional life. (Apologies and gratitude to those I may have accidentally neglected to mention here.) An extra-special shout-out is due Jim Groat, one of the very first furry artists and the man who looked at me and saw an alligator.

The book you're holding (or looking at on a screen) simply wouldn't exist without the perseverance of my wonderful and tireless agent Malaga Baldi, who bought it to the attention of Cleis Press and Stephanie Lippitt, under whose tutelage Furry Nation took root and bloomed. (Thanks too to her associate Allyson Fields.)

Quite a few non-furs lent a hand as well: cartoon maven Jerry Beck, *Jake Long* creator Jeff Goode, Ben Guarino of the *Washington Post*, Jason Fulvi and Craig Davis of VisitPittsburgh and Professor Robert K. Streiffer at the University of Wisconsin-Madison.

Personal thanks go to Peter Stoller who dragged me to my first furry convention, wrapped me in duct tape and helped facilitate my furriness in 1,001 different ways, and to Oliver Coombes, Goldie's creator and Circe's Funhouse's biggest fan. And finally (after my sons Max and Ben), the man I love more than anyone else in the world: "Walrus Royce," aka Furio, who once upon a time called me a "sexy gator" and changed my life.

Printed in the United States
By Bookmasters